THE INTERNATIONAL FINANCIAL ARCHITECTURE

WHAT'S NEW?

WHAT'S MISSING?

PETER B. KENEN

INSTITUTE FOR INTERNATIONAL ECONOMICS
WASHINGTON, DC
NOVEMBER 2001

Peter B. Kenen is Walker Professor of Economics and International Finance at Princeton University. He is the author of many books and articles, including *The International Economy* (fourth edition, 2000), *Economic and Monetary Union in Europe* (1995), *Managing Exchange Rates* (1989), and *Exchange Rates and Policy Coordination* (1989), and was the editor of *Managing the World Economy: Fifty Years after Bretton Woods* (1994). He is a member of the Group of Thirty and serves on the Advisory Committee of the Institute for International Economics.

INSTITUTE FOR INTERNATIONAL ECONOMICS
1750 Massachusetts Avenue, NW
Washington, DC 20036-1903
(202) 328-9000 FAX: (202) 328-5432
http://www.iie.com

C. Fred Bergsten, *Director*
Brigitte Coulton, *Director of Publications and Web Development*
Brett Kitchen, *Director of Marketing*

Typesetting and printing by Automated Graphic Systems, Inc.

Printed in the United States of America
03 02 01   5 4 3 2 1

Library of Congress Cataloging-in-Publication Data

Kenen, Peter B., 1932–
  The international financial architecture : what's new? what's missing? / Peter B. Kenen.
    p. cm.
  Includes bibliographical references and index.
  ISBN 0-88132-297-0
    1. International finance. 2. Financial institutions, International. I. Title.

HG3881 .K438 2001
332.1′5—dc21   2001039471

For
Jacques de Larosière
with admiration and affection

Contents

Preface

The functioning and reform of the international monetary system have been among the central foci of the Institute for International Economics since its creation in 1981. Our very first publications, by Senior Fellow John Williamson, included *The Lending Policies of the International Monetary Fund* (1982) and *IMF Conditionality* (1983). Most recently, Dennis Weatherstone Senior Fellow Morris Goldstein directed the Council on Foreign Relations' Independent Task Force Report on *Safeguarding Prosperity in a Global Financial System: The Future International Financial Architecture* (September 1999) and Barry Eichengreen authored *Toward a New International Financial Architecture: A Practical Post-Asia Agenda* (February 1999). Specialized aspects of the topic have been addressed in *Exchange Rate Regimes for Emerging Markets: Reviving the Intermediate Option* (September 2000) by Williamson and in *Assessing Financial Vulnerability: An Early Warning System for Emerging Markets* (June 2000) by Goldstein, Graciela Kaminsky, and Carmen Reinhart.

This new study traces the evolution of the debate on the international financial architecture through the middle of 2001. In addition to analyzing the substance of the key reform issues, it describes the evolving attitudes of the major players—the finance ministries and central banks of the most important countries, the relevant international institutions, and the private groups and individuals that have participated in the debate. It also draws attention to the interplay between the course of the debate and lessons learned from the currency crises of the late 1990s. Finally, it attempts to explain the outcomes, or absence thereof, on the various issues being debated, and to explain what remains to be done to solidify the system's defenses against future crises and its ability to respond effectively to those crises that do occur.

Professor Peter B. Kenen of Princeton University is one of the most eminently qualified observers to conduct such a study. He has been among the most perceptive and innovative analysts of international monetary affairs for over 40 years, including during several stints in the recent past as an adviser to the US Treasury. He was for many years the director of the International Finance Section at Princeton. His *Essays in International Finance* and other publications have been one of the leading sources of wisdom on these topics.

The Institute for International Economics is a private nonprofit institution for the study and discussion of international economic policy. Its purpose is to analyze important issues in that area and to develop and communicate practical new approaches for dealing with them. The Institute is completely nonpartisan.

The Institute is funded largely by philanthropic foundations and private corporations. Major institutional grants are now being received from the William M. Keck, Jr. Foundation and the Starr Foundation. A number of other foundations and private corporations contribute to the highly diversified financial resources of the Institute. About 31 percent of the Institute's resources in our latest fiscal year were provided by contributors outside the United States, including about 18 percent from Japan. The Rockefeller Brothers Fund provided generous support to this project.

The Board of Directors bears overall responsibilities for the Institute and gives general guidance and approval to its research program, including the identification of topics that are likely to become important over the medium run (one to three years), and which should be addressed by the Institute. The Director, working closely with the staff and outside Advisory Committee, is responsible for the development of particular projects and makes the final decision to publish an individual study.

The Institute hopes that its studies and other activities will contribute to building a stronger foundation for international economic policy around the world. We invite readers of these publications to let us know how they think we can best accomplish this objective.

C. Fred Bergsten
Director
October 2001

Acknowledgments

In the autumn of 1995, I began to serve as a consultant to the US Treasury and continued in that position for four years, working largely on issues relating to the reform of the international financial architecture. Soon thereafter, Fred Bergsten invited me to distill my own views on that subject, and this book is the result. Readers will soon see that I disagree with some of the Treasury's decisions and views. Nevertheless, I am deeply indebted to the officials who took time to discuss the issues with me, especially Jeffrey Shafer, David Lipton, Timothy Geithner, and Caroline Atkinson. I am also indebted to fellow members of the Group of Thirty, the Task Force on the Future International Financial Architecture sponsored by the Council on Foreign Relations, and the Bellagio Group of officials and academics, which discussed the issues intensively.

I owe an equally large debt to the members of the study group convened by the Institute of International Economics to review the manuscript and to all of the readers of the manuscript who took time to write out their comments and suggestions—Alan Blinder, Ralph Bryant, Bill Cline, Jerry Cohen, Barry Eichengreen, Tim Geithner, Ellen Meade, Brad Setser, Jeff Shafer, Ted Truman, and John Williamson.

I am indebted to Patrizia Baudino for producing the charts and to Kathleen Hurley for preparing the final version of the manuscript under very tight time constraints. I am also indebted to the Institute's publications staff, especially Brigitte Coulton, Madona Devasahayam, and Marla Banov.

My work on this book began in the spring of 2000, when I was a visiting scholar in the Centre for Economic Performance at the London School of Economics, and I am grateful to Richard Layard for that opportunity.

Acronyms

BCBS	Basel Committee on Banking Supervision
BIBF	Bangkok International Banking Facility
BIS	Bank for International Settlements
CCL	Contingent Credit Line
CFF	Compensatory Financing Facility
CFR	Council on Foreign Relations
CPSS	Committee on Payment and Settlement Systems
ECB	European Central Bank
EFF	Extended Fund Facility
EFM	Emergency Financing Mechanism
EMS	European Monetary System
ESF	Exchange Stabilization Fund
FATF	Financial Action Task Force
FSA	Financial Sector Assessment (World Bank)
FSAP	Financial Sector Assessment Program
FSF	Financial Stability Forum
FSSA	Financial Sector Stability Assessment (IMF)
GAB	General Arrangements to Borrow
GDDS	General Data Dissemination Standard
GDP	Gross Domestic Product
GKO	The Russian language abbreviation for Russia's treasury bill
HIPC	Highly Indebted Poor Countries
IAIS	International Association of Insurance Supervisors
IASC	International Accounting Standards Committee
IFAC	International Federation of Accountants
IFIAC	International Financial Institution Advisory Commission
IIF	Institute of International Finance

IMF	International Monetary Fund
IMFC	International Monetary and Financial Committee
IOSCO	International Organization of Securities Commissions
LIBOR	London Interbank Offered Rate
LLR	lender of last resort
NAB	New Arrangements to Borrow
NAFTA	North American Free Trade Agreement
NAMU	North American Monetary Union
OECD	Organization for Economic Cooperation and Development
PRI	Partido Revolucionario Institucional (Institutional Revolutionary Party)
ROSC	Report on the Observance of Standards and Codes
SDDS	Special Data Dissemination Standard
SDR	Special Drawing Right
SRF	Supplemental Reserve Facility
UDROP	Universal Debt Rollover Option with a Penalty
WTO	World Trade Organization

Introduction

Speaking at the Brookings Institution in April 1998, Robert Rubin, the US secretary of the treasury, explained the need to strengthen the "architecture" of the international financial system (Rubin 1998). Although he gave a new name to that need, it had been identified three years earlier, shortly after the Mexican crisis of 1994-95, when the governments of the major industrial countries proposed a number of reforms aimed at preventing future crises and resolving more effectively the crises that do occur. This book describes the evolution of that reform effort. It explains how the challenges posed by the emerging-market crises of the late 1990s affected the course of the architecture exercise and how the exercise itself affected the ways in which the official community sought to resolve those crises. It also proposes further changes in the international financial architecture intended to strengthen the financial systems of emerging-market countries, limit the use of large-scale official financing, and foster the involvement of private-sector creditors in the resolution of financial crises.

The Origins of the Architecture Exercise

The Mexican crisis of 1994-95 is discussed fully in chapter 2, along with the Asian crisis of 1997-98. But a brief account must be given here to explain the origins of the architecture exercise.

The Mexican crisis began in March 1994, when capital inflows came to a sudden stop after the assassination of Luis Donaldo Colosio, presidential candidate of the Partido Revolucionario Institucional (PRI), the leading political party. Betting on an early resumption of those inflows, the Mexican authorities declined to take corrective action—to tighten monetary policy or devalue the peso. But subsequent capital inflows were too small to cover the country's large current account deficit, and Mexico's reserves began to fall. To limit the loss of reserves, the Mexican government issued large quantities of *tesobonos*, short-term debt instruments repayable in pesos but indexed to the US dollar. In September 1994, however, a second assassination—this time of the PRI's secretary general—was followed by a sharp drop in the Mexican stock market and more reserve losses. The newly elected Mexican government therefore sought to engineer a modest devaluation. On 20 December, it widened the band within which the exchange rate was allowed to fluctuate. But the peso fell promptly to the weak edge of the band, and Mexico's reserves were too small to defend it. The Bank of Mexico had to let the peso float, and it depreciated rapidly, losing half its dollar value in less than two weeks.

At that point, Mexico's currency crisis turned into a debt crisis. The depreciation of the peso implied a huge increase in the dollar value of the outstanding *tesobonos* and thus jacked up the budgetary cost of redeeming them. Had investors been willing to roll them over, the immediate budgetary burden—the increase in the peso value of the interest payments on the *tesobonos*—might have been manageable. But Mexico could not readily redeem the whole stock of *tesobonos* and could not possibly convert the pesos paid to holders of maturing *tesobonos* into US dollars. Hence, investors were unwilling to roll over their holdings.

Early in 1995, the US Treasury sought congressional support for financial assistance to Mexico, but that effort failed. Faced with the rising risk of a Mexican default, not unlike the one that touched off the debt crisis of the 1980s, the US Treasury and the International Monetary Fund (IMF) assembled $50 billion of official financing, including $20 billion from the US Exchange Stabilization Fund (ESF) and $18 billion from the IMF itself. The package made it possible for Mexico to redeem the whole stock of *tesobonos*—which is precisely what it did during the next several months. The Fund's contribution to the package was the largest in its history, more than twice as large as the normal limit on a member country's *cumulative* use of IMF resources. For its part, Mexico adopted a set of policy changes aimed at cutting the current account deficit in 1995 and reducing the inflation rate to single-digit levels by 1997.[1]

Although it averted a damaging default, the Mexican "bailout" was severely criticized. It was seen by some to increase moral hazard, because debtors and creditors might conclude that they would not be penalized for making mistakes. It was seen by some to be unfair, because it protected

---

1. On the failed attempt to obtain congressional support for unilateral US assistance to Mexico and details of the subsequent financial package, see Henning (1999); on Mexico's policy changes and the markets' response, see Leiderman and Thorne (1996).

from losses one class of investors—those who had bought *tesobonos*—but not investors who had bought Mexican equities and other peso-denominated claims.[2] And it was widely seen as a worrisome precedent, even by those who endorsed it, because the IMF did not have sufficient financial resources to offer large-scale assistance to other crisis-stricken countries.

At the Halifax Summit in June 1995, the governments of the G-7 countries[3] sought to address these objections. They called for measures to reduce the risk of future crises and for steps to strengthen the IMF itself—to augment its resources and improve its procedures—in order to deal decisively with those crises that could not be prevented. The Halifax communiqué (Group of 7 1995) made several recommendations.

In aid of crisis prevention, an "early warning system" should be developed, based in part on strengthened IMF surveillance and the disclosure of more information to market participants. To this end, the IMF should establish benchmarks for the timely publication of economic and financial data and should identify publicly those countries that adopt them. It should also provide sharper policy advice to individual governments and deliver franker messages to those that appear to be avoiding necessary actions.

In aid of crisis resolution, official financing should be made available quickly in amounts sufficient to manage shocks effectively. The IMF should therefore design an Emergency Financing Mechanism (EFM) to provide faster access to Fund financing when crises occur and should make larger up-front disbursements in such situations. To backstop these efforts, the network of credit facilities available to the Fund, the General Arrangements to Borrow (GAB), should be doubled in size by raising the lending commitments of existing participants and adding new participants.

The Halifax communiqué also called for further work on two broad issues. First, it asked that efforts be made to safeguard the financial system by strengthening international cooperation in supervising financial institutions and markets. Countries should still be encouraged to remove capital market restrictions, but the international financial institutions

---

2. In Washington, moreover, critics charged that the Treasury's use of the ESF defied the intent of Congress, which had refused to endorse unilateral US assistance to Mexico. Congress responded by restricting subsequent use of the ESF for loans to foreign governments. As the restrictions were still in force in mid-1997, the United States could not contribute significantly to the financial package assembled for Thailand in July 1997. But they expired later that year, allowing the United States to contribute to the financial packages for Indonesia and Korea.

3. The G-7 countries are Canada, France, Germany, Italy, Japan, the United Kingdom, and the United States. The G-10 countries, mentioned below, actually total 11; they comprise in addition Belgium, the Netherlands, Sweden, and Switzerland.

should help them design appropriate supervisory structures. Second, it called for a review of the legal and other issues posed by debt crises—issues made more complex in the 1990s by the large number and heterogeneity of the private-sector creditors that could be involved in a crisis. Third, it called for an examination of "other procedures" to aid in the orderly resolution of future debt problems.[4]

Some of these recommendations were implemented rapidly. The IMF was quick to adopt an EFM to foster prompt and continuing consultations between the Fund's management and its Executive Board during discussions with governments that have an unusually urgent need for IMF assistance—consultations that had been short-circuited during the Mexican crisis. The Fund also began to develop statistical standards to foster prompt publication of economic and financial data: a Special Data Dissemination Standard (SDDS) for countries that participate in global capital markets and those that aspire to do so, and a less demanding General Data Dissemination Standard (GDDS) for all other countries.

By the end of 1996, moreover, agreement had been reached on a scheme to augment the credit facilities available to the IMF. Instead of enlarging the GAB, a group of 25 countries, including several emerging-market countries, agreed to surround the GAB with another network of credit facilities: the New Arrangements to Borrow (NAB). The GAB remains in place, but the NAB is now the Fund's primary source of credit.[5] The Fund's managing director can ask for activation of the NAB when the IMF requires supplementary resources "to forestall or cope with an impairment of the international monetary system or to deal with an exceptional situation that poses a threat to the stability of that system" (IMF 1999g, 455).

The request for new work on financial stability and the supervision of the financial system did not lead quickly to visible results, but the issue was not dropped. At the Lyon Summit in 1996, the G-7 governments called for "maximum progress" on three fronts:

- enhancing cooperation among the authorities responsible for the supervision of internationally active financial institutions, importantly by clarifying their roles and responsibilities;

- encouraging stronger risk management and improved transparency in the markets and connected activities, especially in the innovative markets;

---

4. The reference to "other procedures" was, I am told, intended to express guarded interest in the proposal by Sachs (1995) for an international bankruptcy regime to deal with sovereign debt problems.

5. The decision to create the NAB, not enlarge the GAB, addressed the concern of some G-10 governments that adding new participants to the GAB would dilute their control over its use.

- encouraging the adoption of strong prudential standards in emerging economies and increasing cooperation with their supervisory authorities; international financial institutions and bodies should increase their efforts to promote effective supervisory structures in those economies. (Group of 7 1996, para. 11)

By that time, moreover, Morris Goldstein had proposed the development of an international banking standard (Goldstein 1997), and that task was taken up by the Basel Committee on Banking Supervision. In April 1997, it issued the first draft of *Core Principles for Effective Banking Supervision* and published the definitive version a few months later (BCBS 1997).[6]

The Rey Report and Private-Sector Involvement

The final recommendation of the Halifax Summit—that there be a review of the issues posed by debt crises—led to the creation of a G-10 working party chaired by Jean-Jacques Rey of Belgium. Its report (Group of 10 1996), often called the Rey Report, was issued a full year before the Asian crisis, was formally endorsed by the G-10 governments, and can fairly be regarded as the point of departure for the subsequent architecture exercise. Its recommendations are discussed later in this study, but some of its main findings deserve mention here.

Although the Rey Report did not rule out large-scale financial assistance to a sovereign debtor—the strategy adopted in the Mexican case—it said that this sort of support is warranted only under exceptional circumstances. The use of official funds to repay private-sector claims is inconsistent with the principle of equitable burden sharing and with the need to conserve official financial resources. Furthermore, frequent use of large-scale financing could give rise to moral hazard on the part of both debtors and creditors. It would insulate debtors from the costs of poor debt management, and it would insulate creditors from the costs of inadequate risk assessment.

The Rey Report rejected radical innovations, such as the proposal by Jeffrey Sachs (1995) for an international bankruptcy regime to meet the needs of sovereign debtors. It cited the legal and practical problems involved, but it also found fault with the implicit analogy between sovereign and private debtors. The report praised the work of the Paris Club, which restructures sovereign debt to official creditors, and that of the London Club, which restructures sovereign debt to commercial banks. It noted, however, that achievements of those groups owed much to the

---

6. There was other work in progress at that same time; see Working Party on Financial Stability in Emerging-Market Economies (1997) and Folkerts-Landau and Lindgren (1998).

fairly small number of creditors involved, which simplified management of the free-rider problem. That problem, it said, will be harder to solve now that the debts of sovereign borrowers consist largely of bond issues, not bank loans, with many of the bonds held by investors who have no enduring links with the debtor countries. Nevertheless, it concluded that debt workouts will be necessary, because large-scale official financing is not the right way to deal with debt crises. That indeed was its main message:

> [I]t is essential to maintain the basic principle that the terms and conditions of all debt contracts are to be met in full and that market discipline must be preserved. However, in exceptional cases, a temporary suspension of debt payments by the debtor may be unavoidable as a part of the process of crisis resolution and as a way of gaining time to put in place a credible adjustment program.
>
> [N]either debtor countries nor their creditors should expect to be insulated from adverse financial consequences by the provision of large-scale official financing in the event of a crisis. Markets are equipped, or should be equipped, to assess the risks involved in lending to sovereign borrowers and to set the prices and other terms of the instruments accordingly. There should be no presumption that any type of debt will be exempt from payments suspensions or restructurings in the event of a future sovereign liquidity crisis. (Group of 10 1996, i)

But the Rey Report dealt mainly with sovereign debt, not private-sector debt. In fact, it expressed strong reservations about interrupting debt payments by private-sector debtors. Trade credits and interbank lines, it said, are crucial links between a country and the world economy. Furthermore, a suspension of private-sector payments could require the use of exchange controls, which might impair a country's access to international capital markets, might not be feasible after a country has dismantled its exchange control regime, and might induce market participants to rush for the exit before controls can be imposed.

The Asian Crisis and the Architecture Exercise

If the Asian crisis of 1997-98 had been—or become—a sovereign debt crisis of the Mexican sort, the findings of the Rey Report would perhaps have influenced the policy response. But there were two crucial differences between the Asian and Mexican crises.

First, the Asian crisis did not start with a sudden shock like the Colosio assassination. There was instead a gradual deterioration of economic and financial conditions in Thailand—the country in which the crisis began—that started more than a year before Thailand ran out of reserves and, like Mexico before it, sought to devalue its currency but was forced to let it float. But the collapse of the Thai baht sent a sudden sharp shock to other Asian countries. The Philippines, Malaysia, and Indonesia were the first to be affected. And when Taiwan devalued its currency to ward off the crisis, the "Asian flu" migrated to Hong Kong and Korea.

Second, Asian governments did not have large foreign currency debts, so there was no risk of a sovereign debt crisis. Instead, short-term foreign lending to the stricken countries' banks suddenly stopped and was reversed. The resulting reserve loss was very rapid and was compounded by capital flight and speculation. The problems of the banks and other private-sector debtors were then exacerbated by the huge depreciations of their countries' currencies.

Unlike the collapse of the Mexican peso, the collapse of the Thai baht was seen at first to be a "glitch" rather than the harbinger of much larger problems. Yet the official response was similar in both cases, and in subsequent cases as well—massive official financing orchestrated by the IMF. The package assembled for Thailand amounted to $17 billion, the one for Indonesia was more than twice as large, and the one for Korea was even larger (see table 1.1).[7]

There was a late and limited attempt to roll over the foreign currency debts of Thai banks; Japanese banks agreed informally not to reduce their remaining claims on their Thai affiliates. There was a more comprehensive effort to roll over and restructure the short-term debts of Korean banks. Even after the first tranche of official financing had arrived in Seoul, foreign banks continued to run down their claims, and Korea's reserves were falling by $1 billion per day. In fact, the first tranche of official financing vanished in a fortnight. To avert a de facto default, the central banks and governments of the major industrial countries urged their own banks to roll over the rest of their claims on Korean banks, and the banks agreed to do so. In addition, they agreed thereafter to swap $24 billion of their short-term claims for one- to three-year obligations, most of which were guaranteed by the Korean government (see, e.g., Eichengreen 2000b). More on this episode later.

The Asian crisis led to innovations at the IMF. Having had to declare that Mexico and Thailand faced "exceptional" problems to enable them to obtain unusually large amounts of IMF credit, the Fund sought to normalize large drawings of that sort. In December 1997, it established a Supplemental Reserve Facility (SRF) with which to provide large-scale assistance to a country faced with a "sudden and disruptive loss of market confidence reflected in pressure on the capital account and the member's

---

7. The 1995 package for Mexico was equivalent to 12 percent of 1994 GDP and to 82 percent of 1994 merchandise exports. The 1997 package for Thailand was smaller by both measures: it amounted to 9 percent of 1996 GDP and 32 percent of 1996 exports. The 1997 package for Korea fell between the two on both measures, at 11 percent of 1996 GDP and 45 percent of 1996 exports. But the 1997 Indonesian package was the largest relative to GDP (16 percent of 1996 GDP) and only slightly smaller than the Mexican package relative to exports (72 percent of 1996 exports).

Table 1.1 Official financing for Thailand, Indonesia, and Korea (billions of dollars)

Country and source	Original package	Disbursed as of March 1999
Thailand		
IMF	4.0	3.1
World Bank and ADB	2.7	2.0
Other	10.5	8.0
Total	*17.2*	*13.1*
Indonesia		
IMF	10.1	9.2
World Bank and ADB	8.0	2.5
Other	18.0	2.6[a]
Total	*36.1*	*14.3*
Korea		
IMF	21.1	18.8[b]
World Bank and ADB	14.2	9.6
Other	23.1	—
Total	*58.4*	*28.4*

ADB = Asian Development Bank.

a. Includes $1.0 billion under the Miyazawa Initiative.
b. Before deducting $4.8 billion repaid by Korea.

Source: International Monetary Fund.

reserves" (IMF 1999g, 276). Drawings on the SRF must be repaid more rapidly than other drawings, and the interest rate charged on those drawings is higher.

In 1999, moreover, after the Russian crisis and the turmoil it produced, the Fund undertook to provide Contingent Credit Lines (CCLs) to help countries cope with contagion—what it described as "circumstances largely beyond the control of the member" caused mainly by "adverse developments in international capital markets consequent upon developments in other countries" (IMF 1999g, 280). To qualify for a CCL, however, a country would have to meet several tests,[8] and it could not use its CCL until the IMF had completed an "activation review" to satisfy itself that

8. A country could prequalify for a CCL if its policies obtained a "positive assessment" from the IMF and were unlikely to cause balance of payments problems for which it might need Fund financing; if it subscribed to the SDDS and other relevant standards such as the Basel Core Principles and was making adequate progress in meeting those standards; if it was maintaining constructive relations with its private creditors and managing its external debt and reserves in a manner conducive to limiting its external vulnerability; and if it submitted a satisfactory policy program, including a quantified policy framework. Recently, however, the Fund sought to make CCLs more attractive by relaxing these requirements. These changes, described in chapter 4, led Fischer (2001b) to predict that countries will soon start to apply for CCLs.

the country's need for financing was indeed due to contagion and that it was ready to adjust its policies to deal with "any real economic impact that may follow from contagion" (IMF 1999g, 280). Thus, when the new window was opened, no one was waiting outside to apply. The preconditions were daunting, and activation was not automatic.

The institutionalization of large-scale financing may have been the most fundamental result of the Fund's involvement in the Asian crisis, but it was not the most controversial aspect of that involvement. The policy commitments the Fund extracted in exchange for its assistance have been strongly criticized by many economists, including some who disagree on many other matters.

When a government seeks to draw on the IMF, it must submit a letter of intent describing the policies it will pursue to solve its balance of payments problem and listing a set of quantitative performance criteria that can be used to monitor the country's progress. If the criteria are not met, Fund financing is suspended until they are met or are renegotiated. Although a letter of intent is, in principle, a unilateral declaration by the government concerned, it reflects the outcome of negotiations between the government and the Fund. The number and scope of the policy commitments contained in the typical letter of intent have increased appreciably, causing a marked increase in the number of performance criteria. But the commitments made by the Asian countries at the Fund's behest were extraordinarily comprehensive, sparking controversy about their nature as well as their number.[9]

Some critics insist that the Asian countries should not have been told to tighten their fiscal and monetary policies. Their policies, these critics say, were far superior to those of countries that typically draw on the Fund; they were the victims of creditor panic, not misguided domestic policies. Furthermore, they had begun to experience dramatic reductions in output, rising unemployment, and ominous social unrest, and economic austerity would have aggravated those grave afflictions.[10]

Other critics accuse the Fund and Western governments of mounting an opportunistic attack on "Asian capitalism" and they argue that many of the policy commitments extracted from the Asian countries had no bearing whatsoever on their urgent problems. Why should Indonesia be made to eliminate food subsidies, reduce its tariffs, and abolish domestic monopolies, such as those dealing in garlic and cloves? Why should Korea be forced to agree that foreigners be allowed to acquire domestic financial

---

9. On the long-term evolution of Fund conditionality, see Polak (1991); on recent developments, see Goldstein (2000).

10. For this view, see Jeffrey Sachs ("The Wrong Medicine for Asia," *New York Times*, 3 November 1997; "IMF Is a Power unto Itself," *Financial Times*, 11 December 1997), Radelet and Sachs (1998, 2000), and Blinder (1999).

institutions? Why must it eliminate "directed lending" by Korean banks and move swiftly to strengthen corporate governance? Each nation is entitled to choose its own economic structure, and its need for short-term financial assistance "does not give the IMF the moral right to substitute its technical judgments for the outcomes of the nation's political process" (Feldstein 1998, 27).

The Fund was prepared to acknowledge mistakes. As it did not expect output to fall so sharply in the Asian countries, its fiscal-policy targets had been too tight. In fact, it relaxed those targets rather quickly. It also agreed that the closing of 16 Indonesian banks had been mismanaged in that, on the advice of the Fund, the Indonesian government had not guaranteed large deposits in those banks or in other privately owned banks. But the Fund defended its demand for the speedy pursuit of far-reaching reforms in the financial and corporate sectors of the Asian countries. It would have been wrong, the Fund said, to clean up or close insolvent banks without addressing immediately the fundamental defects of the financial system: "strengthening weak institutions to continue business as usual in a poorly regulated system would have given at best temporary relief" (Lane et al. 1999, 69). In short, far-reaching structural reforms were essential to start and sustain recovery in the crisis-stricken countries.

These and other issues raised by the critics of conditionality were revived in 2000 by the Meltzer Report, commissioned by the US Congress, which described conditionality as being both intrusive and ineffective.[11] The Fund began to address those issues in 2001, when the managing director, Horst Köhler, issued new guidelines to limit the number and scope of policy conditions in individual IMF programs. Conditionality did not find its way onto the agenda of the architecture exercise, despite the increasing attention it gave to the need for structural reform in emerging-market countries, especially financial-sector reform. Rather than implicitly endorsing the Fund's remedial argument that recovery could not occur without fundamental reform, that attention reflected the ongoing emphasis of the architecture exercise on the need for all emerging-market countries—not just crisis-stricken countries—to reduce their vulnerability to future crises.

The importance attached to crisis prevention became very visible in early 1998, when the US Treasury convened an ad hoc group of 22 "systemically significant" countries, and that group then issued three reports: on transparency and accountability, on strengthening national financial systems, and on managing international financial crises (Group of 22 1998a, 1998b, 1998c). In early 1999, moreover, the G-7 governments estab-

---

11. International Financial Institution Advisory Commission (2000), cited hereafter as IFIAC (2000).

lished the Financial Stability Forum (FSF) to promote international cooperation and the exchange of information among national and international bodies involved in supervising and regulating the financial sector. Participants in the FSF include representatives of the national agencies responsible for financial stability in major financial centers, the international financial institutions, and other international bodies concerned with regulation and supervision. The FSF began its work by creating three working groups of its own—on the issues and risks arising from international capital flows, the issues posed by the activities of hedge funds and other highly leveraged institutions, and the prudential problems posed by offshore financial centers (FSF 2000c, 2000d, 2000e).[12]

What Lies Ahead

The ongoing work of the architecture exercise was distilled in reports made annually to the G-7 summits, most notably the report prepared for the Köln Summit in 1999 (Group of 7 1999b). It is discussed at length in subsequent chapters. Those chapters also examine the ways in which the architecture exercise was influenced by the Russian crisis of 1998, the resulting "flight to quality" in international and national markets, the Brazilian crisis of 1998-99, and the debt problems of four other countries—Pakistan, Ukraine, Romania, and Ecuador.

Chapter 2 looks more closely at the Mexican and Asian crises, in an effort to answer three questions: (1) Were the crises caused by deep-seated flaws in the economic and financial systems of the crisis-stricken countries, by defective policies, or by an inherent instability of international capital flows? (2) Why were the crises so contagious? (3) Why did they lead to deep recessions? The chapter examines the links between banking and currency crises and the roles of exchange rate regimes; and, with the benefit of hindsight, asks whether there were better ways to deal with those crises.

Chapter 3 seeks to clear away some fundamental misconceptions that get in the way of clear thinking about crisis prevention and crisis management. It argues, for example, that an intergovernmental institution like the IMF is ill-suited to serve as a "lender of last resort" to sovereign states, and that the recent debate about the exchange rate regimes and policies of emerging-market countries has been framed in an overly simplistic way. It also examines the principal recommendations of the Meltzer Report, which called for sweeping changes in the mandate of the IMF and for the substitution of prequalification for conventional conditionality.

---

12. Another new body, the Group of 20, was established in 1999. It includes most of the countries represented in the Group of 22, and it has the same aim—to involve emerging-market countries in the effort to reform the international financial architecture.

Chapter 4 traces the evolution of the architecture exercise. It starts once again with the Rey Report, asks how its findings and recommendations fared at the hands of the Group of 22, and asks what was added and subtracted by the reports to the Köln Summit in 1999 and the Okinawa Summit in 2000. It also shows how the evolution of the architecture exercise was influenced by the emerging-market crises discussed in chapter 2 and asks what the architecture exercise has achieved thus far.

Chapter 5 focuses on unresolved issues, paying particular attention to two questions: How can emerging-market countries be induced to adopt the standards and codes that have been developed under the aegis of the architecture exercise and that have been its main contribution to crisis prevention? How can private-sector creditors be involved more quickly and decisively in crisis resolution? It also draws together conclusions and recommendations scattered through earlier chapters.

Some who read the first draft of this book asked why it did not deal with some of the proposals for radical reform of the international financial system, such as the one by John Eatwell and Lance Taylor (1998) for the creation of a global regulatory authority, or the one by George Soros ("Avoiding a Breakdown" *Financial Times*, 31 December 1997) for the creation of an international agency to insure investors against debt defaults. They also asked why it did not deal with a wider range of issues, including the governance of the IMF, new ways of funding the IMF to sever the constraining link between its members' quotas and the financial resources available to it, and the case for redrawing the boundary between the tasks of the IMF and of the World Bank Group.

These are very important issues—more important, perhaps, than some of the issues to which the architecture exercise devoted a great deal of attention. But my objective here is narrower. I aim at assessing the architecture exercise on its own terms, by asking how well the architects met the objectives they set for themselves. By that test, I argue, they did fairly well, but they have more work to do—and some work to be undone. The architecture exercise is not finished and should not be allowed to succumb to fatigue or to be crowded out by other urgent issues.

2

Causes and Consequences of the Recent Crises

It is impossible to explain the evolution of the architecture exercise without first examining the emerging-market crises of the 1990s, especially the Mexican and Asian crises, with particular attention to the explanations given for them and the responses of the international community. Others have already reviewed those crises in detail;[1] this chapter focuses on the features that set them apart from earlier currency crises and on the unusual nature of the official response.

As both crises began when large capital inflows came to a sudden stop and gave way to large capital outflows, this chapter starts by asking why emerging-market countries started to experience large capital inflows in the early 1990s. It then examines the policy problems posed by those inflows—the macroeconomic problems that used to be the main focus of concern, and the microeconomic problems that help explain the vulnerability of the Asian countries and the virulence of the Asian crisis.

The chapter then turns to the Mexican crisis to ask how it began, what might have been done to contain it, and why it was transformed from a currency crisis into a sovereign debt crisis. Although the Mexican crisis had some unusual features and the official response to the crisis was controversial, there was comparatively little debate about the causes of the crisis and no perceived need for a new set of currency-crisis models to explain the onset of the crisis.[2]

---

1. On Mexico, see IMF (1995), Edwards (1997), and Boughton (2000); on Asia, see IMF (1997b, 1998b, 1998c, 1998d), Bosworth (1998), and Eichengreen (1999a, appendix C).

2. See, however, Cole and Kehoe (1996), who model the *tesobono* crisis.

Table 2.1 Private capital flows to developing countries, 1977-95
(billions of dollars)

Type and region	1977-82[a]	1983-89[a]	1990	1991	1992	1993	1994	1995
All developing countries								
By type								
Direct investment	11.2	13.3	18.6	28.4	31.6	48.9	61.3	71.7
Portfolio investment	− 10.5	6.5	18.3	36.9	47.2	89.6	50.4	37.0
Other[b]	29.8	− 11.0	8.5	88.5	51.5	34.6	40.6	72.9
By region								
Asia	15.8	16.7	25.6	47.9	30.8	69.9	81.9	105.9
Western Hemisphere	26.3	− 16.6	17.3	24.0	54.7	64.2	48.5	48.9
Other developing countries	− 11.6	8.7	2.5	82.0	44.8	38.9	22.0	26.7
Total net capital inflow	*30.5*	*8.8*	*45.4*	*153.8*	*130.2*	*173.1*	*152.4*	*181.5*

a. Annual average.
b. Includes bank loans.

Note: Because of rounding, details may not add to totals given.

Source: International Monetary Fund.

The Asian crisis generated much more disagreement. Some blamed it on policies and private-sector practices that were once widely praised as important contributors to the "Asian miracle" but had outlived their usefulness. On this view, the Asian crisis was foreordained. Had it not started in Thailand, it would have been triggered elsewhere in Asia. And once it began, it was bound to spread, because it drew attention to fundamental flaws in the economic and financial systems of several Asian countries. Others saw the Asian crisis as an avoidable accident resulting from policy mistakes in Thailand, and they blamed its subsequent spread on investor panic and the complex workings of financial markets. On this view, Indonesia, Korea, and other Asian countries were the innocent victims of the Thai crisis and could have coped pragmatically with their homegrown problems had that crisis not occurred. These two explanations of the Asian crisis led to a debate about the right remedies and inspired a new set of currency crisis models.

The Capital Inflow Problem

Private capital flows to developing countries grew dramatically in the first half of the 1990s (see table 2.1). Their growth reflected the "push" of events in the major industrial countries and the "pull" of events in the developing countries. In the words of a World Bank report,

> In industrial countries two key developments have increased the responsiveness of private capital to cross-border investment opportunities. First, competition and rising costs in domestic markets, along with falling transport and communications costs, have encouraged firms to look for opportunities to increase efficiency by

producing abroad. This is leading to the progressive globalization of production and to the growth of "efficiency-seeking" FDI [foreign direct investment] flows. Second, financial markets have been transformed over a span of two decades from relatively insulated and regulated national markets toward a more globally integrated market. This has been brought about by a mutually reinforcing process of advances in communications, information, and financial instruments, and by progressive internal and external deregulation of financial markets.

In developing countries, the environment is also changing rapidly. Since the mid-1980s, several countries have embarked on structural reform programs and increased openness of their markets, through progressive lowering of barriers to trade and foreign investment, the liberalization of domestic financial markets and removal of restrictions on capital movements, and the implementation of privatization programs. There have also been major improvements in fiscal performance and the sustainability of external debt.

Although the perceived risks of investing in emerging markets remain relatively high, the more stable macroeconomic environment, growth in earnings capacity (both output and exports), and a reduction in the stock of debt in many countries (following the implementation of the Brady Plan) are leading to a decline in such risks and an increase in the expected rates of return in the major recipient countries. (World Bank 1997, 13-14)

The Bank's report acknowledged that individual countries had suffered reversals, but these, it implied, were due in the main to the countries' own policy errors. Therefore, it was optimistic about the outlook for globalization and financial integration:

The sustained increase in private capital flows in the face of recent shocks suggests that markets have entered a more mature phase. . . . Governments have demonstrated an awareness and ability to respond promptly and aggressively to changes in market conditions. And markets have become more able to discriminate among countries on the basis of their underlying fundamentals. This does not mean that there will not be year-to-year fluctuations in private flows in response to changes in international financial conditions. But private flows to developing countries in the aggregate are less likely to suffer from a widespread or prolonged decline of the kind seen after the debt crisis. (World Bank 1997, 25)

The Fund's assessment of the outlook was somewhat more guarded. It described the revival of capital flows as a "surge" and gave as one of the main causes the "push" of cyclical developments in the industrial countries during the early 1990s—the economic slowdown in the United States and the resulting fall in interest rates (IMF 1995).[3]

---

3. The Fund's more cautious account appeared just after the Mexican crisis and may have been influenced by it; the Bank's account appeared two years later, after that shock had worn off but before the Asian crisis. Nevertheless, the Fund's caution was not new. Early in the 1990s, IMF staff had drawn attention to the volatility of capital flows and to the cost of coping with abrupt reversals; see, e.g., G. Calvo, Leiderman, and Reinhart (1993). There is still disagreement, moreover, about the influence of push and pull factors on capital flows to developing countries. Fernandez-Arias and Montiel (1996) conclude that the push of low foreign interest rates was more powerful than the pull of domestic conditions and policies, but Bacchetta and van Wincoop (1998) reach the opposite conclusion. Nevertheless, most studies show that changes in US interest rates strongly affect those capital flows; see S. Calvo and Reinhart (1996) and Eichengreen and Rose (1998).

What can a capital inflow do for you—and to you? This question is narrower than the one posed by Maurice Obstfeld (1998); he surveys the whole set of benefits conferred by international capital mobility, including benefits that do not require any *net* capital inflow, such as the risk-reducing effects of portfolio diversification.

Whether to Bank or Spend an Inflow

Consider a country that starts to attract foreign capital. The relative contributions of pull and push factors do not matter here, although they may have a bearing on the sustainability of the capital inflow—a point to which we will return. To make use of the extra purchasing power supplied by the inflow, the country should import more or export less and let its trade balance deteriorate. It should also try to ensure that the capital inflow is used for investment, not consumption, so as to raise real output; otherwise, it may not be able to make the requisite income payments to its foreign creditors.

In some cases, a capital inflow will lead directly to an increase in imports; that will happen, for example, when an inflow is used to build a new factory and the equipment needed for the factory has to be imported. But the resulting increase in imports may not be as large as the capital inflow itself, and the government of the capital-importing country must then decide what to do with the rest of the foreign currency counterpart of the capital inflow—whether to "bank" or "spend" it.

When a capital inflow is deemed to be temporary, it is prudent to bank a large part of the inflow in order to guard against its cessation. A government can do that by intervening on the foreign exchange market to prevent its currency from appreciating under the influence of the inflow and, in the process, accumulate foreign exchange reserves. But it must also "sterilize" the monetary impact of its intervention. Otherwise, bank lending will rise and stimulate spending, and the increase in spending will have much the same effect as an appreciation of the country's currency. It will raise imports, reduce exports, and thus spend the proceeds of the capital inflow.[4]

---

4. When a government or central bank intervenes to keep its currency from appreciating, it buys foreign currency with newly created domestic currency, raising the liquidity of the banking system. To offset this monetary effect, a central bank can sell domestic securities, reduce its own lending to the banking system, or impound the increase in liquidity by requiring banks to hold larger cash balances at the central bank. These techniques have different side effects. Sales of domestic securities are costly to the central bank and government; interest rates on domestic securities sold to the public are usually higher than interest rates on reserve assets. Kletzer and Spiegel (1998) find that this quasi-fiscal cost may have deterred some central banks from full-fledged sterilization. A mandatory increase in the banks' cash balances does not have this effect, but it reduces the banks' earnings; see Reinhart and Reinhart (1999). For these and other reasons, countries that seek to keep capital inflows from raising domestic spending are often advised to tighten their fiscal policies instead of

A number of emerging-market countries sought to bank capital inflows in the 1990s. They were concerned to guard against a cessation of the inflows but had additional objectives. Because those countries depended heavily on export-led development, the countries sought to preserve the price competitiveness of their export industries—to hold down the prices of their currencies and the domestic currency prices of their exports. In several cases, moreover, intervention to keep the exchange rate stable was seen as a way of conferring credibility on the central bank's commitment to combat inflation.

When a capital inflow is expected to endure, a strong case can be made for spending the inflow by letting the trade balance deteriorate. Two strategies will accomplish that end: letting the domestic currency appreciate, or intervening to prevent it from appreciating but letting domestic prices rise by allowing the monetary effects of intervention to fuel an increase of lending and spending. Both strategies involve an appreciation of the price-adjusted or *real* exchange rate, but an appreciation of the *nominal* rate may be the better strategy. It is easier to reverse if the capital inflow ends unexpectedly. Furthermore, a onetime increase in domestic prices can ignite an inflationary spiral.

The Crucial Question of Sustainability

It is, of course, impossible for a government to know whether to bank or spend a capital inflow without knowing how long it will last—something no one can know with certainty. Therefore, a prudent government will do some of both; and that was the strategy adopted by many developing countries in the 1980s and early 1990s (see Bosworth and Collins 1999). It is nevertheless essential to form some sort of judgment about the sustainability of a capital inflow in order to assess the long-term viability of a country's policies, its real exchange rate, or its current account deficit. This obvious point is often ignored, however, even by many economists. They still tend to equate appreciation with overvaluation, to treat a current account deficit as a symptom of unsound domestic policies, and thus to regard a capital inflow as a dubious substitute for the elimination of a current account deficit.

These views may have been sensible in the 1970s and 1980s, when capital flows were driven by trade flows. Developing countries sought capital inflows to cover their trade deficits—and most of the inflows went directly to the countries' governments. But in the 1990s, trade flows were driven by capital flows. Emerging-market countries ran current account

---

relying mainly on sterilized intervention; see, e.g., Schadler et al. (1993) and Montiel (1996). Sterilization is sometimes said to raise domestic interest rates, but that is not strictly true. More accurately, it will prevent interest rates from falling, as they would as the result of nonsterilized intervention; see Kenen (1981, 1993) and Frankel (1997).

deficits because they were attracting capital inflows—and most of the inflows went directly to the private sector.[5] In these new circumstances, it was no longer possible to assess the viability of a country's situation without first assessing the long-term outlook for the capital account.

All too often capital inflows end abruptly, for unanticipated reasons. That is what happened to Mexico in 1994. But something can perhaps be learned about the medium-term outlook by assessing the relevant pull and push factors and by examining the composition of the capital inflow itself. During the Asian crisis, for example, flows of foreign direct investment were remarkably stable, whereas interbank flows were very volatile. Pondering the long-run implications of an ongoing capital inflow may also yield clues. Will a country be able to service its external debt, given the rate at which the capital inflow is adding to that debt compared to the rate at which it is raising the country's capital stock and its future output?[6] Has the real appreciation of the country's currency depressed the level or the growth rate of domestic output? If so, confidence in the continuity of the country's policies may be undermined, making it less attractive to foreign investors.[7]

To assess sustainability one must also ask how capital inflows are used. It is not enough to favor investment over consumption. The quality of the investment matters too, as it affects not only future output but also the domestic financial system. When banks and other domestic lenders are flooded with loanable funds, thanks to a capital inflow, they are apt to behave imprudently, and that temptation may be irresistible when lenders are protected by governmental guarantees—explicit or implicit—and are not closely supervised. Under those circumstances, a large capital inflow is likely to reduce the quality of loans and the productivity of the

---

5. Bosworth (1998) makes the same point. Nevertheless, the old view crops up repeatedly; see, e.g., Feldstein (1998), who says that Thailand had to attract foreign capital to cover its current account deficit. It has been equally hard to banish the so-called Lawson Doctrine, which holds that a capital inflow should not cause concern when it offsets a private-sector deficit (an excess of private investment over private saving) but should cause grave concern when it offsets a public-sector deficit. Although the Asian countries did not have large public-sector deficits, we know now that they should have been concerned about the size of the capital inflows they were experiencing in the mid-1990s.

6. For theoretical and empirical work on the dimensions of sustainability, see Milesi-Ferretti and Razin (1996, 2000); for applications, see Edwards (1999b) on Mexico, and Corsetti, Pesenti, and Roubini (1998b) on the Asian countries.

7. Dornbusch, Goldfajn, and Valdés (1995) focus on this question in their analysis of the Mexican crisis; in their view, the slow growth of the Mexican economy in the mid-1990s was due largely to the real appreciation of the peso, and slow growth would lead eventually to a reduction of capital inflows. Yet they are unduly dismissive of the point made here. Without running a large current account deficit and, to that end, letting the peso appreciate in real terms, Mexico could not have spent a very large part of the capital inflow it attracted in the early 1990s.

projects they finance. This moral hazard problem will be compounded when lenders believe that their debtors are likewise protected by governmental guarantees—that they are too big to fail or too well-connected politically. It will also be compounded when capital inflows reflect the relaxation of restrictions on the activities of banks and other lenders unaccompanied by an intensification of prudential supervision. Facing new opportunities on both sides of their balance sheets, new ways of obtaining loanable funds, and new ways of using them, lenders may abuse those opportunities if they are not properly supervised. Taken together, these institutional shortcomings can cause a banking crisis that can lead, in turn, to a currency crisis that aggravates the banking crisis.[8]

The Mexican Crisis of 1994-95

Banking crises often come before currency crises, but that was not true in the Mexican case. Although Mexican banks were in trouble before the onset of the crisis, the currency crisis came first. It began to build up in the spring of 1994, with the assassination of Luis Donaldo Colosio, the presidential candidate of the PRI.[9] Net portfolio investment in Mexico fell from $8 billion in the first quarter of 1994 to $1.5 billion in the second quarter, and it did not recover thereafter (see table 2.2). In the fourth quarter, moreover, there was a large capital outflow that led to a sharp drop in reserves, and the Mexican authorities sought to engineer a modest devaluation of the peso. But the devaluation did not restore confidence; on the contrary, it led to more capital outflows. Mexico's reserves fell by $4 billion in the two days following the devaluation, and its remaining

---

8. Kaminsky and Reinhart (1999) examine the links between financial liberalization and banking crises and the connections between banking and currency crises; they find that the majority of banking crises covered by their study led to currency crises. See also Demirgüç-Kunt and Detragiache (1998) and Goldstein (1998). Adapting a model developed by Kiyotaki and Moore (1997), Edison, Luangaram, and Miller (2000) show how volatile capital flows and exchange rate changes amplify procyclical swings in credit flows and asset values and how this phenomenon helps explain the severity of the Asian crisis.

9. There were other political shocks in 1994: rebels in Chiapas seized six towns in January; the secretary general of the PRI was assassinated in September; and fighting erupted again in Chiapas on 19 December, one day before the devaluation of the peso. But Agénor (1995) found that the Colosio assassination was the only political shock that generated expectations of a devaluation; he also found that changes in economic fundamentals did not significantly affect those expectations. Yet Mexico's reserves started to fall steeply in October, well before the devaluation, and there is reason to believe that residents began to fear a devaluation before foreigners did; see IMF (1995) and Frankel and Schmukler (1996). And in the Mexican and Asian crises alike, the abrupt depreciations right after the crises began were due largely to foreign currency purchases by residents, including domestic banks that were trying to cover their foreign currency debts, not to currency speculation by hedge funds and other foreign investors; see Garber (1996), Garber and Lall (1998), and Eichengreen et al. (1998b).

Table 2.2 The balance of payments of Mexico, 1993-96 (quarterly data, millions of dollars)

Item	1993	1994:1	1994:2	1994:3	1994:4	1995:1	1995:2	1995:3	1995:4	1996:1	1996:2	1996:3	1996:4
Exports of goods FOB	12,972	13,776	15,068	15,064	16,974	18,787	19,631	20,087	21,036	21,870	23,607	24,247	26,275
Imports of goods FOB	16,342	18,073	19,618	19,859	21,796	18,190	17,033	17,873	19,358	19,936	21,410	22,835	25,288
Trade balance	−3,370	−4,297	−4,550	−4,794	−4,822	597	2,599	2,215	1,678	1,934	2,197	1,413	987
Balance on goods, services, and income	−6,760	−7,593	−8,503	−8,957	−8,391	−2,228	−726	−1,525	−1,057	−1,106	−935	−2,019	−2,799
Current account balance	−5,850	−6,782	−7,476	−7,908	−7,496	−1,355	356	−450	−128	−105	296	−829	−1,691
Direct investment (net)	1,097	3,152	3,283	2,814	1,723	1,983	2,914	2,255	2,375	2,028	1,780	2,004	3,374
Portfolio investment (net)	7,089	7,983	1,540	3,257	−5,364	−7,517	−3,998	−414	1,552	1,303	2,913	9,007	738
Other investment (net)	254	664	−1,743	−1,635	113	−3,185	−1,447	−4,165	−840	−3,826	−3,322	−8,687	−1,179
Monetary authorities	—	—	—	—	—	—	—	—	−788	−1,459	—	—	—
Government	−284	−1,471	−343	−262	−310	−863	−117	−2,477	47	145	−329	−8,308	−330
Banks	485	350	321	−953	2,196	−3,633	−1,741	−2,216	784	−1,900	−1,369	−1,313	804
Other sectors	53	1,785	−1,721	−420	−1,774	1,311	412	528	−883	−612	−1,624	934	−1,653
Financial balance	8,440	11,799	3,080	4,436	−3,528	−8,719	−2,531	−2,324	3,088	−496	1,371	2,324	2,933
Net errors and omissions	−782	−4,534	−3,909	3,903	1,217	−1,924	690	543	−3,557	629	−1,479	−70	978
Overall balance	1,808	484	−8,305	430	−9,808	−11,998	−1,484	−2,232	−597	29	188	1,426	2,221
Increase (−) in reserve assets	−1,514	−107	8,654	−140	9,991	−691	−3,229	−4,666	−1,062	224	75	−175	−1,930
Use (+) of IMF credit	−294	−377	−348	−290	−183	7,452	−287	3,416	1,369	−253	−263	−1,250	−291
Exceptional financing	—	—	—	—	—	5,237	5,000	3,482	291	—	—	—	—

FOB = free on board

Note: Because of rounding, details may not add to totals given.

Source: International Monetary Fund.

Figure 2.1 Mexican exchange rate, 1994-97

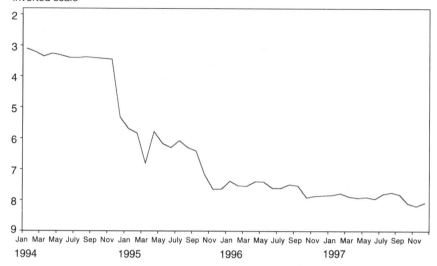

pesos per dollar,
inverted scale

Jan Mar May July Sep Nov | 1994
Jan Mar May July Sep Nov | 1995
Jan Mar May July Sep Nov | 1996
Jan Mar May July Sep Nov | 1997

Source: International Monetary Fund.

reserves were too small to defend the new exchange rate. Therefore, the peso was set free to float, and it began to depreciate rapidly (see figure 2.1).

The Transformation of the Crisis

The currency crisis turned quickly into a debt crisis. The short-term dollar-indexed *tesobonos* were designed to protect investors against exchange rate risk, but the methods by which they were issued and redeemed provided only imperfect protection (see Garber and Lall 1998). This was not a serious problem before the devaluation, when the day-to-day changes in the peso-dollar rate were quite small; it loomed very large, however, as soon as the peso was floated. At the first *tesobono* auction after the float began, investors bid for only $28 million of the $600 million on offer, and outcomes thereafter were not much better. Yet $9.8 billion of *tesobonos* were due to mature in the first three months of 1995, and another $6.4 billion in the following three months. Hence, the Mexican government faced a huge problem. If it could not roll over the *tesobonos*, the budgetary cost of redeeming them would be enormous; the cost of redeeming the $9.8 billion due to mature right away would have exceeded 50 billion pesos—an amount close to a quarter of the government's revenues in 1994.[10] And that was just part of the trouble. The maturing *tesobonos*

10. This calculation uses the exchange rate prevailing at the end of 1994, and the peso continued to depreciate thereafter; it also ignores the $6.4 billion of *tesobonos* maturing in the second quarter of 1995.

were held mainly by foreigners, who would have wanted to convert the proceeds into dollars, and Mexico did not have enough dollars. Its official reserves had fallen to $6.3 billion at the end of 1994. The result was a self-fulfilling debt crisis. As no holder of *tesobonos* could be sure that the rest would roll over their holdings, no one wanted to hold them.[11]

The rest of the story was told in chapter 1. After failing to obtain congressional support for US financial assistance to Mexico, the US Treasury joined with the IMF in assembling $50 billion of official financing.[12] Soon thereafter, the Mexican government announced a number of policy changes, including a tightening of fiscal policy and measures to combat inflation by limiting wage increases.

The official financing for Mexico was unique in more than its unprecedented amount. Although other crisis-stricken countries obtained large-scale official financing in subsequent years, the amounts involved were not intended—nor were they sufficient—to pay off those countries' short-term foreign debts. The size of the Mexican package, by contrast, was meant to extinguish the whole stock of *tesobonos*, to help Mexico cope with large dollar withdrawals from its banking system, and to help it rebuild its reserves.

Mexico's banking system was fragile before the currency crisis. In fact, its fragility is often cited to explain why the Bank of Mexico failed to raise interest rates in 1994, when US short-term rates were rising. But the currency crisis made matters worse. Mexican banks had large foreign currency debts, as well as large foreign currency claims on domestic firms that could not meet their obligations after the peso began to depreciate. Furthermore, Mexican interest rates soared during the currency crisis, doing great damage to debtors, as most bank loans in Mexico have variable interest rates. In the Mexican case, then, the currency crisis was due in part to financial fragility; but it produced a full-fledged banking crisis that led to a sharp contraction of domestic lending and a very large fall in output in 1995.[13] Real gross domestic product fell by 15 percent from

---

11. In the model proposed by Cole and Kehoe (1996), cited above, there are two equilibria—one in which all investors roll over their *tesobonos* and one in which they try to redeem them. The shift from the first to the second is triggered by a "sunspot" variable. The real-world counterpart of that adverse shock was, of course, the December devaluation, which led to the unsuccessful *tesobono* auctions. See also Sachs, Tornell, and Velasco (1996b).

12. This total included $7.8 billion already committed by the IMF. It also included $10 billion from the Bank for International Settlements (BIS) and $3 billion from commercial banks, but those parts of the package were never utilized.

13. See Mishkin (1996, 1999) for ways in which the interest rate and balance sheet effects of a currency crisis disrupt domestic credit flows, causing a financial crisis and depressing economic activity. The same sorts of disruption occurred during the Asian crisis. In fact, the balance sheet problems of the Asian banks are given a very prominent role in most accounts of the Asian crisis—a much larger role than the comparable troubles of the Mexican banks, which were overshadowed by the urgency and size of the *tesobono* problem. In the Asian case, however, the banks' difficulties played a major role in triggering the crisis.

the fourth quarter of 1994 to the third quarter of 1995, although it recovered rapidly thereafter.

An Explanation of the Crisis

Capital flows to Mexico began to grow rapidly in the early 1990s. In fact, net capital flows to Mexico accounted for roughly a fifth of total net flows to developing countries in 1990-93 (IMF 1995). Mexico had been the first country to issue Brady bonds, which reduced, consolidated, and partially collateralized Mexico's debt to foreign banks—the overhang from the debt crisis of the 1980s. Mexico had also embarked on ambitious reforms— deregulation, privatization, and trade liberalization—and would soon subscribe to the North American Free Trade Agreement (NAFTA). Furthermore, it had dismantled most of its capital controls in order to qualify for membership in the Organization for Economic Cooperation and Development (OECD). Finally, Mexico had adopted a comprehensive strategy for reducing inflation, based on a commitment to exchange rate stability and on the annual *pacto*—an agreement involving the government, business, and the trade unions, which aimed at coordinating wage, price, and exchange rate developments. By most measures, moreover, Mexico was following a prudent fiscal policy.[14] There was thus much talk of a "Mexican miracle," although Mexico's performance was less impressive than its reform program promised.[15]

Because of its commitment to exchange rate stability, the Bank of Mexico did not let capital inflows drive up the price of the peso in the foreign exchange market; it engaged in sterilized intervention and built up its reserves. But as the capital inflow continued, a growing share was offset by Mexico's trade deficit, which rose from less than $1 billion in 1990 to $18.5 billion in 1994. Furthermore, the peso was appreciating in real terms—a familiar characteristic of an exchange rate-based stabilization. Although the inflation rate was falling steadily, the inertial nature of inflation, reinforced by backward-looking wage indexation, prevented it from falling fast enough to preclude a large cumulative increase in the Mexican price level and a significant appreciation of the real exchange rate.

For Rudiger Dornbusch, Ilan Goldfajn, and Rodrigo Valdés (1995), who describe this process, the real appreciation of the peso, taken together with the growing trade deficit, proved that the peso was hugely overvalued by

---

14. Leiderman and Thorne (1996) argue, however, that lending by the Mexican development banks should be treated as quasi-fiscal spending and that the increase of that lending in and after 1993 had weakened the country's fiscal stance.

15. On the "invention" of the Mexican miracle, see Edwards (1997, 1-4), who describes the large gap between promise and performance and the more dramatic gap between "modern Mexico, on the verge of entering the first world" and "quasi-feudal Mexico, with its sorrow and frustration."

the mid-1990s; this, they say, was the main cause of the peso crisis. Although the real appreciation was indeed a by-product of the exchange-rate-based stabilization, not of the capital inflow itself, one cannot definitively conclude that the peso was overvalued. Recall the point made earlier: normative judgments about the real exchange rate and the current account balance cannot be made in isolation. One must also ask whether a country should bank a large part of a capital inflow, because the inflow is unlikely to continue, or spend a large part of the inflow (as Mexico did) by letting its real exchange rate appreciate and causing its current account to deteriorate.

One can perhaps argue that the Mexican authorities should have been less optimistic about the sustainability of the capital inflow (see Edwards 1997). Had they taken a more cautious view, however, they would have been forced to devalue the peso in, say, 1993, in order to reduce the current account deficit and bank a bigger portion of the capital inflow. They could not have allowed the peso to float; it would have appreciated in nominal terms instead of depreciating, thereby causing an even larger real appreciation.[16] They might have tried to limit the capital inflow by reimposing the capital controls that they had just dismantled, but that would have jeopardized Mexico's membership in the OECD. They should perhaps have tried less hard to propagate faith in the Mexican miracle. But politicians—least of all fervent reformers like those on the Mexican team—are never willing to sell their own policies short.

It may be more useful to ask what could have been done in 1994, when rising interest rates in the United States and political uncertainties in Mexico itself combined to call into question the sustainability of the capital inflow. The Bank of Mexico should have let Mexican interest rates rise, not with the aim of sustaining the inflow but rather to check the growth of domestic demand and thus slow the growth of imports. At the very least, the central bank should have refrained from sterilizing fully the liquidity-reducing effects of its dollar sales in the foreign exchange market during the spring of 1994, when it intervened to support the peso.[17] It was unwise, moreover, to issue additional *tesobonos* when foreigners started to run down their holdings of peso-denominated government debt. And Mexico should have devalued the peso in October, when it weakened

---

16. The same point is made by Fischer (1996), and I am inclined to agree with his general judgment that Mexico might have come through unscathed had it not suffered a run of bad luck—the set of political shocks that began with the Colosio assassination and continued until the day before the devaluation.

17. This point also is made by G. Calvo and Mendoza (1996), who carry the argument further. Having found that rising US interest rates reduce the demand for money in Mexico, they conclude that additions to the domestic assets of the Bank of Mexico did not merely offset contemporaneous reserve losses but led to further reserve losses.

again, as Mexico still had sufficient reserves to defend a new, lower exchange rate.[18]

It would have been hard to take these steps, however, during the run-up to a national election; and it was not much easier right after the election, when the outgoing government was still in charge and was loath to countenance an implicit repudiation of its previous policies.[19]

The Tequila Effect

The Mexican crisis was contagious. Stock prices fell sharply in Argentina and Brazil after the Mexican devaluation; spreads on Brady bonds rose abruptly, especially those of Argentina, Brazil, and the Philippines. The Argentine peso and Thai baht came under attack, along with the Brazilian real, Philippine peso, and Hong Kong dollar. Argentina was the principal victim of the "tequila effect," losing more than a third of its currency reserves in the three months following the Mexican devaluation. There were large flows of funds out of Argentine assets and out of Argentine banks, and one bank was shut down. And though the so-called tequila effect wore off rather rapidly in most of the affected countries, Argentina suffered a full-fledged banking crisis and had to seek assistance from the IMF and World Bank.

Previous empirical research on contagion had emphasized trade links among the affected countries.[20] But these cannot possibly account for the strength of the tequila effect on Argentina; it does not trade much with Mexico, and the two countries are not close competitors in third countries' markets. And the same can be said of Mexico's trade links with the other victims of the Mexican crisis.[21] It would thus appear that the tequila effect

---

18. On the case for an earlier devaluation and the debate about it in academic and official circles, see Delong and Eichengreen (2001).

19. There is indeed a clear link between the uncertainties surrounding elections and the incidence of financial crises. Mei (1999) examines nine crisis in 1994-97 and finds that eight of them occurred just before or after an election, and the election effect is significant even after controlling for the influence of economic vulnerability. It is also easy to find sources of political uncertainty in most of the countries hit by the Asian crisis: in Thailand, the fall of the government and the rapid turnover of finance ministers; in Indonesia, the illness of President Suharto; in Korea, the statements of the incoming President, Kim Dae-jung, before and after his election. No IMF program, even one flawlessly designed and fully financed, could have produced a rapid revival of confidence amidst those uncertainties.

20. See, e.g., Eichengreen, Rose, and Wyplosz (1996) and Eichengreen and Rose (1999).

21. Glick and Rose (1999) find that trade links do indeed help account for the tequila effect, but their results may reflect their ways of measuring contagion. When they measure contagion by the size of the depreciation in the victim's currency, they find that trade links play a major role; when they measure it by the amount of exchange market pressure, they find that those links play a minor role. Their analysis of the case of Argentina, with weak trade links to Mexico, is consistent with those findings. When they use their first definition of contagion, they find that Argentina was unaffected (because its currency did not depreci-

traveled mainly through asset-market channels. Investors retreated from many emerging-market countries, but mainly from countries with vulnerabilities resembling those of Mexico—pegged exchange rates, weak banks, and low reserves.[22]

The Asian Crisis of 1997-98

Many attempts have been made to blame the Asian crisis on some fatal defect in the public policies and private-sector practices of the Asian countries. Most have focused on the use and abuse of government guarantees, explicit or implicit, to domestic banks and their corporate customers. Michael Dooley (1999, 2000b) argues that a crisis had to occur as soon as the governments' contingent liabilities implied by those guarantees came to exceed the governments' assets. At that point, the guarantees ceased to be credible, and capital inflows gave way to capital outflows.[23] Craig Burnside, Martin Eichenbaum, and Sergio Rebelo (1998) add one step. When guarantees get very large, the government cannot honor them without running a budget deficit; and when the prospective deficit gets very big, the government must switch from debt financing to money financing. There will then be inflation and currency depreciation. But the anticipation of those events will trigger a currency crisis before they have run their course.[24]

Ronald McKinnon and Huw Pill (1998, 1999) and Paul Krugman (1998b) also emphasize the role of guarantees but tell a different story. Instead

---

ate); when they use their second definition, they find that Argentina suffered severely (because it experienced severe exchange market pressure). But Glick and Rose deserve much credit for being among the first to stress the regional nature of contagion.

22. See Sachs, Tornell, and Velasco (1996a). Frankel and Schmukler (1998) also stress the adverse shift in investors' views, but they find that views about a particular country reflect the country's fundamentals. They also find that the Mexican crisis directly affected investors' views about other Latin American countries but only indirectly affected their views about Asian countries, via its impact on Latin America. Tornell (1999) makes a related point: as lending booms occurred in Latin America before they occurred in Asia, the Mexican crisis hit Latin American countries harder than Asian countries, whereas the Thai crisis hit Asian countries harder than Latin American countries.

23. See also Dooley and Walsh (1999) and Chinn, Dooley, and Shrestha (1999). Irwin and Vines (1999) enrich the story by adding a point ascribed below to McKinnon and Pill and to Krugman. The excessive investment induced by guarantees has two crisis-inducing effects: it raises the government's contingent liabilities and also raises the probability that the government will have to honor them.

24. For similar stories, see Corsetti, Pesenti, and Roubini (1998a) and Calomiris (1998a). Buch and Heinrich (1999) tell a different forward-looking story: the expectation of a devaluation or depreciation reduces the expected net worth of domestic banks having large foreign currency debts, making it harder for those banks to roll over their debts and raising the risk of a banking crisis along with a currency crisis.

of assuming with Dooley and others that foreign investors can keep close track of a government's contingent liabilities and will therefore flee a country as soon as those liabilities exceed the government's assets, they stress the effects of guarantees on capital formation and the realized rate of return. As firms will be encouraged to undertake projects likely to yield low rates of return (what Krugman describes as "Panglossian investment"), the guarantees will have to be honored eventually. When the government cannot honor them fully, confidence and capital formation will collapse and capital inflows will be reversed.

These stories help us understand aspects of the Asian crisis. They can explain why the productivity of new investment fell in several Asian countries during the years before the crisis (see Corsetti, Pesenti, and Roubini 1998b). They can also explain why the Asian crisis led to a sharp contraction of capital formation and a large fall in output. Finally, they help explain why the IMF and others responded to the crisis by calling on Asian governments to end what the various models describe generically as implicit guarantees—to eliminate government-directed lending that was by its nature guaranteed, to sever incestuous links between borrowers and lenders, and to introduce and enforce bankruptcy regimes so as to keep insolvent firms from walking away from their debts. Pedro Alba et al. (1999) provide a long list of the objectionable policies and practices.

It is very hard to believe, however, that the Thai crisis erupted simply because foreign investors realized suddenly that the Thai government's contingent liabilities were too big to be honored—or that the attempt to honor them would lead to budget deficits, inflation, and currency depreciation. In fact, it is hard to believe that foreign investors were able to measure and thus add up the government's liabilities. Some liabilities, such as subsidies, had well-defined cash values, but it would have been impossible to attach cash values to other important forms of preferential treatment. What would be the ultimate cost of regulatory forbearance or, for that matter, the cost of future guarantees for some or all of the liabilities of some or all of the Thai banks? No one could know precisely when the Thai government's contingent liabilities had outrun its assets.

The Asian crisis must therefore be explained as the joint result of premature capital account liberalization, inadequate policy responses to the ensuing capital inflow and buildup of foreign currency debt, faulty exchange rate policies, and—last but not least—faith in the immortality of the Asian miracle that led to excessive investment in a handful of cyclically sensitive export industries and in commercial construction. And the subsequent spread of the crisis, first from Thailand to its neighbors, then northward to Korea, can best be explained by panic and herd behavior, when foreign investors began to see that countries quite different in many respects had bad things in common.

Without prejudging the issue raised at the start of this chapter—whether the Asian crisis was inevitable and would have started elsewhere had it not started in Thailand—let us look first at events in Thailand, then track the spread of the crisis to other Asian countries. What were the proximate causes of the Thai crisis? Why was it so contagious? Why did it do so much damage to the real economies of the crisis-stricken countries?

How the Crisis Started

Thailand began to experience a capital inflow in the early 1990s and, like Mexico, started out by banking a large portion of the inflow. It held the baht-dollar exchange rate virtually constant after 1990 and built up its foreign exchange reserves, which rose from $9.5 billion at the end of 1989 to $28.9 billion at the end of 1994. But the capital inflow rose hugely in 1995; and though there was another big increase in reserves, there was also a large increase in the current account deficit, which rose to 8 percent of GDP. Beginning in 1994, moreover, there was a significant change in the composition of the capital inflow. The net foreign currency debt of Thai banks grew by only $3.3 billion in 1993 but rose by $13.3 billion in 1994 and by another $10.5 billion in 1995. This surge followed the opening of the Bangkok International Banking Facility (BIBF), which was ostensibly meant to attract offshore banking to Thailand but served mainly as a vehicle for channeling foreign currency credit to domestic borrowers.[25]

---

25. On the role of the BIBF, see Alba et al. (1999). Thai banks were not allowed to incur unhedged foreign currency debts, but they could treat foreign currency claims on Thai residents as offsets to their foreign currency debts; see Brealey (1999). Thai branches of Japanese banks played a large role in this process. A similar process was at work in Korea, where the foreign branches of Korean banks served as conduits for foreign currency loans to Korean firms; see Dooley and Shin (2000). Bernard and Bisignano (1999) note that these forms of intermediation altered fundamentally the character of interbank lending. Previously it had served as a marginal funding source for large banks in the industrial countries, but in the 1990s it became a principal funding source for Thai and Korean banks. Those banks had low credit ratings, even before the Asian crisis (Bosworth 1998), but the suppliers of interbank credit behaved as though there had been no change in the riskiness of interbank lending. Giannini (1999) suggests that the surge of interbank lending was due partly to the statement in the "widely read" Rey Report (Group of 10 1996) that interbank credits should be excluded from any future restructuring of private-sector debt. But the growth of interbank lending began before the Rey Report appeared—which was, in fact, *not* widely read. Bordo and Schwartz (1998) are among those who take the opposite tack, asserting that foreign investors ignored the main message of the Rey Report, which warned that large-scale official financing would not be forthcoming routinely; others have argued that the fall in spreads on emerging-market debt after the Mexican crisis reflected the effect of moral hazard. Zhang (1999) argues, however, that the fall in spreads reflected a general shift in capital-market conditions, as there was also a fall in spreads on corporate debt in the industrial countries. After controlling for that shift and for economic fundamentals in emerging-market countries, Zhang finds that there was a residual *increase* in spreads on emerging-market debt and no significant impact of the Mexican crisis itself. For other reasons to doubt that the Mexican rescue led to the subsequent Asian crisis, see Mussa (1999) and Mussa et al. (2000). But see Dell' Ariccia, Godde, and Zettelmeyer (2000), who raise serious questions about previous work on this issue.

There was, as a result, an acceleration of credit creation, despite attempts by the Bank of Thailand to sterilize the monetary impact of the capital inflow.[26]

Although capital inflows peaked in 1995, they stayed at high levels in 1996, despite a deterioration in economic and financial conditions. Thai equity prices fell sharply in 1996, followed by property prices, and the fall in property prices was—or should have been—a warning of trouble ahead. Large amounts of lending by Thai banks and finance companies had been secured by real estate. There was, in fact, pressure on the baht in mid-1996, after one Thai bank collapsed. And there was trouble looming on the real side, too. After rising rapidly for several years, the dollar value of Thai exports fell in 1996, because of the recession in Japan, the appreciation of the baht (caused by the appreciation of the dollar vis-à-vis the yen), the global glut in markets for computer chips, and new Chinese competition in some of Thailand's export markets.[27] The reduction in Thai exports reflected falling export prices as well as falling volume, and it cast doubt on the outlook for export-led growth.

The situation in Thailand did not go unnoticed. The managing director of the IMF expressed his concern to the Thai authorities, and IMF officials traveled to Bangkok to convey the same message (see Eichengreen 1999b). In Thailand itself, moreover, there was growing concern about the banks and finance companies. In February 1997, the largest finance company, Finance One, sought a merger with a bank to stave off collapse. In March, the government suspended stock-market trading in the shares of financial institutions but failed to take stronger measures. Even after the baht collapsed in July, it did not move decisively to close insolvent institutions (see, e.g., Haggard 2000).

Pressures on the baht built up in May 1997, and the central bank responded by intervening heavily on the spot and forward markets. It also introduced capital controls to segment domestic and offshore markets. Foreigners, including hedge funds, took on short positions; but much of the pressure on the baht reflected foreign currency purchases by Thai residents, who were seeking to cover their foreign currency debts (which they continued to do after the baht was set free to float, prolonging

---

26. It should be noted, moreover, that sterilization could not keep foreign currency inflows passing through the BIBF from causing domestic credit creation. A foreign currency loan to a Thai resident made by a bank in the BIBF could not raise the reserves of the Bank of Thailand until that Thai resident sold the foreign currency proceeds for domestic currency. Hence, a full round of credit creation had to occur before the central bank had any reason to sterilize the monetary impact of the foreign currency inflow.

27. Diwan and Hoekman (1999) emphasize the impact of Chinese competition and the weakness of the yen but argue that the latter affected Korea and Taiwan more severely than the Southeast Asian countries. Baig and Goldfajn (1999) argue that the weakening of the yen came too early to bear responsibility for the deterioration in the export performance of Thailand and its neighbors.

Figure 2.2 Asian exchange rates, 1996-2000

national currency units per US dollar (1996:1=100),
inverted scale

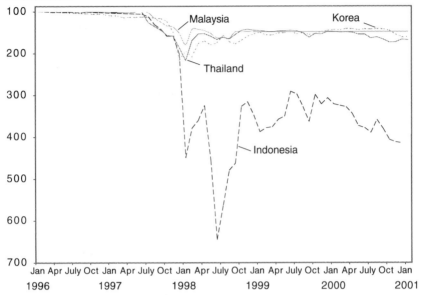

Source: International Monetary Fund.

the depreciation of the currency).[28] By the beginning of July, Thailand's reserves were all but exhausted; those that remained were barely sufficient to match the forward contracts made by the Bank of Thailand.[29] Therefore, the baht was cut loose from the dollar on 2 July and allowed to float. It depreciated promptly by more than 10 percent and, like the Mexican peso before it, continued to depreciate for several months thereafter (see figure 2.2). Having announced a policy package that failed to halt the depreciation, Thailand turned to the IMF. After arduous negotiations, the Fund approved a three-year standby arrangement amounting to $4 billion; funding was also provided by the World Bank, Asian Development Bank, and a group of governments led by Japan.[30]

The large amount of official financing—it totaled $17.2 billion—came as a surprise to those who had read the Rey Report (Group of 10 1996)

---

28. Ito (1999) asserts that hedge funds led the attack on the baht, but Eichengreen et al. (1998b) find that they played a small role—and an even smaller role in subsequent attacks on other Asian currencies. For more on the role of hedge funds in these and other episodes, see De Brouwer (2001), who attaches more importance to them.

29. The central bank's forward commitments were not made public at the time, but well-informed market participants must have been aware of the bank's high-risk strategy; they bet against it heavily.

30. The Thai policy package approved by the Fund is summarized in Lane et al. (1999), together with those for Indonesia and Korea.

and taken it seriously. Why did the official community decide to provide large-scale financing after having warned investors not to count on it again? Four reasons have been given. First, there was fear of contagion. If foreign banks and other foreign creditors had been forced to roll over their claims on Thailand, they might have begun to withdraw from other Asian countries. Second, the Rey Report had dealt mainly with sovereign debt, not private-sector debt, and it would have been hard to compel private-sector debtors to halt their debt payments; the Rey Report itself had warned that capital controls might be needed to enforce a suspension of private-sector payments. Furthermore, the Rey Report had explicitly advised against interfering with interbank debt, which was the largest and most volatile component of Thailand's short-term foreign debt.[31] Third, there were worries about the fragility of the Japanese banks, which were large lenders to Thailand. Fourth, it would have taken time to devise and implement a suspension of debt payments—and time was running out for Thailand, because its currency was depreciating rapidly and it had virtually no reserves.[32]

How the Crisis Spread

The problems faced by Thailand in 1996 and early 1997 had little effect on other emerging-market countries, even within Asia. Some of its neighbors did not suffer a similar slowdown of exports, few of them had overvalued currencies, and none had a comparable current account deficit.[33] Equity prices were still rising in most other Asian countries, and

31. In mid-August, Japanese banks promised informally that they would refrain from reducing their claims on their own Thai branches—but those promises were not honored fully, and Thailand obtained no such promises regarding Japanese claims on the Thai banks themselves; see Lane et al. (1999), who note that creditors' decisions in matters of this sort will always depend on their views about the various debtors involved as well as about the debtor country itself. (In the case of Korea, discussed later, the government solved this problem by guaranteeing the banks' debts.) Despite the informal promises just mentioned, interbank claims on Thailand fell by almost $16 billion in the second half of 1997 and by $12 billion more in the first half of 1998 (BIS, *International Banking and Financial Market Developments*, November 1998).

32. Some of those close to the negotiations give a fifth reason for the decision to provide large-scale official financing: the Japanese government wanted to demonstrate that it could mobilize support for Thailand, much as the United States had mobilized support for Mexico. (They also note that the Thai authorities said at the time and thereafter that the amount of official financing was too small, given the size of Thailand's short-term external debt—that Thailand had been underfinanced relative to Mexico.)

33. Using purchasing-power-parity calculations, Chinn (1998) found that the Thai baht, Malaysian ringgit, and Philippine peso were overvalued in mid-1997, but by small amounts. Using model-based calculations, he found that the ringgit and baht were overvalued, along with the currencies of Singapore and Taiwan. But none of his calculations showed that the Indonesian rupiah was overvalued, and they all showed that the Korean won was

their currencies were still strong. Equity prices were falling in Korea, however, because corporate bankruptcies were rising and the won was being allowed to depreciate gradually. In fact, Korea was starting to lose reserves (but was concealing its losses).

Some countries' currencies came under pressure as the Thai crisis approached, but the pressures were contained by intervention, higher interest rates, and, in the Malaysian case, restrictions on nonresidents' use of swap transactions. Once the baht started to depreciate, however, other Asian currencies came under severe pressure, starting with the Philippine peso. On 11 July, less than two weeks after the baht was set free to float, the Philippine central bank widened the band within which the peso was allowed to fluctuate; three days later, the Philippines became the first crisis-stricken Asian country to receive financing from the IMF. On that same day, the Malaysian central bank ceased to defend the ringgit, but Malaysia did not seek help from the IMF.

The crisis continued to spread in August. There was a brief but sharp attack on the Hong Kong dollar, which was tied tightly to the US dollar by a currency board regime, and it led to a very sharp spike in short-term interest rates. On 14 August, moreover, the Indonesian central bank allowed the rupiah to float and adopted a tight monetary policy.[34] In light of what happened later, it is worth quoting the following assessment of Indonesia's initial response:

> [President] Suharto's initial approach to the crisis appeared both more decisive and coherent than the Chavalit or Kim government's [in Thailand and Korea, respectively] and more cooperative than the bellicose policy pronouncements of [Malaysian] Prime Minister Mahathir. In contrast to Thailand's costly and futile effort to defend the baht, Indonesia's response to regional contagion was to quickly widen the band within which the rupiah traded, and when this proved inadequate, to initiate a float. When the rupiah continued to fall, the central bank adopted an extremely tight monetary stance—well before going to the IMF—in a bid to support the currency. This policy had severe consequences for the already-fragile banking sector.
>
> Suharto's Independence Day speech in mid-August provided a sober assessment of the country's problems, and was followed by the creation of a special crisis management team headed by the widely respected technocrat Widjoyo Nitisastro. A wide-ranging set of policy measures followed in September. In early October,

---

undervalued. Other studies, however, reached different conclusions; see the survey in Edwards (1999b).

34. As Indonesia still had large reserves, the decision to let the rupiah float came as a surprise. In fact, Indonesia's involvement in the crisis was itself surprising. The model of currency and banking crises developed by Kaminsky (1998), drawing on work by Kaminsky, Lizondo, and Reinhart (1998), predicted the involvement of Thailand, Malaysia, and the Philippines, but not Indonesia. Ito (1999) described the decision to float the rupiah as precautionary. Williamson (1998) first called it unnecessary, but later (2000a) wrote that most of those familiar with events in Indonesia believed that the country's crawling-band regime could not withstand the pressure to which it was exposed.

two months after floating the rupiah, the government turned to the IMF. Although the negotiations were not without conflict, Indonesia was able to conclude an agreement much more rapidly than the Thai government. (Haggard 2000, 65)

Indonesia's initial agreement with the IMF provided $36 billion of official financing—including $10 billion from the Fund, $8 billion from the multilateral development banks, and $18 billion from foreign governments.[35] Indonesia agreed to maintain a tight monetary policy to stabilize the rupiah and limit the inflationary impact of the previous depreciation. It also agreed to tighten its fiscal stance, close insolvent banks, and adopt other measures designed to revive the financial sector and reform the corporate sector.

The rupiah strengthened in response to these commitments and to concerted intervention by Asian central banks, but it began to weaken again as bad news arrived. The closing of insolvent banks was poorly handled and undermined confidence in the banking system, as the government shut down 16 small banks without promising not to close others.[36] Furthermore, the central bank diluted its tight monetary policy by creating a special facility to inject liquidity into the banking system. And Suharto made matters worse by reversing his earlier decision to defer 15 large investment projects and by producing a new budget based on rosy suppositions about Indonesia's economic prospects. Markets expressed their doubts, as did the IMF, and the rupiah plummeted.[37] There was a bout of panic buying as food and fuel prices soared.

A new IMF program was signed by Suharto in mid-January, with the managing director of the IMF looking on. It was extraordinarily comprehensive and was clearly aimed at dismantling the economic empire of Suharto's family and friends. But it was attacked by his critics as well as his cronies, and Suharto started to backpedal again. Implementation lagged, and economic conditions worsened; inflation soared and output fell. The IMF program was suspended in March and revised in May, but the newly modified program was undermined by civil unrest and political turmoil.[38] As the rupiah continued to depreciate, moreover, Indonesian

---

35. In this and the subsequent Korean case, however, the bilateral money was meant to provide a second line of defense, whereas the bilateral money for Thailand was used in tandem with disbursements from the IMF; see Lane et al. (1999).

36. See Lane et al. (1999) and Haggard (2000). Caprio and Honohan (1999) believe that this step should have been taken sooner and that more banks should have been closed, so as to draw a clear line between sound and bad banks and to restore confidence in the former. De Gregorio, Eichengreen, Ito, and Wyplosz (1999) take the same view but praise the Indonesian approach, imperfect as it was, as having been better than the vacillating stance of the Thai authorities.

37. But see Radelet and Sachs (1998) for a more favorable assessment of Suharto's budget.

38. For more on these and subsequent events, see Haggard (2000).

corporations faced a gargantuan increase in the domestic currency cost of servicing their foreign debts. Unlike Thai firms, which had borrowed dollars from domestic banks, Indonesian firms had borrowed dollars from other countries' banks, including banks in Hong Kong. They tried at first to cover their forthcoming payments by selling rupiah for dollars, a tactic that inevitably served to hasten the collapse of the currency. And when they could no longer afford to do that, they defaulted on their debts. The resulting corporate debt problem has not been fully resolved, despite attempts to organize a comprehensive settlement.

And How the Crisis Went on Spreading

Meanwhile, the Asian crisis had migrated northward. On 20 October 1997, the Taiwan dollar was allowed to depreciate by about 6 percent. As Taiwan was not gravely affected by the Asian crisis, this event is sometimes ignored (but see Chote et al. 1998; Masson 1999). The reasons for it, moreover, remain rather obscure. The IMF mentions "exchange market pressures" (IMF 1997b), which Giancarlo Corsetti, Paolo Pesenti, and Nouriel Roubini (1998c) attribute to worries about a loss of competitiveness due to the large depreciations of other Asian currencies. Yet Taiwan might have resisted the attack on its currency, as it had huge reserves, and its decision had unfortunate consequences. The depreciation of the Taiwan dollar led immediately to an attack on the Hong Kong dollar. That attack was repelled by the workings of Hong Kong's currency board regime, but the resulting increase in short-term interest rates caused the Hong Kong stock market to fall precipitously, triggering a worldwide fall in stock prices. Furthermore, and more important, the depreciation of the Taiwan dollar drew attention to the vulnerability of Korea, which is closely competitive with Taiwan.

Several large Korean firms had run into serious problems early in 1997, and they were deeply indebted to Korean banks—which were, in turn, deeply indebted to foreign banks. Indeed, it can be argued that Korea was due for a homegrown currency crisis sooner or later. But the timing of the actual crisis can be ascribed to events elsewhere. At the end of October, shortly after the attack on the Hong Kong dollar and the worldwide fall in stock prices, the Korean won came under heavy pressure. Foreign banks ran down their claims on Korean banks and on their foreign branches, forcing those banks to buy dollars with which to repay their debts. The central bank came to their aid by selling them dollars directly and by depositing dollar reserves with their foreign branches. As a result, Korea's reserves, net of those deposits, fell by $15 billion during November (Hahm and Mishkin 2000).

On 20 November, the Korean authorities widened the band in which the won was allowed to fluctuate, and the won fell quickly to the edge of the new band. On the next day, Korea sought help from the Fund—which came through two weeks later. The IMF committed $21 billion (more than ever before), the multilateral development banks put up $14 billion, and foreign governments pledged an additional $23 billion as a second line of defense for the won. Korea undertook to tighten its monetary policy, abolish the band for the won, and introduce comprehensive reforms, including financial-sector reforms and further trade liberalization.

Nevertheless, foreign banks continued to run down their claims on Korea, and the first tranche of IMF credit, amounting to $9 billion, was used up in two weeks.[39] Accordingly, the Korean authorities asked the IMF to speed up the disbursement of the second tranche, and it also sought to draw down the bilateral credits set up by the major industrial countries. But the Fund and industrial countries refused to provide additional money until the major foreign banks had agreed to roll over the rest of their claims—and urged those banks to do that quickly. In a matter of days, the banks agreed and rolled over their interbank claims for three months, through the end of March, in exchange for a commitment by the Korean government to guarantee the ultimate repayment of those claims. A debt-monitoring system was set up at the Bank of Korea to police the agreement, and rollover rates rose "significantly" (Lane et al. 1999). At the end of March, moreover, the Korean government reached an agreement with 134 creditor banks from 32 countries, covering close to $22 billion of the short-term debt owed by the Korean banks. It was converted into government-guaranteed bonds with maturities ranging from one to three years and interest-rate spreads running from 2¾ percent over LIBOR (the London Interbank Offered Rate) for the one-year bond to 2¼ percent for the three-year bond.

More could be said about the evolution of the crisis, but narrative is not the main aim of this chapter. We turn instead to the other questions posed at the start of this section. Why was the crisis so contagious? Why did it cause so much damage to the Asian economies?

Contagion, Exchange Rates, and Output Effects

Contagion is not unusual and tends to be regional. Morris Goldstein (1998) points out, however, that the Asian case had a peculiar feature. It

---

39. The net claims of foreign banks fell by almost $12 billion during the fourth quarter of 1997 and by almost $16 billion during the first quarter of 1998 (BIS, *International Banking and Financial Market Developments*, December 1998). The 1998 rundown occurred despite the rollover agreement reached at the beginning of 1998. A significant part of the rundown represented attempts by Japanese banks to cut back their total loans, as they were incurring loan losses at home and abroad.

began in a fairly small country, Thailand, but infected a number of larger countries, such as Korea and Indonesia. Furthermore, the Asian currencies depreciated hugely—by more, for example, than the lira and the pound when they left the European Monetary System (EMS) in 1992.

Analyzing Contagion

A simple taxonomy provided by Paul Masson (1999) can help us sort out the reasons. There are, he says, monsoonal effects, spillover effects, and expectational effects.

Monsoonal effects are the manifestations of shocks coming from the outside world, mainly from developed countries. Because they can affect several countries simultaneously, producing co-movements in exchange rates, interest rates, equity prices, and other variables, their manifestations resemble contagion.[40] To identify true contagion, however, we must clearly distinguish between the common effects of shocks originating in the outside world and the effects of shocks originating in one of the affected countries.

Spillover effects are the manifestations of economic interdependence and represent true contagion. They can take several forms. A contraction of output and income in a crisis-stricken country will reduce its imports from neighboring countries. A depreciation of the country's currency will reinforce the import-reducing effect of the contraction in its income, and it will also have export-raising effects: first, it will stimulate the country's exports to its neighbors, depressing their import-competing industries; second, it will stimulate the country's exports to the outside world at the expense of its neighbors' exports.[41] Interdependence can operate through asset-market channels, too. When foreign or domestic investors suffer losses in one country, they may run down their claims on other countries, even when they have no reason to believe that they will suffer losses on those other claims; they may have to sell them merely to meet margin calls. Furthermore, investors may try to hedge against prospective losses in one vulnerable country by running down more liquid claims on other,

---

40. On asset price behavior during the Asian crisis, see Baig and Goldfajn (1999), who find that cross-country correlations of exchange rates and interest rate spreads rose significantly during the crisis. When they then allow for the effects of own-country news and of changes in economic fundamentals, they find strong cross-country effects on exchange rates and equity prices (but not on bond spreads). Forbes and Rigobon (1999) show, however, that changes in cross-country correlations may merely reflect the increased volatility of all asset prices, including the prices of commonly held assets, that often occurs during a crisis; they may not reflect an increase in the underlying interdependence of those asset prices.

41. Diwan and Hoekman (1999) examine the bilateral and third-country trade of the various Asian countries but do not assess the impact of the actual trade-flow changes on the spread of the Asian crisis.

similarly situated countries—a practice known as proxy hedging (see, e.g., BIS 1998; G. Calvo 1998; Goldstein 1998; White 1999).

Expectational effects are the manifestations of changes in investors' views. They may involve residents, as well as foreigners, and can take two forms. First, a crisis in one country may lead investors to reassess the economic outlook for seemingly similar countries. Second, a crisis in one country may reduce investors' tolerance for risk and thus cause them to run down their claims on many other countries. Masson describes the first phenomenon as a shift in a unique equilibrium, and the second as a jump between multiple equilibria.[42]

But we also need to distinguish between two quite different ways in which investors may be led to revise their views about a particular country. First, a crisis in one country can serve as a "wake-up call" (Goldstein 1998), causing investors to reassess the existing situation in some other country: it can draw their attention to vulnerabilities they have not noticed before. Second, a crisis in one country can cause investors to predict harmful spillover effects on some other country: they may conclude, for example, that a crisis-stricken country will reduce its imports and thereby reduce some other country's exports. This *anticipation* of spillover effects may have been the strongest cause of contagion during the Asian crisis— more powerful than the actual spillover effects. It may indeed afford the only plausible explanation for the speed with which the crisis spread across the region.

There were some monsoonal effects at the start of the Asian crisis: the Japanese recession, the appreciation of the dollar vis-à-vis the yen, and the fall in demand for Asia's electronic exports. But research on the migration of the crisis has focused mainly on true contagion—the spillover and expectational effects—rather than the common shocks.

Studies of earlier crises, including the EMS crisis of 1992-93, have found that trade-related spillover effects help explain contagion.[43] Two widely cited studies of the Asian crisis also stress trade effects. Reuven Glick and Andrew Rose (1999) show that one country is more likely to import a crisis from another if they have similar trade links with the outside world, and this result holds for the Asian crisis as well as for earlier crises.[44]

---

42. Note that herding can reinforce both of these expectational effects. When some investors start to sell off their claims on a particular country because they have grown more wary of its fundamentals or more risk averse, other investors may mimic them. Furthermore, G. Calvo and Mendoza (2000) have shown how globalization can raise the payoff from this behavior. By increasing the number of readily available country-specific assets, globalization reduces an investor's incentive to acquire costly information about a particular country or asset; the investor is more likely to act on the basis of free information alone—including unverified rumors and observed price changes reflecting the decisions of other investors (who may, of course, be doing the same thing).

43. See the studies cited in n. 20, above.

44. But see the comment on their methodology in n. 21, above.

Graciela Kaminsky and Carmen Reinhart (2000) devise country clusters based on the strength of countries' bilateral trade links and the extent to which they compete in third countries' markets. They find that two countries' membership in the same trade cluster raises the probability that one of them will import a crisis from the other.[45] In the same paper, however, Kaminsky and Reinhart formed other sorts of clusters, including clusters based on creditor-bank links, and they found that the creditor-bank clusters did better than the trade clusters in predicting the actual path of contagion during the Asian crisis. For this and other reasons, they conclude that financial-market links played a larger role than trade links in propagating the Asian crisis.[46]

Other studies stress expectational effects. Michael Bordo and Anna Schwartz (1998) and Morris Goldstein (1998) emphasize the wake-up call sent by the Thai crisis; investors were made to recognize the common and worrisome characteristics of several Asian countries—the sizes of their current account deficits and of their foreign currency debts, the flaws in their banking systems, and the pervasive effects of corruption (see also Chote et al. 1998; Eichengreen 1998; Kaminsky 1998). Henri Bernard and Joseph Bisignano (1999, 20) attribute the spread of the crisis to a shift in market sentiment "relatively unrelated to any change in fundamentals or arrival of new information." Taimur Baig and Ilan Goldfajn (1999) detect in their own empirical results "an element of financial panic" at the start of the crisis. Most of these accounts, however, focus on the attitudes and actions of foreign investors, especially those of the foreign banks that ran down their interbank claims. They pay insufficient attention to the activities of Asian banks and firms, which rushed to cover their foreign currency debts as soon as they saw what was happening in Thailand. We may never know which came first—the exit of the foreign banks or the scramble by Asian debtors to buy foreign currencies with which to repay their debts. But together, the two provide a parsimonious yet attractive explanation for the rapid migration of the Asian crisis and the huge depreciations of the Asian currencies.

---

45. When forming the clusters, moreover, Kaminsky and Reinhart study the commodity composition of the countries' exports as well as the countries to which they export.

46. Three other studies also emphasize trade links. Barth and Dinmore (1999) show that there was a large drop in the dollar prices of the Asian countries' exports and suggest that it may have been due to an intensification of competition among the crisis-stricken countries. Their finding, however, may say more about the effects than the causes of contagion. White (1999) concludes that third-market competition played a nontrivial role in propagating the Asian crisis; but like Kaminsky and Reinhart (2000), he appears to attach more weight to expectational effects and to asset-market spillover effects. Finally, Forbes (2001) shows that countries competing with exports from a crisis-stricken country or exporting heavily to it had lower stock-market returns. Insofar as stock-market returns are forward-looking variables, however, this result may reflect the *anticipation* of trade effects rather than their actual impact—the point made in the text above.

The Role of Exchange Rate Regimes

The exchange rate regimes of the Asian countries and their subsequent collapse played key roles in the crisis. At the end of 1996, the Philippine peso was listed by the IMF as floating independently; the Indonesian rupiah, Korean won, Malaysian ringgit, and Thai baht were listed as having "other managing floating" regimes. In fact, the ringgit and baht had been tied tightly to the US dollar for some years before the crisis; the peso and won had fluctuated modestly vis-à-vis the dollar; and the rupiah had been allowed to depreciate gradually in order to offset domestic inflation.[47]

Five features of the Asian crisis are often blamed on these exchange rate regimes. First, they exposed the Asian countries to large fluctuations in the yen-dollar rate; the appreciation of the dollar in 1995-97 is cited as having been especially harmful to the Asian countries' exports. Second, Asian banks and firms took the commitment to exchange rate stability as an invitation to engage in unhedged foreign currency borrowing; it was, in effect, an implicit guarantee of the sort so often cited in discussions of the Asian crisis. Third, Asian central banks were firmly committed to exchange rate stability and therefore had to intervene on foreign exchange markets to keep their currencies from appreciating, but they could not prevent the resulting increase in bank liquidity from fueling domestic lending and producing the property boom that weakened the balance sheets of the financial sector. Fourth, the Asian countries made the same mistake that Mexico had made in 1994: Thailand and Korea, in particular, defended their dollar exchange rates tenaciously until they ran out of reserves and could not prevent their currencies from depreciating hugely. Fifth, the depreciations of the Asian currencies were the immediate cause of the financial crisis—the implosion of bank lending and of other credit flows that depressed domestic investment and led to the steep fall in Asian output.

---

47. The IMF's characterization of exchange rate regimes was based at the time on each country's description of its own regime; the Fund did not start to make judgments of its own until 1999. McKinnon (1998, 2000) treats the five Asian countries as adhering to a dollar standard: their monetary policies stabilized their dollar exchange rates, and their link to the dollar was the nominal anchor for their domestic price levels. Others, such as Frankel and Wei (1994) and Takagi (1999), treat them for analytical purposes as "basket peggers" that put high weights on the dollar and low weights on the yen; see also Ito, Ogawa, and Sasaki (1998). McKinnon argues, however, that big dollar weights made sense, because much of Japan's trade with Asia is dollar-denominated. In fact, he recommends the restoration of the Asian dollar standard at the purchasing-power parities prevailing before the Asian crisis; otherwise, he warns, Asian countries might engage in predatory devaluations. He readily concedes that an Asian dollar standard cannot be robust unless Japan and the United States undertake to stabilize the yen-dollar rate, but that's what he would like them to do in any case.

The first assertion is rarely challenged, although questions can be raised about the extent to which the appreciation of the dollar slowed the growth of Asian exports and the extent to which the slower growth of exports contributed to the financial-sector problems that triggered the Thai crisis.[48]

The second assertion is made by Barry Eichengreen (1998), Morris Goldstein (1998), Pedro Alba et al. (1999), and others, and it is rarely challenged. But there are two objections to it. First, the foreign currency debts of Thai banks were covered in large part by their foreign currency claims on domestic firms; the firms were the ones with the unhedged debts. Yet Indonesian and Korean firms also took on large amounts of unhedged foreign currency debt, though the rupiah and won were less tightly tied to the dollar than was the Thai baht.[49] Second, some unhedged debt was yen debt, not dollar debt, and no Asian currency was pegged to the yen.[50]

---

48. See the papers cited in n. 28, above; see also Barth and Dinmore (1999), who emphasize the role of the Japanese recession rather than the depreciation of the yen vis-à-vis the dollar.

49. From 1992 to 1995, however, the standard deviation of the monthly percentage changes in the baht-dollar rate, at 0.47 percent, exceeded that for the rupiah-dollar rate, at 0.16 percent, and was not much smaller than that for the won-dollar rate, at 0.58 percent (Williamson 2000a). A similar result is obtained by G. Calvo and Reinhart (2000a), who compute the probability that the absolute monthly change in the dollar value of a country's currency will fall within various limits. These are their results for a set of 19 countries with "other managed floating rates" and for the three Asian countries individually:

| Country | Period | Probability that change will not exceed | |
		1.0 percent	2.5 percent
19-country average	Various	60.0	87.5
Indonesia	11/78-06/97	96.4	99.1
Korea	03/80-10/97	80.1	97.6
Thailand	01/70-06/97	93.6	98.5

The three Asian currencies have higher-than-average probabilities. Here again, however, the rupiah is the most stable in terms of the dollar; the baht is next; and the won comes last.

50. A third objection is raised by McKinnon (2000) and is echoed by Furman and Stiglitz (1998), as well as by Frankel, Schmukler, and Servén (2000). McKinnon points out that the cost of hedging should be low when a country's currency is credibly pegged. Conversely, it should be high and thus a deterrent to hedging when the peg is not credible—what McKinnon describes as a "bad" fix—or when the exchange is flexible and fluctuates widely. Therefore, he says, the failure by Asian firms to hedge foreign currency debt should not be blamed on exchange rate pegging per se; it should be blamed instead on the actual levels at which Asian rates were pegged, which raised the cost of hedging. However, there is a serious flaw in McKinnon's reasoning. If Asian exchange rates were bad fixes and this fact was reflected in the cost of hedging, market participants must have known that they were bad fixes and that the cost of hedging was not unreasonably high (given the risk that such fixes won't survive for long). But McKinnon makes another, more plausible point: Asian banks may have been induced to take on excessive risks, including exchange rate risks, because they believed that they were protected by broad guarantees. Giannini (1999, 36) makes the same point but stresses a different set of broad guarantees: "All arguments emphasizing local guarantees . . . run up against the difficulty of explaining how sophisticated international investors could be made to believe in [local] guarantees when they knew

Although these are valid objections, they do not banish the belief, shared by most observers, that greater exchange rate flexibility might have induced Asian borrowers—firms as well as banks—to hedge more of their foreign currency debts.

The third assertion made above is less controversial. If the Asian countries had let their currencies appreciate before the crisis, in response to the capital inflow, instead of intervening on foreign exchange markets, the capital inflow might not have caused the surge in domestic lending that led to the property boom. Furthermore, the inflow itself might have been smaller. Insofar as the central banks sterilized the effects of their interventions on the currency markets, they prevented domestic interest rates from falling. By seeking to peg their currencies, they thus sustained the interest rate differences that brought on the "carry trade" and the surge of interbank borrowing.

Regarding the fourth effect, the tenacity with which some Asian countries defended their currencies until they ran out of reserves, we should distinguish between the Thai case and all others. Pressures on the baht emerged months before the acute crisis of mid-1997. Accordingly, the Thai authorities might have engineered a modest devaluation and defended the baht thereafter (see Radelet and Sachs 1998). And had they done so, other Asian countries might have been able to defend their currencies. Once the baht had depreciated hugely, however, none of the neighboring countries could expect to engineer a small devaluation or contain a floating rate within a narrow range. The losses incurred by those who had to sell baht, in order pay off their dollar debts, served as a warning to the residents of other countries that they should move quickly to cover their own dollar debts. The result was an extremely inelastic demand for foreign currency that inevitably produced a sharp depreciation of the domestic currency once it was set free to float.[51] In December 1997, after the won was set free to float, Korea's attempt to limit the depreciation of the won exhausted its reserves in a couple of weeks, and even the arrival of IMF money did not stem the reserve loss.

---

that the respective country's external liabilities were denominated mostly in foreign ... currency." To an important extent, he says, imprudent borrowing by Asian banks must be blamed on their foreign counterparties and the guarantees available to them, not the guarantees enjoyed by the Asian banks.

51. See Grenville and Gruen (1999) for a similar interpretation. Corbett and Vines (1999) believe that the Asian countries could have stabilized their currencies had they followed the British example of 1992 and substituted inflation targeting for exchange rate targeting after letting their currencies float. But sterling had ceased to depreciate rapidly before Britain adopted inflation targeting. Similarly, in the case of Brazil the central bank did not start to pursue inflation targeting until the depreciation of the currency had slowed from a crash to a crawl.

Table 2.3 Change in real GDP of Indonesia, Korea, Malaysia, and Thailand, 1996-99 (percent)

Country	1996	1997	1998	1999
Indonesia	8.0	4.5	− 13.0	0.3
Korea	6.8	5.0	− 6.7	10.7
Malaysia	10.0	7.3	− 7.4	5.6
Thailand	5.9	− 1.7	− 10.2	4.2

Source: IMF (2000f).

Exchange Rates, Balance Sheets, and the Collapse of Investment

The final feature of the Asian crisis, the large fall in output, is commonly attributed to the collapse of domestic lending.[52] The output loss was very large indeed. Table 2.3 shows the percentage changes in real GDP.

Most analyses, moreover, blame the fall in output on the banking-sector problems that were an important cause of the Thai crisis, and a major consequence of other countries' crises.[53] But they disagree about the reasons for those banking-sector problems. Martin Feldstein (1998) and others point to high interest rates—which they blame on the IMF. As interest rates rose, they say, firms could not continue to service their debts. Bad loans built up on the books of the banks, which had to curtail their lending. Although all of this happened in Asia, it has also happened elsewhere without causing comparable damage. The unique feature of the Asian crisis was, once again, the huge depreciation of the Asian currencies, which had a devastating impact on the balance sheets of firms with large foreign currency debts. Firms that failed to cover them quickly, before their countries' currencies began to depreciate, could not afford to cover them later. And that, in turn, was one reason for their governments' reluctance to let go of their pegged exchange rates.

The balance sheet effects of high interest rates were featured initially in work by Ben Bernanke and Mark Gertler on the role of the so-called credit channel in transmitting the effects of monetary policy.[54] The corres-

---

52. The collapse of domestic credit flows also prevented Asian firms from exploiting the export opportunities afforded by the depreciations of their countries' currencies; see White (1999). This effect is often invoked to explain why the improvement in the current account balances of the Asian countries during 1998 resulted mainly from import contraction rather than export expansion. Barth and Dinmore (1999) show, however, that Indonesian, Korean, and Thai export volumes rose in 1998 and that the fall in their export receipts was due to a large fall in export prices; see also IMF (1998b).

53. See, e.g., Dekle and Kletzer (2001), who contrast Thailand and Korea, which had very serious banking-sector problems, with Malaysia, Taiwan, and Singapore, which did not. They attach particular importance to the differences between the supervisory regimes in the two groups of countries.

54. See Bernanke and Gertler (1995) and the earlier papers cited there.

ponding effects of currency depreciations have been featured in papers by Guillermo Calvo and Carmen Reinhart (2000c), Paul Krugman (2000), and others.[55] The Calvo-Reinhart and Krugman papers argue that a currency depreciation occurs endogenously when a capital inflow stops or gives way to a capital outflow and a country must therefore shift from current account deficit to current account surplus. In these equilibrium models, moreover, the depreciation is just large enough to make the necessary shift in the current account balance. But it does not operate in the usual way, by switching expenditure from foreign to domestic goods or from traded to nontraded goods—effects that stimulate output and income. Instead, it operates in a dysfunctional way by impairing the creditworthiness of firms with big foreign currency debts, preventing those firms from borrowing, and reducing capital formation—effects that depress output and income. Furthermore, the depreciations of the Asian currencies were far larger than those needed to make the necessary shifts in current account balances. Korea began to accumulate reserves early in 1998, Indonesia and Thailand in 1999. Therefore, the adjustment process was doubly dysfunctional.

What Happened Thereafter

The architecture exercise began in the wake of the Mexican crisis, but it was heavily influenced by the Asian crisis:

- It led to the creation of two new facilities in the IMF—the Supplemental Reserve Facility (SRF) and the Contingent Credit Line (CCL).

- It encouraged more intense international efforts to strengthen the financial and corporate infrastructure in emerging-market countries.

- It strongly influenced the ongoing quest for the most effective ways to involve the private sector in resolving debt-related crises.

- It touched off a vigorous debate about the scope and character of IMF conditionality—whether the Fund should always insist on "orthodox" austerity, and whether crisis-stricken countries should be made to pursue far-reaching structural reforms in the midst of a crisis.

- It inspired the attempt to promote regional monetary cooperation in Asia—an effort that began inauspiciously, when the United States

---

55. See, in particular, Corsetti, Pesenti, and Roubini (1998c), Mishkin (1998), Brealey (1999), and Schneider and Tornell (2000). I also emphasized these effects soon after the Asian crisis began (Kenen 2000b). For empirical work on balance sheet effects in Asia, see Agénor, Aizenman, and Hoffmaister (2000) and other papers cited there. Krugman (1998b) notes that implicit guarantees play no role in his model, though they played a key role in his previous work on the Asian crisis.

quashed a Japanese attempt to create an Asian Monetary Fund, but has since produced a network of credit arrangements linking China, Japan, and Korea with the Southeast Asian countries.

The architecture exercise was also shaped by subsequent events—and they were shaped in turn by the exercise itself. Some of them will be discussed in later chapters, but four deserve to be mentioned here.

Malaysia's Capital Outflow Controls

One event happened in Asia itself. Having declined to seek assistance from the IMF, Malaysia went on to adopt a strategy radically different from those followed by its neighbors. In September 1998, it pegged the ringgit to the US dollar and introduced capital controls in an effort "to insulate the domestic economy from international financial volatility, to curb capital flight and speculation against the ringgit, and eliminate off-shore transactions in the domestic currency" (IMF 1998b, 22). Proceeds from sales of domestic securities had to be deposited for one year in a local currency account, lending to foreign banks was forbidden, and transfers between offshore accounts could not be made without permission. The new restrictions disrupted offshore markets, especially in Singapore, by forcing the liquidation of swap positions and the repatriation of offshore ringgit accounts. They also led, not surprisingly, to dire warnings that Malaysia would pay for its sins—that it would be cut off indefinitely from international capital markets.

Russia's Unilateral Default

The second event happened earlier. In July 1998, the IMF had approved an $11.2 billion drawing by Russia, and $4.8 billion was made available immediately. The Russian government promised to reduce its budget deficit from 5.6 percent of GDP to 2.8 percent in 1999, relying heavily on measures to increase tax collections. It also undertook to overhaul its banking system and lengthen the maturity of its domestic debt by offering holders of treasury bills (GKOs) an opportunity to exchange them for long-term foreign currency bonds. In light of Russia's previous perfor-mance, there were reasons to question the credibility of these commit-ments, but the program was approved despite reservations within West-ern governments. Outsiders explained that "Russia is too nuclear to fail." Insiders seemed to be making a more subtle bet: the money might not buy much real reform but might buy the survival of the reformers themselves.

Unhappily, it did not even buy time. The voluntary debt exchange did little to reduce the stock of short-term government debt, and foreign investors began to wonder whether that debt could be rolled over. They had taken the IMF's decision in July as proof that Russia would be bailed out and had therefore continued to buy high-yielding GKOs, in what traders themselves described as the "moral hazard play." Many had covered their foreign exchange risks by selling rubles forward to Russian banks, but they began to realize that they faced another risk—Russia might default. And that is what happened in August. When Russia failed to honor the promises made in July, the IMF refused to disburse the next tranche of the $11.2 billion drawing. Therefore, Russia announced a unilateral restructuring of its ruble-denominated debt, suspended trading in that debt, and imposed a 90-day moratorium on private debt payments, including forward foreign exchange contracts; it also devalued the ruble— which was allowed to float less than two weeks later. And soon thereafter, Russia sought to restructure its foreign currency debt.

The Russian crisis had an extraordinary impact. This is how the Fund described it in a special issue of its *World Economic Outlook*:

> The recent turbulence in global financial markets was unusual for a period characterized by relatively strong macroeconomic policies and conditions in many of the advanced economies. The volatility reflected a sudden heightened perception of, and aversion to, risk following Russia's effective default in August and an associated flight to quality. Emerging markets were particularly seriously affected as interest rate spreads on their external debt increased significantly and new private financing virtually ground to a halt. But the repercussions were not limited to these countries, as the global flight to quality led to sharp increases in spreads on financial assets in some of the deepest capital markets in the world, especially in the United States, and to sharp volatility in the dollar-yen exchange rate.
>
> Subsequent actions by the Federal Reserve and other central banks to lower short-term interest rates have helped to alleviate fears of a deepening global credit crunch, as has the international support package for Brazil. However, the process of deleveraging and portfolio rebalancing in response to heightened risk aversion may not have run its course, and the situation remains fragile. . . .
>
> The severe reaction to the Russian default was partly due to the sizes of the losses on Russian exposures and positions, but these were not in aggregate large enough to account fully for the ensuing turbulence. More important was the role of the Russian default as a defining event that challenged widely held views about the default risks associated with *all* emerging market investments, and the willingness of the international community to provide assistance to countries in difficulty. . . .
>
> A second issue concerns the sources of the vulnerabilities that led to the Russian default producing severe liquidity problems in some of the deepest capital markets, and prompting action by a major central bank to facilitate the private rescue of a hedge fund [Long Term Capital Management]. The drying up of liquidity resulted mainly from many investors attempting at the same time to rapidly unwind highly leveraged positions, built either to arbitrage mature market credit spreads or to exploit perceived differences in funding costs between major currencies, most notably the dollar-yen carry trade. (IMF 1998b, 14-15)

In short, the remarkable impact of the Russian crisis reflects effects discussed above: the spillover effects across financial markets resulting from losses, margin calls, and the unwinding of positions, and the expectational effects resulting from a sudden increase of risk aversion.[56] And the fear cited by the IMF—that the official community might refuse to rescue every sovereign debtor—would soon be confirmed.

Brazil's Soft Landing

The third major event, however, sent a different signal. The Brazilian crisis of 1998-99 appeared to reaffirm the commitment to rescue every sovereign debtor. One wonders, however, whether Brazil would have received a massive amount of official financing if it had run into trouble at a less turbulent time. Even those who are usually critical of large-scale official financial packages concede that the $41 billion mobilized for Brazil served to postpone the devaluation of the Brazilian real to a more tranquil time (see, e.g., Bordo and James 1999).

Brazil's problems began long before the Russian crisis. In the four years following the introduction of the Real Plan in 1994, the Brazilian inflation rate had fallen from more than 2,700 percent per year to less than 3 percent, and real GDP had grown by some 4 percent per year. But Brazil was a little bit like Russia. The government had a large domestic debt, and much of it was short-term debt. Most was held by residents, not foreigners, but residents and foreigners alike were worried about the rate at which the debt was growing. Public-sector borrowing had reached 6.3 percent of GDP in 1997 and was expected to reach 8 percent in 1998. Furthermore, efforts to hold the debt down had foundered repeatedly in the congress, courts, and provinces.

Brazil had been sideswiped by the Asian crisis but had been able to stem a capital outflow by raising interest rates and unveiling an ambitious fiscal package. That package was not fully implemented, however, and Brazil was thus very vulnerable to the turmoil triggered by the Russian crisis in 1998. There was a $12 billion capital outflow in August and a $19 billion outflow in September. Official interest rates were raised to 43 percent, new fiscal measures were announced, and Brazil sought support from the IMF, which mobilized a $41 billion package and made much of that money available up front.[57] For its part, Brazil undertook once again

---

56. For a clear account of the interactions between these effects, see G. Calvo (1998). For a detailed account of the Russian crisis, see IMF (1999d), where the Fund was unusually blunt. It called the rush to buy high-yielding GKOs a "feeding frenzy," and it acknowledged that moral hazard was important in the Russian case. But it went on say that "many investors bought securities they did not fully understand, and . . . they did so in the face of circumstances that should have raised concerns" (1999d, 41).

57. Of the $41 billion total, $18 billion was to come from the IMF itself, some $8 billion would come from the World Bank and Inter-American Development Bank, and the rest would come from a group of 20 governments via the BIS. About 90 percent of the $41 billion was to be made available during the first 13 months—an arrangement very different

to tackle its fiscal problems, lengthen the maturity of its public debt, and reduce its reliance on floating-rate debt.

Once again, however, it ran into trouble. In December 1998, congressional opposition blocked the government's plan to reform the social security system. In January 1999, one of the states, Minas Gerais, declared that it would seek to restructure its debt payments to the federal government, and other states followed its lead. Capital outflows resumed, interest rates soared, and Brazil took the familiar two-step path to a floating exchange rate; it began by widening the exchange rate band, then let the real float. It did so, however, before exhausting its reserves or using a very large portion of the $41 billion mobilized by the IMF. And it did so without reviving inflation—the country's chronic nemesis.

A New Set of Sovereign Debt Problems

Finally, a series of debt problems emerged after the Russian crisis. Fearing that its creditors would refuse to roll over a tranche of treasury bills due to mature very soon, Ukraine sought help from the IMF. But the Fund did not want to furnish financing that would, it feared, be used to buy back those treasury bills. Therefore, it required Ukraine to keep its foreign exchange reserves at an abnormally high level—one that would bar it from using them to repay its debt. Forced to find another way of avoiding default, Ukraine persuaded most of its foreign creditors to swap their holdings of treasury bills for zero coupon eurobonds. (Those who refused had to accept Ukrainian currency for their maturing treasury bills and could not then swap it for another currency.)

Four more debt problems arose in 1999, involving Ecuador, Pakistan, Romania, and, again, Ukraine. Romania scraped together the foreign exchange needed to repay its maturing debt. Pakistan did that once but had then to adopt the Ukrainian strategy—exchanging new debt for old— and Ukraine did the same thing again. But Ecuador defaulted on its foreign currency debt, and its debt problem was far harder to resolve. These four cases will be discussed again when we take up the thorniest issue faced in the course of the architecture exercise—the role of the private sector in solving debt-related problems.

---

from those for Indonesia and Korea, which doled out the money more gradually (and did not provide for the scheduled use of the bilateral credits furnished by national governments); see IMF (1998b, 1999h) on which this account draws heavily.

3

Myths and Metaphors

Debates about the causes of recent currency crises, the policy responses to them, and the reform of the international financial architecture have raised complex issues. Too often, however, the issues and options are posed in unduly simplistic ways.

Consider the debate about the Asian crisis. Some blame it primarily on creditor panic and argue that the crisis could have been resolved without requiring the Asian countries to alter their policies or reform their institutions. Others blame it on fundamental flaws in the policies, practices, and institutions of the Asian countries and argue that policy changes and structural reforms were essential.

Furthermore, there is disagreement among those who interpret the Asian crisis as a creditor panic. Some believe that confidence could have been restored by large-scale official financing; they claim that the seemingly large amounts supplied by the IMF and others were too small and were doled out too slowly. In the future, they say, the IMF should act more like a "lender of last resort" to end a creditor panic. Others argue that confidence could have been restored by inducing panicky creditors to pause, reflect, and recognize that they would be better off staying than fleeing if all of them did that together. But they go on to disagree about whether that result would be best achieved by relying on persuasion or on coercion.

Complex issues have also arisen in the ongoing debate about private-sector involvement in the resolution of future crises. To distinguish between possible forms of private-sector involvement, academics and officials alike often invoke the seemingly straightforward distinction between a liquidity problem and a solvency problem. A liquidity problem is said to require temporary financing or, at most, rescheduling of a country's debt, because the country's impending debt payments are too large to be met in full, given the country's current earnings and its liquid assets. A solvency problem is said to require a reduction of a country's debt, because a mere postponement of impending debt payments will not suffice when the whole stream of future payments looks to be too large.

But the solvency of a country is far harder to judge than the solvency of a company. It calls for determining the most appropriate way to divide a country's real resources between debt service payments and domestic use. That judgment has economic dimensions but must, in the end, be left to the country's own political process.[1] When a country is deemed to be solvent, moreover, it should presumably be able to borrow in order to meet its impending debt payments. If it cannot do that, one must ask why not. Have capital markets seized up? Or do potential lenders entertain doubts about the country's solvency—its ability or willingness to meet its future obligations?[2]

The tendency illustrated by these examples—basing strong policy advice on simple binary classifications—has infected the debate about exchange rate policy. Shortly after the European Monetary System (EMS) was beset by the currency crisis of 1992-93, Barry Eichengreen (1995) drew the obvious lesson from that crisis: pegged but adjustable exchange rates are not viable when private capital is highly mobile. It is inexpensive to make large bets against them, and it can be very costly to defend them against speculative attacks.[3] Eichengreen therefore predicted that countries would move inexorably to more flexible exchange rates or to monetary unions. His prediction, however, was quickly converted into a prescription. Countries *must* move to one of two corners. They have either

---

1. See, e.g., Tarullo (2001), who goes on to explain why it would be virtually impossible to design a bankruptcy regime for sovereign debtors, even one modeled on chapter 9 of the US Bankruptcy Code, which deals with municipal bankrupcies; see also Rogoff (1999).

2. Eichengreen (2000a) seeks to sort out these issues by attributing solvency problems to "bad" fundamentals that call for policy changes and attributing liquidity problems to creditor panics, but this taxonomy is misleading. Solvency problems typically arise when feasible improvements in a country's fundamentals cannot be expected to release enough domestic resources to service the country's debts. Another simplistic distinction is drawn by the G-7 governments. They concede that it may be impossible to deal with solvency problems without recourse to coercion but imply that liquidity problems can normally be resolved by voluntary market-based arrangements between a debtor country and its foreign creditors. We will return to this matter in subsequent chapters.

3. The same point was made much earlier, after the collapse of the Bretton Woods system in the early 1970s, and it was made again in the European context by Padoa-Schioppa (1988), even before the EMS crisis; he warned that the abolition of capital controls required by the Single European Act would force the EMS countries to choose between greater exchange rate flexibility and monetary unification.

to adopt flexible exchange rates or to fix their exchange rates firmly. By forming regional monetary unions, converting their central banks into currency boards, or replacing their national currencies with other countries' currencies—the solution known as formal dollarization.[4]

This chapter looks at these matters more closely in an effort to lay out clearly the issues and options that are too often simplified excessively by invoking analogies, metaphors, and myths. It focuses on three issues: the use and abuse of IMF conditionality, whether the IMF should serve as "lender of last resort" to its member countries, and the debate about exchange rate regimes. In the process, it touches on other controversies: whether an interest rate defense should be used to combat a creditor panic, whether prequalification can replace conditionality, and whether contingent credit lines can replace precautionary drawings on the IMF. It also examines the main recommendations of the Meltzer Report. But one of the issues mentioned in this introduction, the problem of private-sector involvement, will be deferred to subsequent chapters, because of its central role in the architecture exercise.

Culpability, Confidence, and Conditionality

Assume for the moment that the Asian crisis was due largely to creditor panic, not to the policies and practices of the Asian countries.[5] Was there no need to modify those policies and practices? Was the Fund wrong to insist that the Asian countries adopt the orthodox remedy for a currency crisis—tightening their monetary and fiscal policies? Was the Fund wrong to insist that they embark on far-reaching reforms during the crisis itself?

The answer resides in the rationale for conditionality. It is not meant to punish countries for their past mistakes. It is meant to make sure that countries adapt to current conditions and can therefore repay the Fund

---

4. Eichengreen has also moved from prediction to prescription, but he does not rule out various ways of managing flexible rates; see, e.g., Eichengreen (1999b). Some others, however, who take this approach to the choice of exchange rate regime rule out all "intermediate" arrangements, not merely pegged but adjustable rates; the only viable options, they say, are free floating or hard fixing.

5. This is the stand taken by Radelet and Sachs (1998, 2000). For a formal model of a currency crisis caused by a creditor panic, see Chang and Velasco (1999), who adapt to an open-economy setting the well-known bank-run model of Diamond and Dybvig (1983). Like Radelet and Sachs, moreover, Chang and Velasco argue that "orthodox" policies are not needed to combat a creditor panic and that conditionality can be counterproductive. (They are especially critical of fiscal conditions that, they say, can lead to two equilibria. A good equilibrium is reached when a government holds down its budget deficit to meet its commitment to the IMF and can then use IMF money to finance the acceptable deficit. A bad equilibrium obtains when the government fails to hold down its deficit and the IMF withholds funding; the fiscal problem is aggravated not only by the large size of the deficit itself but also by the lack of IMF money with which to finance it.)

in a reasonable time. In other words, conditionality is forward looking, not backward looking. It is concerned with sustainability rather than culpability.[6] What, then, is the role of conditionality in the case of a creditor panic? If it were possible to restore the status quo ante by providing large-scale official financing or causing panicky creditors to pause, reflect, and decide to start lending again, there would be no need for the crisis-stricken country to make any policy changes. Capital outflows would cease, and capital inflows would resume. But it would be foolish to bet on this ideal outcome. Capital outflows may cease, but capital inflows may not revive right away and they may not return to precrisis levels for a very long time.

There are two reasons to take this view. First, creditor panics do not occur spontaneously. They may reflect unfounded fears, but these may take time to subside. Second, creditor panics can do grave damage when they are not halted immediately, and some of that damage must be repaired before capital inflows will resume. In the meantime, the crisis-stricken country will have to reduce its current account deficit and may even have to run a surplus in order to rebuild its reserves and pay down its debt to the IMF. And that's where conditionality comes in.

Furthermore, creditors' fears are not always unfounded. They are not caused by "sunspots" of the sort that inhabit economists' models. In many cases, including the Asian case, they reflect plausible concerns about the sustainability of the status quo ante and the quality of precrisis policies. The change in creditors' views about the Thai economy was due in large part to the very visible problems of the Thai banking system. The spread of the crisis to neighboring countries was due in part to the realization that they, too, were vulnerable. Creditors panicked, so did debtors, and the resulting crisis confirmed their worst fears. In this sort of situation, policy changes must be made, if only for the purpose of restoring confidence and undoing the damage done by the crisis itself.

The Fund's Precarious Strategy

Unhappily, the strategy adopted by the Fund was built on precarious suppositions. It assumed that policy changes and structural reforms would be implemented promptly and restore confidence quickly, so that capital outflows would cease. On this assumption, moreover, modest amounts of up-front financing would suffice to achieve and sustain exchange rate stability. This strategy would work if everything went right and these suppositions were therefore fulfilled, but it was apt to fail if anything went wrong—and something was bound to go wrong. That's Murphy's

---

6. I have made the same point elsewhere in a different context. A country that suffers a terms-of-trade shock has to adjust to the shock although it bears no blame for it; see Kenen (1986).

Law. If governments procrastinated, and they did, the restoration of confidence would be delayed, and it was. And if confidence was not restored quickly, capital outflows would continue, and the amounts of official financing would be too small to keep the Asian currencies from depreciating further.[7]

A number of critics go on to argue that the Fund's insistence on far-reaching structural reform during the crisis itself made matters worse by convincing panicky creditors that the Asian crisis was the result of deep-seated structural flaws that had to be corrected promptly; otherwise, the Asian economies could not begin to recover.[8] The Fund was right to insist that some things be done quickly. Insolvent banks had to be closed or recapitalized, and plans to deal with corporate debts had to be devised, even if they could not be implemented speedily. But in calling for other reforms, such as removing restrictions on the foreign ownership of domestic banks, abolishing domestic monopolies, and liberalizing trade, the Fund may have undermined its own strategy by implying that all of these tasks were essential for recovery.

The Fund's strategy had another defect. By insisting on controversial reforms, it created uncertainty about the amounts of official financing that were in fact readily available to the crisis-stricken countries (see Bosworth 1998; Stiglitz 1998; Feldstein 1998). A strong case can be made for doling out IMF credit in tranches. If all of it were made available immediately, the Fund would have no way to punish a government that reneged on its commitments. To put the point differently, the tranching of IMF credit enhances the credibility of a government's policy commitments and, to that extent, may actually contribute to the restoration of confidence.[9] But the availability of IMF credit is itself important for restoring confidence. It is not meant merely to buy time for policy changes to take hold and capital inflows to resume. It has a key role to play in arresting a capital outflow caused by a loss of confidence.

There is, in brief, an inherent conflict between two key objectives. The need to ensure compliance with policy commitments calls for the gradual, conditional disbursement of IMF credit; but the need for exchange rate stabilization and the restoration of creditor confidence call for reliable

---

7. Krugman (1998a) goes further, arguing that the Fund's preoccupation with "the confidence game" led it to insist on policies having little to do with the urgent economic and social needs of the crisis-stricken countries; they were fashioned to appeal to "the prejudices of investors" or, worse yet, "what investors believe are the prejudices of their colleagues." Blinder (1999) uses more measured language but renders a similar judgment.

8. See, e.g., Feldstein (1998) and Radelet and Sachs (1998). Others, however, defend the Fund's approach; Goldstein (1998), Eichengreen (1998, 1999b), Lane et al. (1999), and Ahluwalia (2000) say that far-reaching reforms were required to resolve the Asian crisis.

9. For the first formulation, see Eichengreen (1999b) and Fischer (1999); for the second, see Brealey (1999) and Vines (2000).

up-front financing. At the margin, however, the conflict should usually be resolved in favor of front-loading. In "modern" crises, involving large capital outflows, unlike "old-fashioned" crises, involving large current account deficits, it is hard to estimate the so-called financing gap and thus ascertain the total amount of financing required to buy time for resolving a crisis. The size of the financing gap will depend on the size of the subsequent capital outflow, which will in turn depend on the amount of official financing provided.[10] But the larger the amount of up-front financing, the smaller the risk of a large outflow. Therefore, front-loading can reduce the total amount of financing required. Fortunately, the Fund has moved in this direction. It adopted a more open-handed stance in the Brazilian crisis of 1998-99 than in the Asian crisis of 1997-98, and it has continued to do that.

Interest Rates, Exchange Rates, Confidence, and Output

Several economists have attempted to ascertain the impact of IMF programs on creditor confidence by asking how they affect exchange rates and other relevant variables. One would expect the results to differ from case to case, depending on market participants' views about the credibility of a particular government's policy commitments, and that may explain why these efforts have been disappointingly inconclusive. Richard Brealey (1999) reports that Asian exchange rates, equity prices, and bond prices were not significantly affected by announcements of IMF programs, and Takatoshi Ito (2000) reports mixed results, but Graciela Kaminsky and Sergio Schmukler (1999) find that the announcements of IMF programs tended to have a positive effect on Asian equity prices.

Economists have also attempted to ascertain the impact of interest rate policies on the behavior of Asian exchange rates. Some of the Asian countries started to raise their short-term interest rates soon after their currencies came under pressure, even before they turned to the IMF.[11] They raised them only modestly, however—not as much as other countries facing similar problems, and not by enough to offset the contempora-

---

10. Crockett (2000) makes this point; see also Ahluwalia (2000) and De Gregorio, Eichengreen, Ito, and Wyplosz (1999). The Fund was able to calculate financing gaps in the debt crisis of the 1980s, even though the crisis involved an abrupt cessation of capital inflows. But in that case, the subsequent behavior of capital flows was not nearly as sensitive to the amount of official financing provided, and it was thus comparatively easy to forecast the amount of financing required.

11. The Bank of Thailand raised rates promptly but then pursued a stop-go policy, allowing rates to fall "at the first sign of exchange rate stability" (Lane et al. 1998, 42). The Indonesian central bank also raised rates promptly but reversed course sharply to assist domestic banks. But the Bank of Korea did not raise rates substantially until December 1997, not long before it had to abandon its defense of the won.

neous expectation that their countries' currencies would go on depreciating.[12] They were worried about the effects on their banking systems, as well as the output-reducing effects. But some were then told by the IMF that they must tighten their monetary policies, and this advice was controversial.

Some critics said that high interest rates would make matters worse by damaging the balance sheets of many more firms, aggravating the problems of the banking sector, and producing other effects that would make panicky creditors even more pessimistic about the prospects for the speedy recovery of the crisis-stricken countries. Furthermore, an increase in interest rates is apt to be seen as an attempt to compensate for the failure of other policies, in which case it will damage confidence.[13] Even some who do not deny the efficacy of a conventional interest rate defense criticized its use in the Asian crisis. Its adverse effects on balance sheets, they said, combined with its other output-reducing effects, were more harmful than the larger currency depreciations that would have occurred if interest rates had not been raised (see, e.g., Feldstein 1998). But others took the opposite view, saying that larger depreciations would have done more harm (see, e.g., Cline 2000a).[14]

Empirical work on these issues has not resolved them.[15] Jason Furman and Joseph Stiglitz (1998) examined 13 episodes in which interest rates rose temporarily by unusually large amounts and found that their level and duration affected exchange rates perversely. Aardt Kraay (1998) identified large sets of successful and unsuccessful attacks on countries' currencies (successful attacks being those that produced large depreciations); he found no significant relationship between central banks' interest rate policies and the success or failure of the attacks, even though he sought

12. When a currency is expected to depreciate by 1 percent per day, risk-neutral investors will require an overnight interest rate 1 percent above the international interest rate. Hence, the annualized interest rate difference must exceed 3,600 percent; see Furman and Stiglitz (1998), who note that the rupiah depreciated by an average of 0.8 percent per day between 1 July 1997 and 30 January 1998, so that a risk-neutral investor who had forecast correctly the actual rate of depreciation would have required an annualized interest rate premium of 1,700 percent to hold rupiah-denominated claims.

13. These and other perverse effects of a conventional interest rate defense are set out at length by Furman and Stiglitz (1998). Several recent papers have sought to model formally the effects of an interest rate defense; see, e.g., Lahiri and Vegh (2000) and Flood and Jeanne (2000). But most of those papers use "first-generation" models of currency crises in which the collapse of the currency is inevitable; they are concerned solely with the impact of interest rate policy on the timing and cost of the collapse.

14. Lamfalussy (2000) gives another rationale for a strong interest rate defense: combating the inflationary effects of a large depreciation by limiting the depreciation and reducing aggregate demand.

15. The summary that follows draws heavily on the review and assessment in Lane et al. (1999).

to control for the endogeneity of those policies. But Ilan Goldfajn and Poonam Gupta (1999) obtained different results when they asked a slightly different question: confining attention to cases in which a currency has already depreciated and is clearly undervalued, is there any relationship between interest rate policy and the subsequent path of the exchange rate? They found that higher-than-average interest rates are positively associated with subsequent appreciation. Finally, Goldfajn and Taimur Baig (1998) used daily data to study the Asian story itself. They found that interest rates do not explain exchange rates and that exchange rates do not explain interest rates. In some subperiods, however, increases in interest rates were significantly associated with currency appreciations.

Working with data on individual firms, Stijn Claessens, Simeon Djankov, and Giovanni Ferri (1998) found that the effects of the depreciations of the Asian currencies were larger than those of the interest rate changes; the exchange rate changes, by themselves, drove almost two-thirds of Indonesian firms, one-fifth of Korean firms, and one-tenth of Thai firms into insolvency, and they drove even larger numbers of firms into illiquidity (defined as a state in which the firms' debt service payments exceeded their pretax earnings). The effects of the corresponding interest rate changes were appreciably smaller. But this finding does not resolve the debate about the benefits and costs of an interest rate defense: it says nothing about the extent to which the Asian currencies would have depreciated if interest rates had not been raised.

It is thus hard to quarrel with Barry Eichengreen's summary of the debate about the interest rate defense:

> The effect of interest rates on the exchange rate, while an empirical question, is one on which there exists exactly zero convincing evidence, forcing both the Fund and its critics to rest their cases on arguments rather than statistics. Both sides can agree that in theory there exists an "interest rate Laffer Curve." While modest interest rate increases are likely to strengthen the currency, if taken to excess they may so damage the financial condition of banks and firms that confidence deteriorates and the currency weakens. The empirical question is where the point of inflection lies and whether IMF-inspired policies surpassed it. . . . Assertions that interest rates were pushed to the point where they weakened the exchange rate rather than strengthening it remain just that—assertions. (Eichengreen 1999b, 112)

But agnosticism does not justify imprudence. A sensible economist advising the government of a crisis-stricken country would not tell it to go all out for domestic recovery by cutting its interest rates sharply without also warning that the country's currency is apt to depreciate steeply unless the government suspends debt payments and imposes comprehensive capital controls.[16] And if the government is unwilling to take those steps

---

16. Eichengreen (1999b) makes this point clearly; so does Krugman (1998a).

and fears the consequences of a large depreciation, a sensible economist would tell it to raise interest rates and hold them at fairly high levels unless and until it is quite clear that the gambit is not working.[17]

Can the IMF Function as an LLR?

The IMF has often been described as a lender of last resort (LLR), and that is an apt description—up to a point. Member countries turn to the Fund when no one else will lend to them on affordable terms. Recently, however, the term has been used more strictly to describe the role of the Fund. The IMF should serve as the ultimate bulwark against creditor panic, because no other institution can take on that task. Yet those who use this metaphor have little else in common. Some, like Stanley Fischer (2000), use it to characterize and defend the Fund's recent practices—the increasingly frequent use of large-scale official financing. Others, like Charles Calomiris (1998b) and the Meltzer Report (IFIAC 2000), use it to attack those same practices and to insist that the Fund should redefine its role.

The Classic Case for an LLR

Before examining the merits of these disparate views and their implicit presuppositions, we should revisit the normal meaning of an LLR. There is, as Fischer (2000) notes, no agreed-on definition, but few who use the term could object strongly to this one: an LLR is an institution that is willing and able to supply unlimited amounts of short-term credit to financial institutions when they are threatened by a creditor panic that could cause an implosion of lending or a sharp fall in the money supply, which would do serious damage to the real economy. It can be the central bank, which has the credit-creating power to perform that role, but other institutions, including private institutions, have often served as LLRs; Curzio Giannini (1999) gives examples. An LLR can lend to the market at large or to individual banks.[18] And it may or may not adhere fully to

---

17. This recommendation is broadly consistent with the finding by Eichengreen and Rose (2001): countries that defended their currencies successfully suffered smaller output losses than those that failed to do so. (Their paper, however, does not cross-classify the two groups of countries to distinguish clearly between those that mounted an interest rate defense, successful or otherwise, and those that adopted a different defense.)

18. See, however, Capie (1998), who argues that a well-behaved LLR, true to the principles set out by Thornton (1802) and Bagehot (1873), will lend only to the market at large, not to individual banks. For this reason, he says, and because it cannot create an ultimate means of payment, the IMF cannot serve as an international LLR. But Capie's argument is strongly influenced by Thornton's concern (the need to prevent a large fall in the money supply) and by the peculiar modus operandi of the Bank of England, which did not deal directly with British banks but instead bought up bills offered by the discount houses, leaving it to them to on-lend the proceeds to individual banks. Goodhart (1999) takes the opposite view.

Walter Bagehot's well-known rule—that the LLR should lend freely but at a high interest rate and against good collateral. Some central banks post discount rates that do not differ appreciably from prevailing market rates, and some are prepared or required to lend without demanding collateral.

Why did Bagehot want the LLR to charge a high interest rate and require collateral? Insistence on high interest rates is commonly interpreted as a way to discourage abuse of the credit-creating facility provided by an LLR. It could be abused ex ante if banks were led to act imprudently; it could be abused ex post if banks were led to borrow from the LLR to meet routine liquidity needs. Today, however, the ex ante problem of moral hazard is commonly addressed by "constructive ambiguity." A central bank that is firmly committed to act as an LLR is not necessarily committed to rescue every single bank that runs into trouble.[19] Insistence on good collateral is justified by two concerns: the need to protect the LLR from suffering losses and the need for a way to distinguish between illiquid and insolvent banks, as the LLR should lend freely to illiquid banks but not to insolvent banks.

Under contemporary arrangements, however, these needs can be met differently. Most LLRs are public institutions—which was not true in Bagehot's time—and they can therefore look to their governments for indemnification if they suffer large losses. Furthermore, prudential supervision enables an LLR to distinguish between illiquidity and insolvency, even when the LLR is not directly involved in that supervision. And though bank supervisors are far from infallible, their judgments are apt to be better than those based on a bank's ability to post good collateral; a truly insolvent bank may still possess high-quality assets.

How the Fund Resembles an LLR

Turning now to the question at hand—whether the IMF can be or become an international LLR—consider Fischer's (2000) view that the Fund is

---

Lending to the market, he argues, is observationally equivalent to an open-market purchase made for monetary policy purposes; the LLR should therefore be defined by its willingness to lend to individual banks, even though it may also lend to the market in a particular episode (such as the 1987 stock market crash, in which the Federal Reserve supplied liquidity to the banking system on the understanding that banks would not reduce their lending to market-making securities firms). Fischer (2000) takes Goodhart's side, but for a different reason. Under crisis conditions, he says, market participants cannot distinguish clearly between illiquid and insolvent institutions and may therefore be unable to on-lend efficiently the credit created by an LLR that lends to the market at large. See also Jeanne and Wyplosz (2001), who argue that an LLR cannot assist illiquid institutions by lending to the market at large if that market is perfectly integrated with global markets; the credit it creates will flow out to those global markets rather than remain available locally to illiquid institutions.

19. See, however, Fischer (2000, 15) who warns against undue reliance on constructive ambiguity. There will always be some ambiguity about an LLR's response to a future crisis,

starting to look much like an LLR. He gives four reasons. First, the Fund has institutionalized large-scale lending by establishing the Supplemental Reserve Facility (SRF) and Contingent Credit Line (CCL); the former allows it to make larger amounts of Fund credit available than the usual cumulative limit (300 percent of a country's quota), and the latter allows it to make large amounts of credit available to countries that prequalify, so as to ward off contagion and the effects of other calamities for which they are not directly responsible. Second, the Fund has become an effective crisis manager; it has been able to mobilize consortia of governments to provide financing jointly with the Fund. Furthermore, it has become more nimble; by using the streamlined procedures of the Emergency Financing Mechanism (EFM), it is able to furnish assistance faster than before. Third, the Fund can supplement its financial resources by activating the New Arrangements to Borrow (NAB), as well as the General Arrangements to Borrow (GAB), and can therefore commit itself credibly to make large-scale financing available in the event of a creditor panic; it does not need the power to create international money, although it may be able to do so eventually if there is a relaxation of the rigid restrictions that currently govern the creation of Special Drawing Rights (SDRs).[20] Fourth, the Fund is taking on a new task—monitoring adherence to standards and codes that have been devised to guide and promote the strengthening of national financial systems; no international body is presently engaged in anything like prudential supervision, but the Fund will be able to influence the evolution and functioning of national regimes that oversee banks, securities markets, and other parts of national financial systems.

Fischer goes on to argue that the Fund is moving in the right direction. It *should* evolve into an international LLR, because a national LLR cannot create internationally acceptable money and thus meet its country's needs in an external crisis—one in which the government, the private sector, or both have massive demands for foreign currency. But he also argues that the Fund's ability to perform that special task will depend in large part on the effectiveness of ongoing efforts to involve private-sector creditors in the resolution of external crises—which is not how a national LLR tries

---

but "it is preferable to specify as clearly as possible the general principles under which the lender of last resort will act."

20. Special Drawing Rights are bookkeeping entries on the books of the Fund that can be created periodically under strict rules set out in the Fund's Articles of Agreement. They can be created to meet the "long-term global need" for international reserve assets and must be distributed in proportion to member countries' quotas in the Fund. They cannot be created on an ad hoc basis to finance the activities of the Fund itself. The first allocation of SDRs took place in 1970-72 and the second in 1979-81, but there have been no further allocations, and SDRs play only a marginal role in the international monetary system. They are not likely to become the "principal reserve asset" of the system, which was their original purpose. The SDR is valued in terms of a currency basket comprising dollars, euros, pounds, and yen.

to prevent or stem a creditor panic. Fischer views private-sector involvement as the way in which the Fund should combat creditor moral hazard.

There are, however, obvious objections to Fischer's reasons for claiming that the IMF is evolving into an international LLR.

How the Fund Differs from an LLR

Although the SRF and CCL enable the IMF to provide large-scale financing on a regular basis, without having to decide that each applicant country faces "exceptional circumstances" in order to breach the usual ceiling on quota-based drawings, the IMF does not lend freely in a Bagehot-like manner, against good collateral.[21] Instead, it disburses large-scale financing in tranches to make sure that policy commitments are being fulfilled. It has front-loaded large-scale financing in several cases, but it cannot completely abandon its usual practice without losing its only device for monitoring conditionality. In other words, two sorts of credibility come into conflict: the credibility of the Fund's commitment to furnish adequate financing as an international LLR and the credibility of its client countries' commitments to implement policy changes. Yet both are required to end a creditor panic caused by doubts about the sustainability of a country's policies or the stability of its currency.[22]

Although the IMF has been able to mobilize bilateral financing to supplement its own, the need for it to do that can also be taken to mean that the Fund does not have the resources required to serve as an LLR. Bilateral funding, moreover, comes with its own restrictions and conditions; it could not be used *pari passu* with the Fund's own money in the Indonesian and Korean cases, and there can be little doubt that some of the extraneous policy conditions imposed in the latter case reflected the narrowly national objectives of the governments involved (see Delong and Eichengreen 2001).

Furthermore, the rules governing access to the NAB and GAB are quite restrictive. The NAB can be activated only when the Fund receives a

---

21. In fact, the very concept of "good collateral" becomes rather fuzzy when transplanted to the international context in which the Fund operates. Claims on a crisis-stricken country cannot be deemed to be "good collateral" for the same reason that its "solvency" cannot readily be assessed. A country *can* pledge its reserve assets as collateral, but these are its own first line of defense; no country is likely to ask for Fund credit before it has drawn them down to a level that is not large enough to "back" a big loan from the IMF. A government can also pledge its country's future export earnings, but only if they can be mobilized easily by the country's government. (That is, in fact, what Mexico did in 1995, when it pledged future oil earnings as collateral for its loan from the ESF.) Meltzer (1999) mentions the use of collateral in his own plan for reform of the IMF, but the Meltzer Report does not, because of the "practical difficulties" that it would pose for many countries (IFIAC 2000).

22. Eichengreen (1999b) and Feldstein (1999) both emphasize this point.

request for a drawing and the managing director of the Fund considers that the proposed drawing "is necessary in order to forestall or cope with an impairment of the international monetary system" (IMF 1999g, 423) and that the Fund's resources need to be supplemented in order to finance the drawing. After that judgment is made, moreover, the managing director must consult with the Executive Board of the Fund and with the governments participating in the NAB. In fact, the NAB cannot be activated without the consent of governments accounting for 80 percent of the credit commitments covered by the NAB.[23]

Finally, the ways in which the IMF reviews its members' policies and their compliance with international standards and codes are not even analogous to prudential supervision. The Fund itself has acknowledged that adherence is voluntary, and the official community has backed away from any attempt to penalize individual governments for declining to adhere to them. There are good reasons for that, discussed in subsequent chapters, but they undercut any analogy between the Fund and an international LLR. In fact, the structure of the IMF is based on principles quite different from those that govern the behavior of an LLR.

This point is stressed by Giannini (1999), who invokes my own analogy between the IMF and a credit union in which relations among members are based on reciprocal rights and duties (Kenen 1986). Here is what he says:

> The concepts of reciprocity and lender of last resort are basically at odds with one another. The lender of last resort must either be in a position to create its own resources—which would be incompatible with the credit-union concept— or to channel resources systematically from those who have them to those who do not—the kind of distributive task that eventually brought down the U.S. clearinghouse system in the early 1900s. The framers of the international monetary architecture seem to have been aware of this tension, because they took a number of steps to make sure that the IMF would *not* develop a lender-of-last-resort role, either by statute or by spontaneous endogenesis. (Giannini 1999, 19)

Most important, the Fund is founded on the principle of universality. It can discriminate between cases by crafting policy conditions designed to resolve the particular problems facing one of its members, but it cannot say "yes" to one country and "no" to another simply because the first is well managed and the second is not. And a country is not a bank, which can be shut down completely. The Fund's financial resources are limited— and they come from all of its members. The Fund's punitive powers are

---

23. Giannini (1999) says that unanimity is required to activate the GAB and that the same rule holds for the NAB. In fact, the relevant clause of the GAB says that a proposal by the managing director must be "accepted by the participants," but the so-called Baumgartner letter annexed to the GAB parses that phrase to mean approval by two-thirds of the participants accounting for at least three-fifths of the credit commitments. The corresponding clause of the NAB contains the provision cited in the text (see IMF 1999g, 426, 438, 463).

also limited—and they likewise derive from its members. In short, the IMF is a cooperative institution "whose activity can hardly be based on the tenets of 'pure' central banking" (De Bonis, Giustiniani, and Gomel 1999, 78).[24]

Recasting the Analogy

Fischer sought mainly to stress the similarities between a national LLR, which comes to the aid of stricken banks during a creditor panic, and the IMF, which comes to the aid of stricken countries. Their roles are analogous, albeit distinct. Others have taken a different tack. In open economies, they argue, central banks may be unable to function effectively as LLRs. An increase of central bank credit will lead to a loss of reserves when the exchange rate is pegged and to a depreciation when the rate is flexible.

This problem is not new. Charles Goodhart (1999) reminds us that central bank lending was constrained under the gold standard, as any significant increase of lending could lead to a drastic fall in the central bank's gold holdings, and there were two ways to resolve the problem: borrowing gold from other central banks or having the government step in to confer legal-tender status on the central bank's own liabilities. But it has become important again because banking crises have become so frequent. A run on a country's banks is almost certain to produce a huge demand for foreign currency by the banks' panicky creditors. This outcome is inevitable when some of the panicky creditors are foreigners who have foreign currency claims on the country's banks. That is what happened in Asia. But the same outcome is nearly inevitable when all of the panicky creditors are residents who have domestic currency claims, as they may try to protect themselves by moving their money to foreign banks and thus moving from domestic to foreign currency.[25]

There is thus a functional complementarity between the role of the IMF as the ultimate supplier of foreign currency credit to a member's central bank and the role of the central bank itself as the ultimate supplier of credit to the banking system in the event of a creditor panic.[26] This comple-

---

24. Cline (2000a) and Rogoff (1999) make similar statements, and Goodhart (1999) makes another point. The quota-based currency subscriptions made by the Fund's members represent the full extent of their financial commitment to the IMF. Therefore, the Fund is fundamentally different from a national LLR, which can count on financial support from its government if it suffers losses.

25. The first case, involving foreigners, is cited by Brealey (1999) and by Goodhart (1999) as the rationale for IMF lending to mitigate banking crises; the second is cited by Chang and Velasco (1999) and by Mishkin (1999).

26. Mishkin (1999) carries this point further, asserting that liquidity from a foreign source, such as the IMF, does not lead to inflationary pressures of the sort caused by domestic liquidity creation and thus helps stabilize the domestic currency. Insofar as IMF assistance raises a country's reserves, it does help stabilize the country's currency. But close examination

mentarity holds, moreover, whether exchange rates are fixed or flexible. When they are fixed, a creditor panic will cause a huge loss of reserves; when they are flexible, it will cause a precipitous depreciation of the domestic currency.

Metaphor and Mischief in the Meltzer Report

The observation just made brings us directly to the Meltzer Report (IFIAC 2000).[27] One cannot make much sense of its recommendations without understanding the two-part premise on which they are based: creditor panics experienced by countries are due mainly to creditor panics experienced by those countries' banks, and a national LLR may not be able to stem an attack on its country's banks without foreign currency credit from an international LLR. Hence, the Meltzer Report recommends that the IMF transform itself into an international LLR. It should limit itself to making very short-term loans, base its lending decisions exclusively on preconditions aimed chiefly at appraising the soundness of its member countries' banks, and do little else.

Before examining these recommendations, let us look at their antecedents—the views of Allan Meltzer himself and of Charles Calomiris, whose plan for reforming the IMF is more cogent than the plan offered in the report.

Meltzer and Calomiris both attach great importance to moral hazard. Meltzer (1999) asserts that the Fund's willingness to provide large-scale financing has encouraged too much private-sector lending and allowed too few losses on risky loans. Furthermore, it has encouraged policymakers to postpone reform. Ministers of finance, Meltzer explains, must often choose between allowing more short-term foreign borrowing and adopting policies that would avoid a crisis. "It is sufficient for moral hazard that the existence of subsidized loans from the IMF modifies the finance minister's evaluation of the costs he faces. The very large increase in the number of countries experiencing large crises in recent years suggests

---

of the relevant transactions makes clear that liquidity from a foreign source cannot find its way to a country's banks without crossing the books of the central bank and raising the stock of base money. It is no less inflationary than liquidity provided by the country's central bank.

27. The discussion that follows focuses on the majority report and on its recommendations regarding the IMF. The report also deals with the multilateral development banks, the BIS, and (rather oddly) the World Trade Organization, and its proposals for reforming the multilateral development banks are just as radical as those for the IMF. The majority report was endorsed by eight of the eleven members of the commission, including Allan Meltzer, Charles Calomiris, and Jeffrey Sachs. A minority report was filed by four members (one of whom also endorsed the majority report). The minority report, drafted by C. Fred Bergsten, anticipates many of the criticisms set out in the text below; see also the critique prepared by the US Treasury (2000).

that a change of this kind has occurred" (Meltzer 1999, 252). Calomiris (1998b) goes further. In too many cases, he says, IMF credit has been used to bail out insolvent banks and corporations, shielding them from market discipline.

A Very Different IMF

What, then, did they recommend? Meltzer favored the creation of an international LLR that would follow Bagehot's precept. A central bank could borrow from it only by presenting appropriate collateral—internationally traded assets—and would thus be induced to hold such assets. The central bank would then on-lend to domestic banks in the event of a bank run.[28] Presumably, the new institution would replace the IMF, though Meltzer did not say so explicitly. Calomiris urged the IMF to return to its earlier mission, "advising countries on their macroeconomic policies (to improve exchange rate stability) and serving as an internationally delegated monitor charged with tracking those policies and providing credible information to global capital markets" (1998b, 90). Calomiris said nothing about IMF lending, though he noted cryptically that the Fund has enough capital to carry out these tasks. In another paper, however, Calomiris (1998a) offered a blueprint that reappeared thereafter in the Meltzer Report.

Calomiris would reconstitute the IMF by restricting its membership to countries that adopt "credible" bank regulation. By this, however, he does not mean prudential supervision (though he notes that regulation is required to limit inside lending, monitor market risk exposure, and oversee compliance with capital requirements). Instead, he favors a regime with four components: (1) capital requirements, including a subordinated debt requirement, to guarantee that the banks' uninsured claimants— holders of equity and subordinated debt—will suffer losses whenever the banks suffer losses and will therefore monitor the banks' behavior; (2) conventional reserve requirements that must be satisfied by holding cash and globally traded securities denominated in dollars, euros, or yen; (3) explicit deposit insurance; and (4) the unlimited chartering of banks conforming to common regulatory standards, as well as unrestricted foreign investment in domestic banks to provide adequate capital and foster diversification.

---

28. The notion of on-lending is an odd one in this context, involving a departure from the typical way in which governments and central banks utilize IMF credit. Central banks sometimes lend foreign currency to their commercial banks or deposit it with them (as Korea did in 1998). Normally, however, governments and central banks provide foreign currency to banks and others via the foreign exchange market, selling foreign currency rather than lending it. But others have also proposed that central banks on-lend foreign currency supplied by the IMF when they discuss the role of the Fund as an international LLR; see, e.g., Jeanne and Wyplosz (1999).

This new IMF should impose restrictions on the recapitalization of banks, set standards for the maturity structure of government debt, require countries with fixed exchange rates to let their banks offer deposits in both foreign and domestic currencies, and require those countries' central banks to hold reserves equal to some fixed fraction of the monetary base.[29] Having laid down these requirements, the new IMF would act "to mitigate problems of illiquidity that may arise when a country is pegging its exchange rate" (Calomiris 1998a, 26). It would do that by opening a discount window to lend to central banks in a Bagehot-like manner, demanding collateral, charging a high interest rate, and limiting its loans to 90 days. Furthermore, it would use a market test to assess the quality of a borrower's policies: it could refuse a request for credit if the fundamentals driving the value of the collateral—which would include the country's own securities as well as foreign securities—had deteriorated sharply in the previous week.

Finally, the new IMF would eschew conditionality. Conditionality would not be needed to protect the IMF itself; the collateral requirement would do that. And it would not be needed to induce policy changes by countries with ongoing balance of payments problems; they would be barred from borrowing by the market test (or be cut off later by the 90-day limit on IMF loans) and would then have to rectify their policy errors.

Whatever one's views about the quality of this blueprint, one cannot accuse Calomiris of failing to devise a coherent plan or failing to explain it carefully. Furthermore, it has a well-defined objective—strengthening the banking systems of emerging-market countries—which Calomiris rightly regards as a vital part of a successful development strategy. The Meltzer Report, however, borrows his blueprint as a ready remedy for all the faults and failings of the IMF. Furthermore, its account of those faults and failings is elliptical and tendentious.

From Reform to Rhetoric

In its account of the Mexican crisis, the Meltzer Report implies that the credits provided by the IMF and US Treasury were used to support insolvent banks and protect insolvent borrowers and that the Mexican taxpayer was stuck with the bill. There was a banking crisis in Mexico, its resolution was costly, and the Mexican taxpayer must pay for it eventu-

---

29. Calomiris would not require the IMF to impose any sort of fiscal discipline. "It is too hard," he says, "to design useful, credible, uniform rules about fiscal policy" (Calomiris 1998a, 25). In this respect, his plan differs significantly from the Meltzer Report. But the fiscal requirement proposed in the Meltzer Report seems to have been a last-minute addition. It is indeed the only point at which the report acknowledges that many currency crises are first-generation crises of the type modeled by Krugman (1979); they are caused by bad budgets, not bad banks.

ally. But the report goes further, asserting that Mexico's debt to the IMF and US Treasury represented a net addition to the burden borne by the Mexican taxpayer. Insofar as Mexico used the funds provided by the IMF and US Treasury to redeem the outstanding *tesobonos*, it was left in the end with no more debt than it had before.

The report also claims that the Mexican episode sent the wrong message to foreign lenders, who made the Asian crisis very much worse by providing large short-term loans in the run-up to the crisis, and that "the importance of the moral hazard problem cannot be overstated." But it offers no evidence to this effect. The very next paragraph, moreover, veers off in a different direction: "Whether or not the IMF contributed to moral hazard in Asia, it did little to end the use of the banking and financial systems to finance government-favored projects, eliminate so-called 'crony capitalism' and corruption, or promote safer and sounder banking and financial systems" (IFIAC 2000, 33)—this after saying elsewhere that IMF conditionality is too intrusive and impedes the development of democratic institutions!

The report also wrenches statements out of context. At one point, it quotes an IMF staff study (Ul Haque and Khan 1998) that surveys recent research on the effectiveness of conditionality:

> [I]t is now well accepted that Fund-supported programs improve the current account balance and the overall balance of payments. The results for inflation are less clear cut. . . . In the case of growth, the consensus seems to be that output will be depressed in the short run as the demand reducing elements of the policy package dominate. (IFIAC 2000, 19)

But that's not the end of the passage in the staff study. The rest—not quoted—reads as follows:

> Over time the structural reform elements of the program start to take effect and growth begins to rise. These newer empirical results indicate that, on average, Fund-supported adjustment programs have been more effective in achieving their objectives than earlier analyses would indicate. (Ul Haque and Khan 1998, 19)

And the same thing happens again. Discussing the debt crisis of the 1980s, the report asserts that the Fund's willingness to provide "an apparently unlimited external supply of funds forestalls creditors and debtors from offering concessions" (IFIAC 2000, 38). This is a gross caricature of the Fund's actual policy—its willingness to "lend into arrears" (i.e., before a government has reached agreement with its private creditors concerning the restructuring of its debt and is therefore still in arrears).[30]

---

30. Furthermore, the report quotes Eichengreen (1999b) in support of its interpretation, whereas Eichengreen had cited the Fund's *previous* policy, under which it had refused to lend into arrears.

The Meltzer Report winds up by arguing that the IMF should be restructured as a smaller institution with three responsibilities: (1) to act as a quasi-lender of last resort to "solvent emerging economies" under a mechanism designed to avoid the abuse of liquidity assistance to sponsor bailouts, (2) to collect and publish financial and economic data from member countries and disseminate those data to market participants, and (3) to provide policy advice (but not impose conditions) in the course of its regular Article IV consultations.

The "mechanism" proposed by the report would be based on rules much like those outlined by Calomiris.[31] To draw on the IMF, a country would have to allow foreign financial institutions to enter and operate freely; make sure that its banks are "adequately capitalized" so as to foster market discipline; publish regularly the maturity structure of its sovereign debt, including guaranteed debt and off-balance-sheet liabilities; and meet a "proper fiscal requirement" (the nature of which is not explained). IMF loans would be limited to 120 days with only one permissible rollover, and they would bear a penalty rate—a premium over the sovereign yield paid by the borrowing country one week before applying for an IMF loan.[32] Finally, the report suggests that countries be subject to a borrowing limit equal to one year's tax revenue, which would be very much higher than the Fund's present quota-based ceiling.

The report adopts the two-corner approach to exchange rate policy—exchange rates should be fixed firmly or allowed to float—but does not follow Calomiris, who said that IMF financing should be limited to countries with fixed exchange rates. But like Calomiris, the report concludes that the Fund has sufficient financial resources. Should these not suffice, moreover, the Fund should borrow from the market or from member countries.

The blueprints proposed by Calomiris and the Meltzer Report would presumably meet the need for an international LLR to complement the functioning of national LLRs—to supply foreign currency credit when a national LLR must cope with huge cross-currency flows caused by a run on its banks. But both are seriously flawed because they are based implicitly on both parts of the two-part premise set out at the start of this

---

31. With one small but important difference. Whereas Calomiris would use those rules to govern membership in a new IMF, the Meltzer Report would not disband the existing IMF. Although many of its members would be barred from access to Fund credit, they would still be subject to the data-reporting requirement and to regular Article IV surveillance. (The report does suggest, however, that OECD countries should not be subject to surveillance, because their policies are reviewed by the OECD itself and by other bodies. But Mexico and Korea are OECD countries!)

32. Unlike Calomiris, the Meltzer Report does not call for collateralization (see n. 21, above); but it does insist that IMF loans be given preferred status and be exempted from negative pledge clauses.

discussion—that an international LLR is needed to deal with the external manifestations of a creditor panic, and creditor panics originate in the banking system. That may have been true in the Thai case. It was not true, however, in the Mexican case, where the acute phase of the crisis began when a creditor panic arose in the debt market—when foreign holders of *tesobonos* began to fear that the Mexican government could not roll them over.[33]

There is, we have seen, a close association between banking and currency crises, and there was a banking crisis in Mexico. But causation can run both ways—and does. Emerging-market countries should be encouraged to strengthen their banking systems. But it would be hard to devise a more oblique and hazardous way of achieving that goal than the approach embodied in these blueprints—refusing access to IMF credit until countries have achieved it. Countries are not banks; they face many risks and problems. And the solvency of a country's banks says nothing about the solvency of the country itself—which is, in any case, an elusive concept. Barry Eichengreen (2000a) raises the same objection.

Both blueprints also reflect an obsessive concern with moral hazard and a remarkable faith in the ability of financial markets to make subtle judgments about very complex issues—to process information fully and exercise market discipline in a consistent, timely way. There is, indeed, a paradox here. If financial markets can do that, why should we worry about creditor panics?

Finally, both blueprints reflect a naive belief that an intergovernmental institution like the IMF can be bound by simple, objective rules—whether they are used to govern eligibility for membership, as in the Calomiris blueprint, or eligibility for IMF credit, as in the Meltzer Report. That is unlikely:

> [The authors] seem to believe that by imposing an *ex ante* rule, discretion and political considerations will disappear. To the contrary, everything we know of international relations suggests that discretion will instead migrate to a different decision point, such as whether a country is eligible for IMF assistance. . . . The upshot might be the worst of both worlds—a nominal commitment to rules, which are broken in somewhat regular fashion. (Tarullo 2001, 38)

There may be no need to worry about this possibility, as the recommendations of the Meltzer Report will not be adopted. Some members of the Bush administration have been said to favor them, but they will not find

---

33. Consider, moreover, the case of Argentina in 2000-01. It might have met the preconditions set out in the Meltzer Report but might not have qualified for IMF assistance. It faced an incipient debt crisis—the risk that it would be unable to refinance its external debt—not a banking crisis. Furthermore, the penalty rate proposed by the Meltzer Report would have been extremely high, because the prevailing interest rate on Argentina's sovereign debt had risen hugely, thanks to the country's debt problem.

favor in other countries—least of all those that cannot expect to meet the preconditions for access to IMF credit. But those recommendations may surface again when Congress is asked to adopt legislation approving an increase in IMF quotas or takes up any other matter involving the Fund.

The Right Role for Prequalification

The Meltzer Report proposed that prequalification replace conditionality, and others have made that same recommendation. Here are two examples:[34]

Malcolm Knight, Lawrence Schembri, and James Powell (2000) would reconfigure the IMF to concentrate all of its lending in two facilities. Access to the first facility would be based entirely on prequalification and be limited to 500 percent of a country's IMF quota. Access to the second facility would be based on conventional conditionality and be limited to 300 percent of quota—the normal cumulative limit. A country would prequalify for access to the first facility if it adhered to key standards and codes, such as the Basel Core Principles (BCBS 1997), had a "sustainable" exchange rate regime, and wrote collective action clauses into its sovereign bond contracts.[35] A country that did not prequalify for the first facility would be shunted to the second.

John Williamson (2000b) would eliminate all but one of the Fund's existing facilities and would create a new Crisis Facility. He would retain but liberalize the Compensatory Financing Facility (CFF), which would provide low-conditionality credit to countries afflicted by shocks clearly beyond their control, such as shortfalls in their commodity exports and natural disasters. The Crisis Facility, by contrast, would help countries cope with macroeconomic crises, and access to it would be governed by prequalification. A country would have access to that facility if it adhered to the Basel Core Principles and the Special Data Dissemination Standard (SDDS), wrote collective action clauses into its bond contracts, and, most important, was rated by the IMF as having "good" macroeconomic policies—a finding that the Fund would make at the conclusion of the coun-

---

34. Eatwell and Taylor (1998) provide a third, as part of a radical plan for reforming the international financial architecture. Writing before the Basel Core Principles had become the agreed-on standard for assessing the quality of banking supervision, they proposed that access to IMF credit be made dependent on the quality of financial-sector supervision. To that end, moreover, they urged the establishment of a World Financial Authority to oversee financial-sector supervision in individual countries (and to oversee the IMF itself). No country could draw on the IMF unless it met the standards set by that new institution. But Eatwell and Taylor were less clear on the point at issue here—whether this sort of prequalification would fully replace conventional conditionality.

35. Collective action clauses are discussed in chapter 4; they are aimed at promoting agreements between debtors and creditors when bonded debt must be restructured.

try's regular Article IV consultation. Presumably, this last requirement would replace conditionality.[36]

These sorts of prequalification, however, are not adequate substitutes for conditionality, because they are based on a simplistic supposition. They assume implicitly that countries that prequalify will not need assistance from the IMF unless they succumb to contagion or to other shocks for which they bear no blame. But we have already seen that contagion is not random: the countries most likely to suffer contagion are those that are seen to have defective policies or other vulnerabilities for which they must take blame. Furthermore, countries that suffer long-lasting shocks for which they bear no blame must nonetheless adapt to those shocks and must thus change their policies. Adherence to the Basel Core Principles can perhaps protect a country from banking-sector problems, homegrown or imported, but cannot protect it from other problems. The use of collective action clauses can help a country resolve a debt problem but cannot prevent it from creating a debt problem by running an imprudent fiscal policy. Williamson's suggestion, that Article IV consultations be used to identify countries that have "good" policies, is better than most others. But Article IV consultations take place annually or, in some case, biannually, and a country's policies can go badly wrong between those consultations. Furthermore, his suggestion takes no account of the need for policy changes to adapt to external shocks.

This is not to say that prequalification is a bad idea. Indeed, it is a good idea, if it is combined with conditionality. It can be used to reward a country for doing sensible things—adopting the Basel Core Principles and other key standards and codes, putting collective action clauses into its bond contracts, and adopting devices proposed later in this book to strengthen its financial system and cope with creditor panics. Prequalification should be used as a carrot, not a stick—as a way to reward countries for adopting reforms that reduce the risk and cost of future crises. It should be used to provide them with faster, cheaper, or more generous access to IMF credit. It should not be used to decide whether a country deserves financing because it is an "innocent victim" or does not deserve financing because it has failed to take the steps that might have prevented a crisis or has followed policies that produced the crisis.

The Fund's current use of prequalification does not draw this distinction clearly, and that is one reason why the CCL has not been attractive to countries that might have been expected to apply for it. Because the CCL was meant to help countries cope with contagion or with global shocks beyond their control, a country applying for a CCL runs the risk of being judged by an invidious standard. If it applies and is rejected or, having

---

36. Williamson (2000b) does not say what sort of assistance would be available to a country that suffered a crisis but had not prequalified. His suggestions appear very briefly in a paper that surveys several proposals for reforming the IMF and the World Bank.

been approved for a CCL, is told later that it has ceased to qualify, markets are bound to conclude that its policies are defective and is therefore the wrong place in which to invest. Although the Fund has modified the terms of access to the CCL to give a country "the strong benefit of the doubt" when it seeks to activate its CCL,[37] the country will be stigmatized if its application is refused or its CCL is not renewed.

There is another way to show what is wrong with the CCL. A number of countries have made "precautionary" use of ordinary quota-based drawings. They do not expect to need them. By making the necessary changes in their policies, however, submitting thereafter to the regular quarterly review required of all countries with IMF programs, and making more policy changes when needed, they can obtain an unambiguous, ongoing endorsement of their policies—which is more desirable from their point of view than the promise of obtaining the benefit of the doubt when, at some uncertain future date, they seek to activate a CCL.[38] Furthermore, a country can often obtain an ordinary quota-based drawing and the corresponding "seal of approval" from the IMF as speedily as it can hope to obtain a CCL. As this book went to press, there were reports that three emerging-market countries had sought CCLs but that their negotiations with the IMF had gone on for many months. Finally, a country needing immediate help can presumably count on expedited treatment via the Emergency Financing Mechanism (EFM). It does not need a CCL to obtain Fund credit quickly.[39]

We will return to prequalification at the end of this book, but in the alternative context suggested above—not as a way to determine whether a country qualifies for financing from the IMF or as a substitute for conditionality, but as a way to reward it for adhering to standards and codes, adopting collective action clauses, and introducing other provisions into its public and private debt contracts so that it may qualify for larger amounts of financing and at lower cost.

Can Floating Fix It?

Even before the currency crises of the 1990s, academic economists had begun to recast the debate about the comparative merits of alternative

---

37. This and other modifications in the terms of access are described in chapter 4.

38. Cline (2000a) argues that a country seeking a precautionary drawing can be stigmatized in the same way as a country applying for a CCL, but he misses the crucial distinction drawn in the text. The Fund rarely rejects outright a request for a "precautionary" drawing; instead, it calls on the applicant to modify its policies and adhere thereafter to "performance criteria." By contrast, a country that meets the preconditions for a CCL cannot know in advance what policy changes may be requested when it seeks to activate its CCL. Furthermore, the quarterly reviews required of countries with Fund programs serve to renew periodically the Fund's approval, and markets take notice of those regular renewals.

39. The same point is made by Goldstein (2001).

exchange rate regimes, and the crises themselves revived old objections to exchange rate pegging—even de facto pegging of the sort practiced by Thailand and some other Asian countries. Yet there was little discussion of exchange rate arrangements in the early phases of the architecture exercise. Writing in January 1999, Zanny Minton Beddoes noted that "the official architects are strangely silent about another crucial aspect of global financial reform: exchange rates" (1999).

Exchange Rate Regimes and the Architecture Exercise

There were two reasons for that silence about exchange rates. First, there were disagreements within the G-7 on this and other matters. American officials have long favored floating rates; Europeans, especially the French, have been fond of fixed rates, not only for themselves, as in the EMS, but for other countries too.[40] Second, the Articles of Agreement of the IMF permit individual governments to choose from a wide range of exchange rate arrangements. Article IV.2(b) lists these options:

> (i) the maintenance by a member of a value for its currency in terms of the special drawing right or another denominator, other than gold, selected by the member, or (ii) cooperative arrangements by which members maintain the value of their currencies in relation to the currency or currencies of other members, or (iii) other exchange rate arrangements of a member's choice.

In short, almost anything goes. To be sure, Article IV also requires the Fund to "exercise firm surveillance" over its members' exchange rate policies and "adopt specific principles" for the guidance of its members; that is the legal basis for the Article IV consultations that the Fund holds regularly with its members. Nevertheless, those principles must respect each member's right to choose from the open-ended menu offered by Article IV.[41]

---

40. As recently as 2001, at a meeting of European and Asian finance ministers, the French and Japanese circulated a discussion paper endorsing a hands-on approach to exchange rate management—one quite different from that adopted by the G-7 at the Köln Summit in 1999. For more on European views concerning this and other issues, including German objections to large-scale official financing, as well as differences among the Europeans themselves, see Coeuré and Pisani Ferry (2000). On the evolution of the US role in the architecture exercise, as well as its role in shaping the official response to the Mexican and Asian crises, see Delong and Eichengreen (2001).

41. The Fund adopted a set of "general principles" in 1977 and has reviewed them periodically. They state that the Fund may initiate discussions with a member if it engages in "protracted large-scale intervention" or "an unsustainable level of official or quasi-official borrowing," if it imposes or intensifies restrictions on current or capital transactions, if the behavior of its exchange rate "appears to be unrelated to underlying economic and financial conditions," or if there are "unsustainable flows of private capital" (IMF 1999g, 12-13). But the Fund is not entitled to punish a member when it objects to the member's exchange rate policy. (It should nevertheless be noted that access to IMF resources is not automatic, and

In May 1999, however, the US secretary of the treasury, Robert Rubin, ended the strange silence on exchange rate policy. In a speech at the School of Advanced International Studies, he referred obliquely to the freedom conferred by Article IV but warned against the risks and costs of pegging exchange rates and proposed a big change in the policy stance of the official community:

> The right exchange rate regime is a choice of the individual country. Yet at the center of each recent crisis has been a rigid exchange rate regime that proved ultimately unsustainable. The costs of failed regimes can be significant, not only for the countries involved, but also for other countries and for the system as a whole.... As a matter of policy, we believe that the international community should not provide exceptional large-scale official finance to countries intervening heavily to defend an exchange rate peg, except where the peg is judged sustainable and certain exceptional conditions have been met, such as when the necessary disciplines have been institutionalized or when an immediate shift away from a fixed exchange rate is judged to pose systemic risk. (Rubin 1999)

His statement fell slightly short of endorsing the two-corner approach. Rubin did not say that each country can or should be made to choose between a flexible exchange rate and a firmly fixed rate, and no one in the official community has said that since.

Soon after Secretary Rubin's speech, however, the G-7 finance ministers used very similar language in their report to the Köln Summit. They began with a general observation:

> Some emerging economies have sought to achieve exchange rate stability by adopting peg regimes against a single currency or a basket of currencies, often in the same region, of countries with which they have the closest trade and investment links. Countries choosing fixed rates must be willing, as necessary, to subordinate other policies to that of fixing the exchange rate. If countries choose fixed rates, recent history suggests that arrangements institutionalizing that policy can be useful to sustaining a credible commitment to fixed rates. (Group of 7 1999b, para. 30b)

And they went on to make another general observation:

> We agree that the most appropriate regime for any given economy may differ, depending on particular economic circumstances, such as the degree of integration with its trading partners. Since economic circumstances vary over time, the most appropriate regime for any given country may also vary. In any case, stability depends on the exchange rate regime being backed by consistent macroeconomic policies and supported by robust financial systems. (Group of 7 1999b, para. 33a)

Then they borrowed Secretary Rubin's language, almost word for word, but omitted his qualifying reference to systemic risk:

> We agree that the international community should not provide large-scale official financing for a country intervening heavily to support a particular exchange rate

---

the Fund can always reject a request for a very large drawing—one larger than the usual quota-based limits.)

level, except where that level is judged sustainable and certain conditions have been met, such as where the exchange rate policy is backed by a strong and credible commitment with supporting arrangements, and by consistent domestic policies. (Group of 7 1999b, para. 33b)

They chose to ignore—or did not notice—the conflicting implications of the first two paragraphs quoted above. A commitment to a fixed exchange rate will not be credible unless it is seen to be permanent or, at least, long-lasting; nevertheless, the G-7 ministers declared that the appropriate exchange rate regime is time dependent, because circumstances change. They also ignored the vexed issue of time consistency. What should the official community do when a government *has* intervened heavily to support a pegged exchange rate and has run out of reserves—and should the answer depend on the extent of the systemic risk involved in refusing large-scale financing?[42]

Although the G-7 finance ministers endorsed Secretary Rubin's views, the IMF's Interim Committee did not.[43] This is all it had to say after the Köln Summit:

> The Committee considers that increased mobility of capital has raised the requirements, in terms of both policy adaptability and institutional preparedness, for maintaining a fixed exchange rate regime. That said, members should be able to choose a regime that is appropriate to their particular circumstances and longer-term strategy. The choice of exchange rate regime and the implementation of supporting policies are critical for countries' economic development and financial stability, and in some cases potentially for the world economy. In all cases, IMF programs and surveillance should further focus on consistency of macroeconomic and other policies and institutional arrangements with the chosen exchange rate regime. (IMF 1999a, para. 17)

And it has not said much since—although others have said a great deal.[44]

Classifying Exchange Rate Regimes

To sort out the issues being debated and the actual exchange rate policies of emerging-market countries, we need first to list the options. How best

---

42. A former official who has drafted more communiqués than he cares to remember scrawled a note opposite the first draft of this paragraph: "The fact that communiqués, especially successive communiqués, are not fully rational or consistent should come as no surprise to anyone; they are written by committees, often with late-night compromises to paper over fundamental differences." His point is well-taken and should be borne in mind when reading the next chapter, as well as this one.

43. The Interim Committee was subsequently reconstituted as the International Monetary and Financial Committee (IMFC).

44. Recently, however, the Fund's Executive Board agreed that the IMF should not provide large-scale assistance to countries intervening heavily to support an exchange rate peg that is inconsistent with underlying policies, and it encouraged the Fund's staff to help countries with pegged rates design exit strategies; see IMF (2000e).

can we subdivide the continuum of exchange rate regimes that runs from free floating to firm fixing? Here is a four-part taxonomy that draws on the one used currently by the IMF:[45]

- Under a *free float*, a country's monetary authorities refrain from intervening on the foreign exchange market or altering interest rates for the purpose of affecting the level or path of the nominal exchange rate.

- Under a *managed float*, the monetary authorities do not adopt a particular exchange rate target; nevertheless, they intervene or alter interest rates at their discretion to affect the level or path of the exchange rate.

- Under a *soft peg*, the monetary authorities *do* adopt an exchange rate target and intervene or alter interest rates whenever the market exchange rate strays too far from that target. They may announce the target rate and the width of the band around it (which gives operational meaning to the phrase "too far") or may engage in de facto pegging, without announcing a target rate and without necessarily having in mind a clearly defined band. A target rate may be altered infrequently and, therefore, by relatively large amounts; that is what was done under the Bretton Woods system and in the EMS, which are sometimes described as having horizontal but adjustable pegs.[46] Alternatively, the target may be altered frequently and, therefore, by small amounts; that is what is done with crawling pegs or bands. In addition, the bands are typically wider under those arrangements than those surrounding horizontal pegs, because they must accommodate the changes in the crawling pegs. Soft pegs include single-currency pegs and multiple-currency (basket) pegs.

- Under a *hard peg*, the monetary authorities formally adopt a target rate and bind themselves firmly to maintain it indefinitely. There are three ways to do that: (1) converting the central bank into a *currency board* that must have foreign currency holdings at least as large as its monetary

---

45. On the Fund's taxonomy, see IMF (1999b); it differs in three major ways from the one in the text. First, it does not separately identify freely floating rates but lists them with other independently floating rates. Second, it distinguishes between two types of managed floating: "managed floating with no preannounced path" and "independent floating." Third, it uses a narrower definition of de facto pegging: my taxonomy includes all cases in which governments are committed in practice to a peg but do not announce it, whereas the Fund includes only cases in which governments precommit in practice to a peg surrounded by a narrow band. (Had the IMF been using its present scheme in the mid-1990s, it might not have classified a country such as Thailand as having a de facto peg, although Thailand was often described that way.)

46. The combination of a horizontal peg and narrow band is the "intermediate regime" criticized by Eichengreen (1995) when he predicted that countries with open capital markets would move eventually to one of the two corners. It is especially vulnerable to attack; see, e.g., Obstfeld and Rogoff (1995).

liabilities, must buy and sell foreign currency freely at the target rate, and must abstain from all other transactions (e.g., purchases and sales of domestic securities) that would alter its monetary liabilities;[47] (2) substituting a foreign currency for the domestic currency and thus extinguishing the exchange rate completely—the option described as *formal dollarization*; and (3) entering into a full-fledged *monetary union*, in which the members replace their national currencies with a new single currency and establish a new central bank to manage monetary policy for the union as a whole.

The boundaries between these regimes are clear conceptually but less clear operationally. No country can be deemed to practice free floating if its government or central bank has intervened recently or might do so in the future, and no can one assert with confidence of any central bank that it ignores the exchange rate completely when setting its interest rate policy.[48] The boundary between managed floating and soft pegging is even harder to draw operationally, because soft pegging includes de facto pegging, and one can only infer adherence to it from the observed behavior of the actual exchange rate and of other variables.[49] These difficulties, however, do not diminish the validity of the general conclusion, drawn by Stanley Fischer (2001a) and others, that there has been a discernible trend away from soft pegging. In 1991, only 3 of 34 emerging-market countries had hard pegs (Argentina and Hong Kong, which had currency boards, and Panama, which was formally dollarized), 21 had soft pegs, and 10 had managed floats; by 1999, a fourth country, Bulgaria, had a currency board, 14 countries had soft pegs, and 26 had managed floats,

---

47. On the history, functioning, and uses of currency boards, see Williamson (1995) and Ghosh, Gulde, and Wolf (2000).

48. The United States is often said to have a freely floating rate, which does come closer to free floating than do most other countries. In the 1970s and 1980s, it intervened to influence the value of the dollar in terms of other key currencies taken together (i.e., the dollar's effective exchange rate). Thereafter, it intervened less frequently and mainly to influence the dollar value of the yen or euro, not the overall value of the dollar.

49. For attempts to draw such inferences, see G. Calvo and Reinhart (2000a), Bénassy-Quéré and Coeuré (2000) and Levy-Yedati and Sturzenegger (2000). The same basic strategy is used by Edwards (2000) to absolve Mexico of the charge that it has practiced soft pegging rather than managed floating. It is nevertheless hard to use this technique to monitor exchange rate policies closely. A long span of data may be required to identify the key parameters of a de facto peg, especially one based on a currency basket; see Frankel, Schmukler, and Servén (2000), who go on to argue that the opaque nature of that regime buttresses the case for the two-corner approach. Transparency matters, however, mainly insofar as it enhances the credibility of a pegged rate regime and fosters the stabilizing speculation modeled by Krugman (1991) in his seminal paper on target zones. It is not by itself a reason for choosing or rejecting a particular regime.

including a number of large emerging-market countries, such as Brazil, Korea, Mexico, and South Africa.[50]

Comparing Three Forms of Hard Pegging

All three forms of hard pegging have one common property. The advent of a balance of payments deficit, whether caused by a trade-related shock or by a reversal of capital flows, reduces the domestic money supply automatically, raises domestic interest rates, and thereby imposes deflationary pressures. Furthermore, those pressures will build up for as long as the balance of payments remains in deficit, because the money supply will go on falling. Thus, when wages and prices are sticky, output growth will fall, and there may be an outright recession. With a long-lasting shock, moreover, these painful effects will persist until the gradual fall in the price level—or faster inflation in the outside world—has brought about a real depreciation of the domestic currency large enough to offset the shock and thereby eliminate the balance of payments deficit. The buildup of deflationary pressures will be attenuated if an increase of domestic interest rates can attract capital inflows, as these will reduce the balance of payments deficit, and this is most likely to happen under formal dollarization and in a monetary union. Under both of those regimes, domestic banks are apt to have access to large, liquid interbank markets. Therefore, adjustment to shocks may be less painful than under a currency board, but it may take more time.[51]

Two sorts of hard pegs have other properties in common. A country that replaces its central bank with a currency board or dollarizes formally cannot pursue an independent monetary policy. To that extent, of course, both regimes serve to enhance the credibility of the hard peg itself. Under both regimes, moreover, the country must find a roundabout way to provide its banking system with a lender of last resort. A currency board

50. See Fischer (2001a, figure 2 and table 2). Countries counted here as soft peggers are those listed by the IMF as having conventional fixed pegs (as opposed to hard pegs), with narrow or wide bands, and those having crawling pegs or bands; countries counted here as managed floaters are those listed by the IMF as having managed or independent floats. Recently, one of the 34 countries (Ecuador) switched from managed floating to formal dollarization, and another developing country (El Salvador) has also dollarized. Five more countries have currency boards (Brunei, Bosnia and Herzegovina, Djibouti, Estonia, and Lithuania), and there are two monetary unions in Francophone Africa, both with the same single currency (the CFA franc), which is pegged to the euro. But no large emerging-market country belongs to a monetary union.

51. It is hard to test this conjecture, because there are so few countries with hard pegs. But Fischer (2001a) cites Argentina's experience to illustrate the painful nature of adjustment under a currency board, and Céspedes, Chang, and Velasco (2000) demonstrate formally that the output, employment, and investment effects of real exchange rate adjustment are larger with fixed than with flexible rates.

cannot serve as an LLR because it cannot acquire domestic currency claims, and the same problem arises under dollarization, because there is no domestic institution capable of creating bank reserves. Therefore, the government itself must serve as the LLR and raise the necessary funds by taxation or borrowing.[52] Alternatively, under dollarization, the central bank of the country issuing the foreign currency that has replaced the domestic currency can serve as the LLR to its client country's banks.[53] (Under both regimes, to be sure, foreign commercial banks can serve as LLRs to their local affiliates, but there may be no way of forcing them to do so.)

Nevertheless, there are major differences between these two regimes. A currency board must hold foreign currency reserves and will therefore earn interest on them. A country that opts for formal dollarization must use its reserves to redeem and extinguish its domestic currency (and may even have to borrow if its reserves are small). The resulting revenue loss may not be inconsequential for the government or for the whole country.[54] Furthermore, it is easier to exit from a currency board than from formal dollarization. Like most governmental arrangements, currency boards are creatures of law and can be abolished by changing the law. More important, the durability of a currency board depends entirely on the strength of the commitment to it—whether the government is willing to incur the

---

52. The importance of this problem was illustrated by the banking crisis in Argentina during the 1994-95 Mexican crisis, shortly after the Argentine central bank began to function as a currency board. When large capital outflows led automatically to a sharp fall in bank liquidity, the government borrowed from the IMF and World Bank, used the foreign currency proceeds to buy pesos from the central bank, and lent the pesos to Argentine banks; see Caprio, Dooley, Leipziger, and Walsh (1996). Thereafter, Argentina erected defenses against a repetition of that banking crisis; it set up credit lines with foreign commercial banks and required Argentine banks to hold large amounts of liquid assets. Furthermore, foreign banks have acquired or replaced most of the major Argentine banks and thus strengthened the banking system; see Alston and Gallo (2000) and Edwards (2000).

53. Thus far, however, the Federal Reserve System has been unwilling to assume this role vis-à-vis the banks of countries that use the US dollar to replace their currencies, and the Clinton administration opposed any such foreign entanglement, saying that it would be inappropriate for the US authorities "to extend the net of bank supervision, to provide access to the Federal Reserve discount window, or adjust bank supervisory responsibility or the procedures or orientation of US monetary policy in light of another country deciding to adopt the dollar" (Summers 1999a).

54. Hanke and Schuler (1994) have urged the United States to compensate countries adopting the dollar for this loss of seigniorage, and legislation aimed at allowing it to do so was sponsored by Senator Connie Mack in 1999, before his retirement. Taking a different tack, Robert J. Barro has proposed that the United States print the necessary dollars and hand them over gratis; that would allow a dollarizing country to retain its reserves and use them to support its banks in the event of a future liquidity crisis ("Let the Dollar Reign Supreme from Seattle to Santiago," *Wall Street Journal*, 8 March 1999).

economic and political costs of abiding by the rules.[55] Finally, a country with a currency board retains its own currency and can abandon its hard peg without taking the steps required to introduce a new national currency. A country that has formally dollarized cannot move as swiftly and may be very vulnerable to capital flight and financial disruption if it is thought to be contemplating the introduction of a new national currency. The potential costs of that disruption constitute an additional barrier to exit and thus reinforce the credibility of the commitment to formal dollarization.

From the standpoint of an individual country, a monetary union has properties similar to those of the two unilateral hard pegs, a currency board and formal dollarization. The country gives up the right to pursue an independent monetary policy in return for relief from the need to defend its exchange rate. But there is also a basic difference. A monetary union has a central bank and can therefore pursue an independent monetary policy. Opting for a currency board or formal dollarization thus involves a surrender of monetary sovereignty, whereas membership in a monetary union involves a pooling of monetary sovereignty.[56] Under the two unilateral regimes, the country involved must accept some other country's monetary policy. In a monetary union, by contrast, monetary policy is designed to meet the needs of the entire union. (In the European case, it is aimed at maintaining price stability in the whole euro area, and each member country has a voice in the making of monetary policy, not just because it has a vote in the policymaking body but also because its own price index enters the price index of the euro area.) It is easy to show formally that the asymmetric policy domain of a currency board or formal dollarization is less satisfactory from the standpoint of the country concerned than the multinational policy domain of a monetary union.[57]

A monetary union, however, may afford less protection against currency crises than does formal dollarization. Its members do not have exchange rates of their own, but the union has one, and it has to decide what sort of exchange rate regime to adopt. If it pegs its currency to some other currency, its pegged rate can be attacked. If it adopts a flexible rate, the union and its members still face exchange rate risk, and it will not be negligible unless the union's members trade mainly with each other. Furthermore, its vulnerability to currency crises may not differ greatly

---

55. The importance of this distinction is illustrated by the existence of a spread, which has been very large at times, between the interest rate paid by Argentine banks on peso deposits and the rate paid on dollar deposits; see Edwards (2000).

56. Cohen (1998), among others, has emphasized this point.

57. See Kenen (2000a) on the effects of real shocks under formal dollarization and a monetary union; see also Alesina and Barro (2000), who show that the benefits of dollarization depend on the ability of the client country to bribe the leading country to take explicit account of the client country's inflation rate when the leader sets its monetary policy.

from that of its member countries before they formed the union. Much will depend on its monetary and fiscal policies and on the quality of its financial system. If the union's central bank pursues a lax monetary policy, if its member governments run lax fiscal policies, or if its private sector accumulates foreign currency debt, it may still experience currency crises.

But another difference dominates the rest. A currency board can be introduced unilaterally, as can dollarization. But countries cannot form a monetary union without first agreeing on how it should be governed. If the United States, Canada, and Mexico were to form a North American Monetary Union (NAMU), how would its policymakers be chosen and how would they be held accountable for their performance? Who would draft and enact the legislation required to introduce the union's new currency and govern its subsequent use? The members of the European Union could not have written the Maastricht Treaty in 1991 had they not written the Treaty of Rome in 1958, creating the institutions of the European Union, and learned to use them thereafter.[58]

There has been much talk about regional monetary cooperation in Asia and Latin America, and modest steps are being taken in that direction.[59] But the individual countries of those regions have different political systems and cultures. Furthermore, their regional trading arrangements are less complete and robust than those of North America, let alone those of the European Union. Thus regional monetary unions may be a long way off, and countries that want to adopt hard pegs may have to choose between currency boards and formal dollarization. Hence, the remainder of the chapter concentrates on those two forms of hard pegging and compares them with other regimes. Must emerging-market countries move to one of the two corners? If so, which corner? Or can a solid case still be made for intermediate regimes?

A Closer Look at the Two Corners

At an earlier stage in the debate about exchange rate regimes, economists focused on the effects of various shocks under fixed and floating rates. They distinguished between monetary and real shocks and between domestic and foreign shocks. It was widely agreed that countries faced mainly with domestic monetary shocks should opt for fixed exchange rates, because the intervention on foreign exchange markets needed to keep an exchange rate fixed would have the effect of exporting those shocks to the outside world. Furthermore, a firm commitment to a fixed

---

58. Buiter (1999) makes the same point.

59. See, e.g., Bénassy-Quéré and Coeuré (2000), Park and Wang (2000), and Christopher Swann ("Yearning for Stability Spurs Surge of Regional Harmony," *Financial Times*, 7 March 2001).

exchange rate would constrain the conduct of monetary policy, with the dual effect of conferring credibility on that monetary policy and reducing the size and frequency of the monetary shocks emanating from it. Countries faced mainly with foreign monetary shocks should opt for flexible exchange rates, which would insulate them from those shocks. It was likewise agreed that countries faced mainly with real shocks, whether domestic or foreign, should also opt for flexible rates. Adjustment to a real shock requires a change in the real exchange rate, which is much easier to achieve by changing the nominal rate than by changing the price level. In his review of the literature, however, Barry Eichengreen (1997) noted that this mapping of shocks and regimes is not very helpful when countries confront a variety of shocks or when the dominant type varies across time.

In the 1980s, attention turned to a different issue—the case for using a fixed exchange rate to restore price stability in a country suffering from high inflation. Fixing the exchange rate, it was said, would help in three ways. First, it would harness goods-market arbitrage to stabilize the domestic currency prices of internationally traded goods and thus reduce the inflation rate automatically. More generally, it would exploit the various links between the exchange rate, on the one hand, and domestic prices and wages, on the other. When the exchange rate is flexible, those links tend to produce a wage-price spiral and currency depreciation; when the exchange rate is pegged, the wage-price spiral tends to decelerate. Second, the move to a fixed exchange rate would affect expectations. Once firms and workers were convinced that the domestic currency had ceased to depreciate, they would have little incentive to raise prices and wages. Third, fixing the exchange rate would alter expectations about monetary policy. Instead of accommodating the wage-price spiral or, what is worse, driving that spiral, the central bank would have to defend the fixed exchange rate by reducing the growth of the money supply and keeping it low thereafter.

Unfortunately, these ideal outcomes rarely happen. The wholesale prices of traded goods stop rising quickly, but their retail prices do not. That is because retail prices include distribution costs, which depend on domestic wages and the prices of nontraded goods, and they cannot be stabilized by goods-market arbitrage. In fact, wages and the prices of nontraded goods go on rising for some time, albeit at reduced rates. Therefore, the real exchange rate appreciates gradually and becomes increasingly overvalued, posing a dilemma. If the government changes the fixed nominal rate or moves to a flexible rate, it undermines its credibility and risks reigniting expectations of inflation. If instead it sticks to the fixed rate, it faces a gradual deterioration in the trade balance, a need to attract capital inflows to cover a growing current account deficit, and the prospect of slow real growth in the traded-goods sector. Too often, governments stick with fixed rates, because they put credibility first, and are then forced to abandon them when faced with currency crises. At that point, of course, their currencies depreciate sharply.

In short, fighting inflation may justify the temporary use of a fixed exchange rate, but the intrinsic dynamics of disinflation dictate an early exit, before the domestic currency becomes hugely overvalued. It is not a rationale for a permanently fixed rate, let alone a hard peg such as a currency board regime, from which it is hard to exit. It is indeed wise to exit at an early stage, when capital inflows are large and reserves are rising. The currency is likely to appreciate, not depreciate, when the fixed rate is abandoned. It is also important to adopt a new anchor for monetary policy, such as inflation targeting, to replace the previous exchange rate commitment. But the whole strategy poses a conundrum. Can a fixed rate serve as an anchor for monetary policy during the transition to low inflation, when everyone believes that the rate will be abandoned once it has done its job? A temporarily fixed rate might still promote goods-market arbitrage, stabilizing the prices of traded goods. But a temporary fixing of the exchange rate may not stabilize expectations, especially if, as Lawrence Summers (1999a) suggests, a country using a fixed rate to bring down inflation should disclose its exit strategy. It may be helpful, however, to introduce inflation targeting even before exiting from a fixed rate, whether or not the exit strategy has been disclosed in advance and despite the obvious awkwardness of trying to target the inflation rate as well as the exchange rate.[60]

The two-corner approach to the choice of exchange rate regime can be viewed as a by-product of the previous debate about the efficacy of exchange rate-based stabilizations.[61] Countries with open capital markets cannot sustain pegged but adjustable rates. If rates are adjustable, they can be knocked off their pegs. Thus, when the dynamics of disinflation require the abandonment of a pegged rate, a country cannot move to a new pegged rate and expect to stick to it. That is widely understood. It is equally clear, however, that the old taxonomic approach to the choice of regime cannot give countries adequate guidance. It does not take full account of the complex environment in which regime choices must be made.

---

60. Edwards (2000) surveys the large literature on exchange rate-based stabilizations and draws conclusions similar to those offered here. On exit strategies and the problems involved in switching from exchange rate targeting to inflation targeting, see Eichengreen (1999a) and Eichengreen et al. (1999).

61. In fact, one former US official has described the G-7 endorsement of the two-corner approach and the threat to withhold official financing from a country that intervenes heavily to defend a fixed exchange rate as a device for encouraging countries to exit early from exchange rate-based stabilizations and for prodding the IMF to persuade them to do so.

Three features of that environment have been cited frequently in the debate about the two-corner approach: (1) the extent of de facto dollarization, especially liability dollarization, which is itself a legacy of past inflation and currency depreciation; (2) the limited ability of emerging-market countries to issue long-term debt in their own currencies, which is likewise due to previous depreciations but also reflects the asymmetry between the size of the typical emerging-market country and the size of the global capital market in which it must borrow; and (3) the fact that no country can peg its currency to one key currency without having it float in terms of the rest—and in terms of all other currencies that are pegged to another key currency or float independently.

The first feature is invoked by Guillermo Calvo and Carmen Reinhart to explain why many emerging-market countries evince "fear of floating" and to explain why those countries should move from de facto to de jure dollarization.[62] When firms, banks, and governments have large foreign currency debts, exchange rate fluctuations destabilize cash flows and balance sheets and can therefore produce large output losses of the sort suffered by the Asian countries in 1997-98.

The second feature is invoked by Ricardo Hausmann and others as a more general justification for formal dollarization, even by countries that have not undergone extensive de facto dollarization within their own economies.[63] Currency risk, they argue, has compounded country risk, inhibiting the development of capital markets, limiting the ability of firms and governments to issue long-term debt in domestic currency, forcing them to issue foreign currency debt, and thus perpetuating their exposure to currency risk. Hausmann calls this phenomenon "original sin," and he sees formal dollarization as the path to salvation.

But the third feature of the environment is cited by those who warn that formal dollarization is dangerous for any country that trades extensively with many other countries and is therefore vulnerable to exchange rate changes in the outside world. To be sure, it is technically feasible to base a currency board on a currency basket rather than a single foreign currency. But such an arrangement sacrifices transparency and credibility to trade-oriented optimality, and it may not provide a perfect hedge against exchange rate changes in the outside world.[64]

---

62. See G. Calvo and Reinhart (2000a, 2000b), who also cite econometric studies showing that developing countries are particularly vulnerable to the trade-depressing effects of exchange rate fluctuations.

63. See Hausmann et al. (1999) and Eichengreen and Hausmann (1999). Knight, Schembri, and Powell (2000) point out, however, that Chile and Mexico already have well-functioning markets for domestic currency debt. Furthermore, Larraín and Velasco (1999) raise questions about the statistical evidence offered by Hausmann et al. in support of their assertion that capital markets are deeper in countries that have fixed exchange rates.

64. Domingo Cavallo has said that he considered this sort of arrangement when designing Argentina's currency board. It would have avoided the appreciation of the effective exchange

Crawling Away from the Corners

Where, then, do we wind up? Jeffrey Frankel (1999) is right to conclude that "no single currency regime is right for all countries or at all times." And Stanley Fischer (2001a, 5) has written recently that "proponents of what is now known as the bipolar view—myself included—probably have exaggerated their point for dramatic effect." But we can go further. We can safely say that no single exchange rate will be right for any country at all times. Therefore, the vast majority of countries should shun any regime that promises—or threatens—to fix the exchange rate forever.

There is, to be sure, "fear of floating" and some reason for it, but Calvo and Reinhart may overstate its prevalence and relevance. Two large Latin American countries that used to have pegged rates, Brazil and Mexico, seem now to be comfortable with flexible rates. And some of the Asian countries that seemed to be lapsing back into soft pegging after the Asian crisis allowed their currencies to depreciate substantially when the demand for their exports declined in 2001.

A hard peg may still be appropriate for a very small open economy, which is, for all practical purposes, an economic appendage of a single key currency country and cannot expect to outgrow that status. Formal dollarization, moreover, may be the best form of hard pegging for that sort of country. It is not easily undone and is, by its very nature, immune to attack: no one can short a currency that does not exist. Currency boards can be attacked; and though they have survived attacks, their built-in defense mechanisms have imposed high costs. The attack on the Argentine peso in 1995 began as a currency crisis, but the workings of the currency board transformed it into a banking crisis. The attack on the Hong Kong dollar in 1997 did not lead to a banking crisis, because Hong Kong's banking system was less vulnerable, but it caused a sharp spike in interest rates that deeply depressed equity and property markets.[65]

---

rate for the Argentine peso resulting from the appreciation of the dollar and the depreciation of the Brazilian real. He did not adopt it because his chief concern was to restore public confidence in the Argentine peso, and a one-to-one link between the peso and the dollar looked better from that standpoint than the variable link implied by a one-to-one link with a currency basket. In 2001, however, Cavallo introduced legislation that will tie the Argentine peso to a dollar-euro basket. The value of the peso will equal one-half of a dollar *plus* one-half of a euro, and the legislation will take effect when the euro reaches parity with the dollar (so that the shift to the new valuation will not cause an abrupt change in the dollar value of the peso). Lamfalussy (2000) has also raised the possibility of basing a currency board on a currency basket.

65. It should also be remembered that Argentina and Hong Kong chose hard pegs for very special reasons. Argentina sought to end its long addiction to inflation. Hong Kong sought to preserve financial stability in the face of the grave political uncertainty produced by the start of the very long process that would lead to the transfer of sovereignty from London to Beijing.

Hard pegs are inappropriate for larger countries, especially those with diversified trade or those likely to experience structural change as they develop. Although they may have reason to fear floating, they should be no less fearful of hard fixing. And they have very strong reason to shun soft pegging, even de facto pegging, because it attracts attack. For them, the two-corner approach constitutes a metaphoric warning rather than a menu of viable options. If you need to peg, it says, you must adopt a hard peg, not dwell in the soft peg neighborhood of the exchange rate continuum. But the constraints of a hard peg strongly suggest that you should move the other way, toward managed floating. How far you should go, however, remains an open question. You need not go all the way to free floating. Recall the main point made at the start of chapter 2. When faced with a very big capital inflow, too big to be sustainable, a country should bank a large part of the inflow rather than let its currency appreciate. And there is a sensible case for taking a stronger stand, along lines suggested by John Williamson.

A few years ago, Williamson (1996) favored crawling bands for emerging-market countries. They would adopt exchange rate targets, put wide bands around them, but let the target rates and bands move gradually through time to offset changes in economic fundamentals. This regime, he argued, would reduce the risk of serious misalignments in exchange rates—those that occur with pegged rates when fundamentals change, and those that occur with floating rates when fundamentals do not change but capricious shifts in market sentiment generate exchange rate changes. But when he returned to the subject two years later (Williamson 1998), he began to contemplate a less rigorous regime—a "monitoring band" instead of a "crawling band." Under a crawling band, the monetary authorities must intervene on the foreign exchange market or modify their monetary policies whenever the market exchange rate crosses the edges of its band. Under a monitoring band, there is no such obligation:

> There is a presumption that the authorities will normally intervene to discourage the rate from straying far from the band, but they have an extra degree of flexibility in deciding the tactics they will employ to achieve this. In particular, if they decide that market pressures are overwhelming, they can choose to allow the rate to take the strain, even if in doing so it goes outside the band. (Williamson 1998, 68-69)

What, then, is the operational difference between a monitoring band and a loosely managed float?

> In practice, having a monitoring band may make a difference even if the authorities choose not to intervene, as long as the market knows that the authorities can employ policy weapons to push the rate back within the band, and the limits of the band are known. This knowledge should make the market fearful of pushing the rate so far as to set up the conditions for a bear squeeze (or a "bull squeeze"). Another possible restraint is that the market may believe that the authorities have

correctly estimated the long-run equilibrium rate in their positioning of the band; this again may discourage the market from pushing the rate as far as it would otherwise go. (Williamson 1998, 69)

And when Williamson (2000a) returned to the subject yet again, he urged emerging-market countries to revive the "intermediate option" by using a basket, band, and crawl—his "BBC" proposal—but he favored a monitoring band rather than a crawling band.[66] This proposal has merit. It can allay the fear of floating without drawing an indefensible distinction between an exchange rate change that crosses an arbitrarily fine line and one that is just a bit smaller than that. Furthermore, a monitoring band can be reconciled with inflation targeting under conditions of high but imperfect capital mobility, in which sterilized intervention is not utterly impotent.[67]

What, then, remains of the view taken by the G-7 ministers, that the international community should not provide large-scale official financing to a country intervening heavily in defense of a soft peg? Not much. Very few countries should have hard pegs, and those that should have them will not need large-scale official financing if they dollarize formally rather than rely on a less robust currency board regime. Furthermore, the threat to withhold large-scale financing from countries with soft pegs will not be credible unless and until a large country with a soft peg runs into a currency crisis and is denied financing. It would be far better to devise another way of coaxing such a country off its soft peg before its currency is attacked. For that, of course, the Fund would need an early warning system—a subject to which we will come back.

---

66. The new and most distinctive feature of Williamson's proposal is his recommendation that the East Asian countries adopt a common currency basket rather than the dollar standard recommended by McKinnon (2000).

67. To reconcile it with inflation targeting, however, the crawl of the monitoring band should be based on the authorities' forecast of inflation (or their inflation target) rather than the current inflation rate; this was the strategy adopted by Israel (see Williamson 1996).

4

The Architecture Exercise: What's New?

The origins of the architecture exercise were discussed briefly in chapter 1, which listed the main recommendations of the Halifax Summit in June 1995, soon after the Mexican crisis. The evolution of the architecture exercise is examined more thoroughly in this chapter and the next. This one looks at its achievements; the next looks at its shortcomings and what should be done about them.

We begin with a chronological account. It is meant in part to show how the focus of the architecture exercise was influenced by changes in the character of the financial crises that erupted as the exercise proceeded. Like generals preparing to fight the last war instead of the next one, participants in the architecture exercise seemed sometimes to be trying to ward off the last crisis. The chronology also introduces the key documents, recommendations, and decisions that represent the products of the architecture exercise. The chapter then moves on to an issue-by-issue account. Adopting the distinction often employed in the exercise itself, it looks first at efforts aimed at crisis prevention and then at efforts aimed at crisis management.[1] This review does not examine all of the issues raised in the course of the architecture exercise. The chapter does not discuss IMF lending to low-income developing countries—those that receive subsi-

---

1. A further distinction is often drawn between two types of crisis-preventing measure: those aimed at enhancing transparency and accountability in the public and private sectors of emerging-market countries, and those aimed at reforming the functioning and supervision of their financial and corporate sectors. But there is little to be gained by distinguishing sharply between them, because both types employ the same basic strategy—drafting various standards and codes and then promoting adherence to them.

dized credit from the Fund's Poverty Reduction and Growth Facility—and it does not discuss the HIPC Initiative, the program designed to reduce the debt burdens of highly indebted poor countries. It does not consider the supervision of hedge funds and other highly leveraged institutions, the attempt to enhance bank supervision in offshore financial centers, or the efforts of the Financial Action Task Force (FATF) to combat money laundering. And it does not revisit the exchange rate debate reviewed in chapter 3.

The Evolution of the Architecture Exercise

The history of the architecture exercise can be divided into three phases, each lasting two years. The first began in 1995 and included the Halifax and Lyon Summits. The second began in 1997 and included the Denver and Birmingham Summits. The third began in 1999 and included the Köln and Okinawa Summits. Measured by their contributions to the architecture exercise, some of these G-7 summits were more important than others. But all of them served their usual catalytic purpose—forcing a meeting of minds—and each helped set the next year's agenda.

Halifax and Lyon

The principal recommendations of the Halifax Summit were heavily influenced by the Mexican crisis. Because market participants had accused Mexico of concealing the size of the fall in its official reserves, the Halifax Summit called on the IMF to develop benchmarks aimed at promoting the timely publication of economic and financial data. Because the Mexican "bailout" was brought before the Executive Board of the IMF without prior consultation, on what amounted to a take-it-or-leave-it basis, the Halifax Summit urged the Fund to devise the Emergency Financing Mechanism (EFM)—a set of procedures designed to provide a crisis-stricken country with speedy access to Fund credit without depriving the Fund's board of its rightful role in the decision-making process. Because of the huge size of the financial package required to extinguish Mexico's *tesobonos*, the Halifax Summit called for a doubling of the bilateral credit lines available to the IMF—the recommendation that led eventually to the creation of the New Arrangements to Borrow (NAB) rather than enlargement of the existing General Arrangements to Borrow (GAB).

Finally, the Halifax Summit led to the creation of the working group that wrote the Rey Report (Group of 10 1996). Its main message was quoted in chapter 1. While affirming "the basic principle that the terms and conditions of all debt contracts are to be met in full," it warned that a temporary suspension of debt payments may be required in exceptional cases. Therefore, debtor countries and their private creditors should not "expect to be insulated from adverse financial consequences by the provision of large-scale official financing" and should not expect any type of debt to be exempt from a payment suspension or restructuring in the event of a future crisis. It even declined to rule out a suspension of debt payments on private-sector debt or using exchange controls to enforce it.

The Recommendations of the Rey Report

Having warned that debt suspensions might be needed in the future, the Rey Report made two recommendations aimed at resolving a crisis rapidly after debt payments are suspended.

First, it proposed the inclusion of collective action clauses in international debt contracts. These, it said, could facilitate dialogue between debtors and creditors, promote cohesion among the creditors, and reduce the power of dissident creditors to delay or block an agreement acceptable to the vast majority of creditors. It suggested that three sorts of clauses be included in debt contracts: (1) clauses providing for the collective representation of creditors; (2) clauses permitting a qualified majority of creditors to approve modifications in a debt contract, rather than requiring unanimous approval; and (3) clauses requiring any creditor receiving payments from a debtor to share them with all other creditors, thereby diminishing a creditor's incentive to bring suit against a debtor or seek preferential treatment.[2] As collective action clauses cannot be introduced retroactively into existing debt contracts, it would take several years to include them in the totality of outstanding debt. Furthermore, the Rey Report conceded that no single borrower might want to lead the way, for fear of raising the cost of issuing new debt. Nevertheless, it declined to recommend any concerted official effort to foster the use of such clauses, saying rather lamely that "it would be both natural and appropriate for the private sector to take the lead in the development of new clauses and

2. The case for these clauses was set out initially by Eichengreen and Portes (1995). Bonds issued under UK law already contain clauses providing for collective representation and for qualified majority voting (but do not contain sharing clauses). Furthermore, UK Trust Deed bonds give the trustee the exclusive right to initiate litigation; an individual bondholder cannot do so. Petas and Rahman (1999) give examples of collective action clauses in existing bond covenants and explain in detail the differences between UK and US law on these and related matters. See also the discussion in the *Report of the Working Group on International Financial Crises* (Group of 22 1998a), which addresses common concerns about collective action clauses and notes that the inclusion of majority voting clauses in bonds issued under UK law has not made them more costly to issue. Recent work by Eichengreen and Mody (2000a, 2000b) has refined this result. Classifying issuers by their creditworthiness, they show that the interest rate spreads on UK bonds are smaller than those on US bonds for more creditworthy issuers but larger than those on US bonds for less creditworthy issuers. See also Eichengreen (2000a).

that such efforts should receive official support as appropriate" (Group of 10 1996, para. 65).

Second, the Rey Report proposed a change in IMF policy. Normally, a country in arrears to its private creditors cannot obtain financing from the IMF until there is an actual or imminent agreement on the clearance of arrears. In an effort to resolve the debt crisis of the 1980s, however, the Fund undertook to "lend into arrears" in exceptional circumstances. A country that had not reached agreement with its commercial-bank creditors and was thus running up arrears on its outstanding debt could still obtain financing from the IMF when that was deemed to be essential for the implementation of an adjustment program and when the country was making a good faith effort to reach agreement with its commercial-bank creditors. In the future, the Rey Report said, the IMF "might be well advised to extend this practice to debt owed to other groups of private creditors." Such lending would tell private creditors that the debtor's policies are strong enough to warrant their support, as well as official support, and would also prevent private creditors from delaying an adjustment program. Making the same point more bluntly, the Rey Report stated that IMF financing "can improve the bargaining position of the debtor" while serving as a signal to the unpaid creditors "that their interests are best served by reaching agreement quickly with the debtor country" (Group of 10 1996, para. 94). But the IMF was remarkably slow to adopt this recommendation. It did not do so until 1999, three years after the Lyon Summit had welcomed the Rey Report's recommendations.

The Private Sector's Response

The private sector took less time to make its views known. The Institute of International Finance (IIF), a global association of financial institutions, created its own working group soon after the creation of the G-10 working group that produced the Rey Report. This was its main finding:

> In mid-1996, the international financial system appears relatively immune to systemic defaults by developing countries, and any future crises seem unlikely to be associated with a generalized problem of excessive borrowing by sovereign entities in emerging market countries. Accordingly, the . . . approaches to resolving crises should be case by case and generally ad hoc, without predetermined processes. They should be geared to the expectation of isolated episodes in individual countries, most likely characterized by foreign exchange liquidity problems rather than difficulties with servicing medium-term debt. (IIF 1996, i)

When crises do arise, moreover, the agreed-on international approach should be "market-based." The crisis-stricken country should adopt "extraordinary" fiscal, monetary, and exchange rate measures, but changes in market prices can also play important roles. Reductions in equity prices will tend to attract bargain seekers, and wider interest rate spreads will attract new capital—bank loans and bond issues—if the country's policies are deemed to be credible. As these should stabilize most crises and thus pave the way for restoring market access, there should be no need to reschedule debt. When crises do deepen, moreover, they are likely to be liquidity crises, not debt crises, and "their resolution" will have more to do with further policy action and the gradual rebuilding of confidence than with the rescheduling of debt payments" (IIF 1996, iii). Indeed, rescheduling bonds and other medium-term debt may be counterproductive, because it may lead to an extended workout process that could delay the restoration of market access.[3]

The IIF report did not object to the first recommendation of the Rey Report, that market participants should be free to adopt collective action clauses but should not be forced do so. But it objected vehemently to the second recommendation, that the IMF should broaden its policy on lending into arrears. Such lending, it argued, confers official approval on breaching contractual obligations, and the Fund should *rescind* its existing policy rather than broaden it from bank loans to bonds. The Fund should never lend into arrears unless the debtor has agreed to pay off those arrears.[4]

Crisis Prevention and Financial-Sector Reform

Apart from the change in Fund policy on lending into arrears, most of the reforms proposed or inspired by the Halifax Summit were adopted quickly. The next summit, however, launched another initiative. Recall the passage quoted in chapter 1, in which the 1996 Lyon Summit called for progress on three fronts: enhancing cooperation among the supervisors of internationally active financial institutions, strengthening risk management and enhancing transparency in financial markets, and encouraging emerging-market countries to adopt strong prudential standards (Group of 7 1996).

The last of these three goals was to become the principal crisis-preventing strategy of the architecture exercise. The Basel Committee on Banking Supervision (BCBS) was already working on its *Core Principles for Effective Banking Supervision;* and a new working party, this one including representatives of emerging-market countries as well as G-10 countries, issued a report that called on other groups to draft similar sets of principles (Work-

3. Although the IIF report did not explicitly endorse large-scale official financing, its emphasis on liquidity crises rather than debt crises and its opposition to the mandatory use of collective action clauses suggest that its authors disagreed strongly with the main premise of the Rey Report—that debt restructuring should be employed in lieu of large-scale official financing.

4. See the essays in Kenen (1996) for other assessments of the Rey Report and the recommendations of the Halifax Summit itself.

ing Party on Financial Stability in Emerging-Market Economies 1997). The International Organization of Securities Commissions (IOSCO) was urged to develop standards for regulating securities markets, and the International Association of Insurance Supervisors (IAIS) was urged to do the same thing for the insurance industry; the International Accounting Standards Committee (IASC) was asked to develop high-quality accounting standards; and other public and private bodies were asked to develop standards or codes in their own areas of expertise. Some of those groups were already at work, and the rest rose to the challenge. At last count, 64 standards and codes had been drafted or were being developed.[5]

An Odd Initiative

One more effort got under way late in this first phase of the architecture exercise—a campaign led by the G-7 countries and the management of the IMF to widen the definition of currency convertibility in the Fund's Articles of Agreement.[6] Under Article VIII, members of the IMF must not impose restrictions on payments or transfers for current account transactions.[7] But they may still impose restrictions on international capital flows. (In fact, Article VI forbids countries from using the Fund's resources to finance a large or sustained capital outflow, and it empowers the Fund to request that a country adopt capital controls to keep that from happening.)

To promote and complete the liberalization of international capital movements, it was suggested that Article VIII be revised to prohibit the use of capital controls (and that Article VI be rescinded). There would, of course, be transitional arrangements and well-defined exceptions. As

---

5. The Financial Stability Forum maintains an up-to-date list on its Web site (FSF 2001) and identifies 12 standards and codes as being of key importance for sound financial systems (the names of the issuing bodies are in parentheses): the Special (or General) Data Dissemination Standard (IMF), the Code of Good Practices on Transparency in Monetary and Financial Policies (IMF), the Code of Good Practices on Fiscal Transparency (IMF), the Core Principles for Effective Banking Supervision (BCBS), the Objectives and Principles of Securities Regulation (IOSCO), the Insurance Core Principles (IAIS), the International Accounting Standards (IASC), the International Standards on Auditing (IFAC), the Core Principles for Systemically Important Payments Systems (CPSS), the Principles of Corporate Governance (OECD), the Forty Recommendations of the Financial Action Task Force (FATF), and a set of principles for insolvency regimes being developed under the auspices of the World Bank.

6. Delong and Eichengreen (2001) say that it was initiated by the British and French governments, which feared that the World Trade Organization (WTO) would interpret its mandate to liberalize trade in financial services as a mandate to liberalize capital flows. That task, they believed, belonged to the Fund. The Fund, not surprisingly, climbed onto the bandwagon quickly, and the US Treasury was not far behind.

7. A number of countries, however, including some that have been IMF members for many years, have not yet accepted this obligation; they operate under the "transitional arrangements" of Article XIV.

a matter of principle, however, the concept of currency convertibility would be broadened, and every member of the Fund would have to relax and eventually remove restrictions on capital inflows and outflows. This objective was endorsed in principle by the Fund's Interim Committee at its Hong Kong meeting in September 1997, two months after the collapse of the baht.[8] As the Asian crisis deepened and spread, however, the campaign for capital account convertibility ran out of steam. And this was no bad thing. The objective was not well defined and was fundamentally inconsistent with one of the main aims of the architecture exercise—reducing the worrisome gap between the fast pace of financial liberalization by emerging-market countries and the slow pace of financial-sector reform.

Denver and Birmingham

The Denver Summit took place in June 1997, just before the onset of the Asian crisis, and falls chronologically into the second two-year phase of the architecture exercise. Yet it said very little about the international financial architecture, apart from endorsing the recommendations of the working party that had called for the drafting of standards to strengthen financial systems in emerging-market countries.[9] The second phase of the architecture exercise really began with the outbreak of the Asian crisis and lasted through the Russian crisis, both of which strongly affected the course of the exercise.

The Impact of the Asian Crisis

The Asian crisis refocused the debate about using large-scale official financing to cope with capital outflows from crisis-stricken countries. What had been regarded as exceptional in the Mexican crisis was becoming

---

8. See Fischer (1997) on the case for the proposal and the papers by Cooper, Massad, Polak, and Rodrik in Fischer et al. (1998) for objections. See also Bhagwati (1999), Cooper (1999), and Stiglitz (1999), who reject the implicit analogy between the case for free trade and the case for free capital flows.

9. It also asked international regulatory bodies, the IMF, and the World Bank to report on their efforts to strengthen their roles "in encouraging emerging market economies to adopt the principles and guidelines identified by the supervisory community" (Group of 7 1997, 5). The IMF's reply is noteworthy for stressing the demanding nature of those principles and guidelines. As they draw on the experience of advanced economies to define "best practice," they may need to be adapted to the different circumstances and less sophisticated financial systems of developing countries (Folkerts-Landau and Lindgren 1998). Failure to anticipate this need helps explain why developing countries insist that adherence must be voluntary and why they want to be "graded" in terms of the progress they make rather than their absolute level of compliance. We will come back to these matters later.

ordinary in the Asian crisis. In fact, it inspired the creation of a new Fund facility, the Supplemental Reserve Facility (SRF), which served to institutionalize large-scale financing and was first used to assist Korea. The Russian crisis inflamed the ongoing debate about moral hazard and inspired the creation of another Fund facility, the Contingent Credit Line (CCL), which was designed to combat contagion of the very virulent sort caused by the Russian crisis.

Furthermore, the Asian and Russian crises refocused the debate about private-sector involvement. The Mexican crisis had involved sovereign debt to private-sector creditors, but the Asian crisis involved private-sector debt, including both interbank and corporate debt. It also appeared to vindicate those in the official and private sectors who favor market-based ways of dealing with debt crises: the cooperative strategy adopted by Korea, they said, was vastly superior to the abrupt, disruptive, unilateral strategy adopted by Russia.

Finally, the Asian crisis triggered the debate discussed in chapter 1 about the wisdom of using IMF conditionality to reform the financial and corporate sectors of crisis-stricken countries and, more broadly, about the opportunistic use of conditionality to foster far-reaching reforms that do not clearly contribute to resolving the crisis at hand.

Although the Thai crisis began two months before the IMF's Annual Meeting in Hong Kong and had already spread to other Southeast Asian countries, it was not seen as posing grave problems for the countries already affected or for other countries. The Interim Committee's communiqué devoted just one paragraph to it:

> The Committee noted that recent disturbances in Asian financial markets have again underscored the importance for policymakers in all countries to ensure the internal consistency of macroeconomic policies, strengthen financial systems, and avoid external deficits and reliance on short-term borrowing. Although the impact of the recent financial market turmoil on some of the countries affected is expected to result in a slowdown of growth in the near term, the countries' economic fundamentals remain solid and their longer-term outlook is favorable, provided the required adjustment policies are sustained. (IMF 1997a, para. 5)

The same sentiments were heard in the corridors, where various pundits—including me—noted sagely that the crisis was being contained. Markets, they said, were distinguishing wisely between the two generations of Asian tigers.[10] Three weeks later, however, the crisis jumped generations, spreading northward via Taiwan to Hong Kong and Korea. And in December, the IMF issued a special interim edition of its *World Economic Outlook*

---

10. There was indeed more talk about the insults exchanged by Mahathir Mohamed and George Soros than about the crisis itself. Mahathir blamed the crisis on foreign speculators and called for the abolition of currency trading, and Soros called Mahathir an idiot.

(IMF 1997b), in which it took a grave view of the Asian crisis and its global implications.

The next Interim Committee communiqué, in April 1998, reflected that grave view, and much of the communiqué was devoted to the international financial architecture.[11] It called for the strengthening of financial systems and of IMF surveillance and for broadening the Special Data Dissemination Standard (SDDS) to cover additional financial data, including net reserves and reserve-related liabilities. It also emphasized the need, when warranted by crisis situations, "to involve private creditors at an early stage, in order to achieve equitable burden sharing *vis-à-vis* the official sector and to limit moral hazard" (IMF 1998a, para. 3e).

The Interim Committee's communiqué was strongly influenced by some special features of the Asian crisis. Jack Boorman and Mark Allen (2000) point out that the reference to net reserves and reserve-related liabilities reflected unpleasant surprises that came to light during the Asian crisis. Thailand had encumbered its reserves by huge foreign currency sales in the forward market, and Korea had deposited most of its reserves with the foreign branches of Korean banks, so as to strengthen their balance sheets. In the same vein, the communiqué asked the IMF to develop a "tiered response" under which it would issue "increasingly strong warnings" when it believed that a member's policies were "seriously off course" (IMF 1998a, para. 3b). Recall that Thailand had ignored several warnings from the Fund in the run-up to the crisis. The notion of a "tiered response" reappeared in the report of the G-7 finance ministers to the 1998 Birmingham Summit, and they went much further. "In addition," they said, "it may be helpful for the Fund to make public statements of concern about its assessment of countries' policy making and vulnerabilities" (Group of 7 1998, para. 11). But the US Treasury, among others, had strong reservations about public warnings (Rubin 1998), and the idea died.

Apart from making the suggestion just noted, that the IMF might "go public" by issuing warnings to individual countries, the 1998 Birmingham Summit made no major contribution to the architecture exercise. Nevertheless, it raised an important issue. What can be done to encourage compliance with the various standards and codes already in place or being developed? The report of the G-7 finance ministers attached to the summit communiqué identified a "gap" in the international system:

> We see an urgent need for a system of multilateral surveillance of national financial, supervisory and regulatory systems. This could encompass surveillance of such areas as banking and securities supervision, corporate governance, accounting and disclosure, and bankruptcy. (Group of 7 1998, para. 17)

---

11. It was issued just after the speech, mentioned at the start of chapter 1, in which Secretary Rubin sought to shape the architecture exercise, and it was the first such document to speak about the international financial architecture.

And there is also a need, it said, to find ways of promoting compliance with the relevant standards and codes. But it made only one concrete suggestion: access by foreign financial institutions to major financial centers might be conditioned in part on the quality of prudential and regulatory standards in their home countries. Finally, it declared, there is a need for a framework to ensure continuing private-sector involvement when a country is facing difficulties in meeting its foreign currency liabilities as they fall due, but this matter requires further discussion with other countries and the private sector.

The G-22 Reports

At the time of the Interim Committee meeting in April 1998, the US Treasury invited the finance ministers and central bank governors of 22 "systemically significant economies" to meet for a discussion of issues relating to the stability of the international financial system.[12] The meeting agreed to establish three new working groups, which issued their reports in October 1998. Two groups focused on crisis prevention, and the third group focused on crisis resolution.

The G-22 and Crisis Prevention

The first working group dealt with transparency and accountability. Its report (Group of 22 1998c) stressed the need for transparency in the private sector and, to that end, the need for governments to require compliance with high-quality accounting standards in the corporate sector, as well as sound rules for loan valuation, loan-loss provisioning, and credit-risk disclosure in the financial sector.[13] It discussed at length the ways in which the SDDS might be broadened to furnish more information about official reserves, as well as the need to compile data on the foreign exchange positions of the public, financial, and corporate sectors and on the international activities of investment banks, hedge funds, and other

---

12. The Group of 22 was also known as the Willard Group, because it met at the Willard Hotel near the US Treasury. It was convened to fulfill a promise made by President Clinton to involve emerging-market countries in the architecture exercise. The group grew eventually to 33 countries, but its successor is smaller. The Group of 20, established in 1999 as a forum for consultation on matters relating to the international financial system, includes the G-7 countries and 11 others (Argentina, Australia, Brazil, China, India, Korea, Mexico, Russia, Saudi Arabia, South Africa, and Turkey).

13. Sound rules for loan-loss provisioning are, of course, essential for the proper enforcement of the Basel Capital Adequacy Accord. Alba et al. (1999) point out that Indonesian, Malaysian, and Thai banks adhered to the Basel capital-adequacy standard but underreported their bad loans; see also Caprio and Honohan (1999) and earlier work by Goldstein and Turner (1996).

institutional investors.[14] It urged the international financial institutions to adopt a "presumption" in favor of releasing information unless doing so would compromise confidentiality. Members of the Fund, it said, should permit publication of Letters of Intent, background papers to Article IV reports, and Public Information Notices (PINs) summarizing Executive Board discussions of Article IV reports. Most important, it called for "transparency about transparency." The IMF, it said, should compile "transparency reports" assessing the extent to which each member meets internationally recognized disclosure standards. This was the recommendation that led the Fund to start compiling Reports on the Observance of Standards and Codes (ROSCs).

The second working group dealt with strengthening national financial systems, and its report (Group of 22 1998b) reflected clearly the concerns and reservations of the participants from emerging-market countries— more perhaps than did the reports of the other working groups. It started with recommendations aimed at avoiding reliance on ad hoc measures to resolve financial crises. While favoring "structured early intervention" to deal with troubled banks in normal times, it noted that this strategy may be inconsistent with some countries' legal systems, requires strong supervisory skills, and may be inadequate to resolve systemic crises. Even in crisis situations, however, the use of public money should be strictly limited, the owners of banks should not be bailed out, and banks should be allowed to fail if they would not be viable after recapitalization. The report also proposed sets of criteria for assessing the quality of deposit insurance plans and insolvency regimes.

Although the working group acknowledged the need to foster compliance with international standards and codes, it stopped short of recommending that the international financial institutions assess compliance on a country-by-country basis; it suggested instead that "some type of collective private sector mechanism" might take on that task.[15] It did

---

14. Although the working group favored the publication of comprehensive data relating to official reserves, including data on forward positions, it could not agree on the desirability of publishing data more frequently. The SDDS requires that data on gross reserves be published monthly with no more than one week's lag, and some members of the working group favored more frequent publication. The report of the working group noted, however, that more frequent publication "could restrict the ability of the authorities to intervene discreetly in foreign exchange markets" (Group of 22 1998c, 16).

15. For some countries, of course, assessments of compliance with standards pertaining to financial-sector stability might be riskier than similar assessments of compliance with standards pertaining to transparency, as the former might affect their creditworthiness. That might explain why the first working group could agree to endorse the compilation of transparency reports, but the second working group could not agree to endorse assessments of compliance with financial-sector standards. (The second group also divided on the proposal made at the Birmingham Summit that market access for foreign banks be conditioned on the quality of prudential supervision in the banks' home countries; it suggested instead

endorse the use of IMF conditionality to foster the implementation of financial-sector standards but said that "appropriate time must be allowed for implementation, the right sequencing of measures must be carefully considered, and their impact on social stability should be weighed" (Group of 22 1998b, 43).

The G-22 and Crisis Resolution

The report of the third working group (Group of 22 1998a) had much in common with the Rey Report but took account of issues raised by the Asian and Russian crises. It started, for example, by criticizing the use of government guarantees to the private sector, because they encourage excessive risk taking, but went on to say that the "socialization of risk" might be worthwhile during a crisis to halt a sudden withdrawal of credit or to catalyze orderly agreements with foreign creditors—an obvious reference to the Korean case. Similarly, the report opposed the granting of guarantees to the corporate sector, because corporate financial difficulties rarely constitute a threat to the payments system; but it also noted that widespread insolvencies in the corporate sector can generate problems for the financial sector and may therefore require special arrangements to facilitate rapid economywide restructuring—an equally obvious reference to the Indonesian case. Finally, the report went out of its way to criticize the use of controls on capital outflows to break the link between monetary policy and the exchange rate—a thinly veiled reference to the Malaysian case.[16]

The report recommended various forms of self-insurance against market volatility—holding adequate reserves, issuing long-term debt instruments and spacing the maturity of existing debt, and arranging contingent credit facilities with foreign banks.[17] It also endorsed the inclusion of

---

that industrial and emerging-market countries might jointly devise principles to govern national practices concerning market access.)

16. The working group also commented cautiously on the relative merits of fixed and flexible exchange rates. Relatively rigid rates, it said, can be "an important symbol of policy commitment" and "an integral part of a country's strategy for achieving and maintaining macroeconomic stability," but relatively flexible rates can help to prevent the accumulation of unhedged foreign currency exposure and can permit more macroeconomic policy flexibility. It conceded that countries will differ in the extent of their commitments to rigid rates but suggested that "many would benefit from considering strategies for increasing flexibility during periods of macroeconomic and financial stability, when the costs of introducing increased flexibility may be quite small" (Group of 22 1998a, 13-14).

17. The report noted, however, that these facilities may not provide much new money during a crisis, as banks may engage in dynamic hedging; they may offset the increase in their exposure to a crisis-stricken country by cutting back their other claims on that same country. Others, including Eichengreen (1999b, 2000b), make the same point; and Mussa et al. (2000) warn that this practice can contribute to contagion, as banks can offset their exposure to one country by reducing their claims on other countries. The IMF (1999e) notes

collective action clauses in debt contracts, going a bit further in this regard than the Rey Report. Although collective action clauses cannot by themselves guarantee that a qualified majority of bondholders will agree to restructure a bond issue in time to avoid a crisis, nor guarantee quick agreement on a workout if a crisis does occur, wider use of these clauses would help achieve coordination among the holders of a particular bond. Therefore, the governments of industrial countries should give consideration to (1) engaging in educational efforts to promote the use of collective action clauses in sovereign bonds issued in their markets, (2) identifying sovereign issuers likely to come to their markets soon and encouraging them to use collective action clauses, and (3) examining the use of such clauses when they themselves issue bonds in foreign markets.[18]

The working group devoted much of its report to debt problems and debt workouts. Without actually mentioning Russia, it noted that recent experience has "underscored the fact that unilateral actions, especially if they substitute for reform and adjustment, are highly disruptive" (Group of 22 1998a, x), and it went on to recommend that debt problems be managed cooperatively, in close consultation with the IMF:

> When the government of a country anticipates that the country may have difficulty meeting in full the terms of its contractual obligations, public or private, or that it may face serious balance of payments problems for other reasons, it should initiate a dialogue with the IMF. It should evaluate its policy options and rapidly develop and implement a program of policy adjustments to enhance the country's capacity to meet its obligations and to attract new private capital. . . .
>
> The government of the crisis country is responsible for choosing among its various policy options. A government's choice, of course, will be influenced by the IMF's evaluation of the country's financing need and possible policy adjustments, as well as by preliminary indications from the IMF and other members of the official community of the amount of official support that is likely to be forthcoming if the government adopts strong policy reforms.
>
> In extreme cases when an interruption of payments is unavoidable, a cooperative, orderly restructuring of contractual obligations, combined with the initiation of strong policy reform, could increase the collective welfare of both the debtor

---

that some banks threatened to reduce trade credits to Mexican borrowers when Mexico drew on its contingent credit lines in September 1998; for more on that episode and the banks' objections to Mexico's drawing, see IIF (1999). Mexico has since let its credit lines expire.

18. The report's phrasing was even more guarded. It said, in effect, that members of the working group representing industrial countries would recommend to their governments that they give consideration to examining the use of collective action clauses in their own foreign offerings—and you can't get more guarded than that. This phrasing is sometimes interpreted as a concession to private-sector views—recall the objections of the IIF to the mandatory inclusion of collective action clauses—but two other interpretations are more plausible. Some emerging-market countries feared that writing collective action clauses into their bond contracts might make borrowing more expensive (a matter discussed at length later). And Delong and Eichengreen (2001) suggest that the US Treasury feared that a major campaign on behalf of collective action clauses might crowd out efforts to achieve other, more important objectives.

and its creditors by providing the debtor with the time and incentives needed to make appropriate policy adjustments necessary to enhance its payments capacity and encourage the rapid restoration of market access. (Group of 22 1998a, 24-25)

The report noted, however, that the IMF should not be expected to determine the size or the nature of the contribution to be made by private creditors. Although an IMF-supported program "may implicitly indicate the need for a contribution from the private sector, it is the responsibility of the government of the crisis country and its private creditors to determine the form of this contribution" (Group of 22 1998a, 27).

The report warned repeatedly that countries should avoid "disruptive unilateral action" and extolled the advantages of voluntary negotiations between a crisis country and its private creditors:

In contrast to a unilateral or mandatory suspension of payments, a voluntary approach is less likely to have long-lasting effects on the country's access to international capital markets. It is also less likely to cause contagion. While a mandatory suspension of payments on some debt instruments could activate cross-default clauses in debt instruments not covered by the suspension, a voluntary approach may avoid triggering those cross-default clauses. Finally, a voluntary approach is less likely to generate litigation. (Group of 22 1998a, 29)

But it also conceded that there are "certain extreme circumstances" in which it may be difficult to pursue a purely voluntary approach. A voluntary debt exchange, for example, will necessarily reflect market conditions. A government may not have the bargaining power to obtain sustainable terms for the restructured debt instruments and creditors may then require interest rates so high that they generate destabilizing debt dynamics. Some creditors may refuse to participate in a purely voluntary scheme and thus prevent an overall agreement. Finally, a purely voluntary approach may take too much time and thus lead to an erosion of confidence that worsens the crisis country's problems. But even when a mandatory suspension is unavoidable, "it is crucial for the government of the crisis country to maintain an open, transparent and cooperative approach to the country's creditors in the wake of its decision to interrupt payments" (Group of 22 1998a, 30).[19]

Why devote so much attention to this working group's report? There are three reasons. First, it was drafted by representatives of emerging-market countries as well as industrial countries. Second, it demonstrates clearly the extent to which the course of the architecture exercise has been

---

19. This part of the working group's report concluded with a thoughtful discussion of the problems involved in designing a suspension—the scope of the suspension, whether it should cover private-sector debt payments, and whether those payments can be interrupted without imposing capital controls. The report also repeated the Rey Report's recommendation that the IMF should extend from bank loans to bonds its policy of lending into arrears (an action that the IMF had not yet decided to take).

influenced by the changing nature of financial crises. Third, it foreshadows the framework adopted by the G-7 governments and the IMF itself, as they strove to steer a course between the case-by-case approach favored by the United States and the rule-based approach favored by some other G-7 countries.

Köln and Okinawa

The third phase of the architecture exercise covered two more summits and important developments elsewhere, including attempts to involve the private sector in the resolution of debt-related crises, attempts to encourage adherence to international standards and codes, and changes in the policies and practices of the IMF. To shorten this long chronology, however, we focus here on the two summits and defer discussion of the other developments to the next part of this chapter.

The report of the G-7 finance ministers to the Köln Summit in June 1999 (Group of 7 1999b) devoted a great deal of attention to the roles, policies, and governance of the IMF and World Bank, the further development of standards and codes and the need to encourage adherence to them, and the strengthening of financial regulation in the industrial countries. It also contained the passages quoted in chapter 3, recommending that countries committed to fixed exchange rates "institutionalize" their commitments and endorsing the position taken earlier by Secretary Rubin that the international community should refrain from providing large-scale official financing to a country intervening heavily to support a particular exchange rate unless the rate is judged to be sustainable and is backed by supporting arrangements and policies. But the main contribution came at the end of the report, in a set of recommendations pertaining to private-sector involvement that closely resembled the recommendations in the G-22 report on international financial crises (Group of 22 1998a).

The report acknowledged the need for stronger efforts to broaden the use of collective action clauses. Their use, it said, should be "best practice" in debt management and a "consideration" in determining access to the CCL, and the G-7 governments should consider further "the possible inclusion of such provisions in our own debt instruments and otherwise encouraging the use of such provisions in the debt instruments issued by other sovereigns in our markets" (Group of 7 1999b, para. 42d).[20] The

---

20. Three months later, at the IMF's Annual Meeting in September, it was reported that the G-7 countries had considered a firm commitment to write collective action clauses into their own debt instruments but the United States had opted out. Thereafter, however, three G-7 countries acted unilaterally. Canada and the United Kingdom undertook to include collective action clauses in their international bond issues, and Germany affirmed the validity of the clauses under German law (IMF 2001b).

report also provided a "framework" for involving the private sector in crisis resolution, comprising a set of principles and a set of tools.

The Köln Framework

The principles were not new or controversial, perhaps because they were an attempt to paper over disagreements within the G-7 between governments that favored a case-by-case approach and those that favored a rule-based approach. They can be paraphrased briefly: (1) The approach to crisis resolution must not undermine the obligation of countries to pay their debts on time. (2) Market discipline will work only if creditors bear the consequences of the risks they take. (3) In a crisis, reducing net debt payments to the private sector can help a country meet its immediate financing needs and reduce the amount of financing provided by the official sector, but these effects must be balanced against the potential effect on a country's ability to attract new capital inflows and on other countries, *via* contagion. (4) No class of private creditors should be regarded as inherently privileged; claims of bondholders should not be viewed as senior to those of banks when both are material. (5) Wherever possible, crisis management should aim at cooperative solutions negotiated by the debtor country and its foreign creditors.

The report listed five tools that might be used to promote private-sector involvement: (1) The provision of official support can be linked to appropriate efforts by the recipient: efforts to initiate discussions with its private creditors to explain its policy program; efforts to elicit voluntary commitments of support, including commitments to provide new money and specific commitments by existing creditors to maintain exposure levels; and efforts to restructure or refinance existing obligations. (2) When a country's official debt needs to be restructured, Paris Club principles require a comparable restructuring of the country's debt to private creditors, but the Paris Club should adopt a flexible approach to comparability. (3) When official financing is provided, a reserve floor can be imposed to ensure that the recipient secures an adequate contribution from its private creditors, rather than using reserves to repay them. (4) In exceptional cases, a country may be unable to avoid the accumulation of arrears, and IMF lending into arrears may be appropriate if the country is seeking a cooperative solution with its private creditors. (5) In exceptional cases, a country obtaining IMF support may impose capital or exchange controls to implement a payments suspension or standstill needed to buy time for an orderly debt restructuring.

The finance ministers emphasized that the appropriate role for private creditors and the best ways of inducing them to play that role will depend on the circumstances of each case, and they dwelt on this theme in language that would be repeated in subsequent G-7 and IMF documents:

> There are circumstances where we believe emphasis might best be placed on market-based voluntary solutions to resolve the country's financial difficulties.

There are also cases where more comprehensive approaches may be appropriate to provide a more sustainable future payments path. Where a country falls on this spectrum will help to determine the policy approach best suited to its particular circumstances. Relevant considerations include the country's underlying capacity to pay and its access to the markets.

In addition, the feasibility of different policy approaches will depend on the nature of outstanding debt instruments. These will influence assessments of which claims need to be addressed to resolve the country's financing difficulties, the magnitude of possible concerns about equitable treatment of various categories of creditors, and the scope for voluntary versus more coercive solutions. (Group of 7 1999b, paras. 47, 48)

Finally, the finance ministers asked the IMF to address the legal and technical questions raised by this framework and to do so within three months—in time for the Fund's next Annual Meeting.

The Fund, however, could not meet that deadline. In his report to the International Monetary and Financial Committee (IMFC), the Fund's managing director said that the Executive Board needed more time to refine the Köln framework and listed some of the unresolved issues, including the role of standstills (IMF 1999f).[21] Hence, the G-7 countries undertook to develop the Köln framework on their own.

Implementing the Köln Framework

In September 1999, the G-7 finance ministers and central bank governors produced a reformulation of the passage quoted above, describing the spectrum of cases in which private-sector involvement would be appropriate (Group of 7 1999a). In April 2000, moreover, they agreed on another reformation and a set of "operational guidelines" for implementing the Köln framework:

With regard to crisis resolution, we agreed that the approach adopted by the international community should be based on the IMF's assessment of a country's underlying payment capacity and prospects for regaining market access.

In some cases, the combination of catalytic official financing and policy adjustment should allow the country to regain full market access quickly. In some cases, emphasis should be placed on encouraging voluntary approaches as needed to overcome creditor coordination problems. In other cases, the early restoration of full market access on terms consistent with medium-term external sustainability may be judged to be unrealistic, and a broader spectrum of actions by private creditors, including comprehensive debt restructuring, may be warranted to provide for an adequately financed program and a viable medium-term payments profile.

In those cases where debt restructuring or debt reduction may be necessary, we agreed that IMF programs should be based on the following operational guidelines:

i.   Put strong emphasis on medium-term financial sustainability, with the IMF determining the appropriate degree of economic adjustment required by the

---

21. These issues are discussed in Boorman and Allen (2000).

country and the IMF and the country agreeing on a financing plan compatible with a sustainable medium-term payments profile.

ii. Strike an appropriate balance between the contribution of the private external creditors and the official external creditors, in the light of financing provided by [the International Financial Institutions]. In cases where a contribution from official bilateral creditors (primarily the Paris Club) is needed, the IMF financing plan would need to provide for broad comparability between the contributions of official bilateral creditors and private external creditors. The Paris Club, if involved, should of course continue to assess the comparability desired and achieved between its agreement and those to be reached with other creditors.

iii. Aim for fairness in treatment of different classes of private creditors and for involvement of all classes of material creditors. The IMF should review the country's efforts to secure needed contributions from private creditors in light of these considerations, as well as medium-term sustainability.

iv. Place responsibilities for negotiations with creditors squarely with debtor countries. The international official community should not micromanage the details of any debt restructuring or debt reduction negotiation.

v. Provide greater clarity to countries at the start of the process about the consequences for their programs, including in terms of official financing, of any failure to secure the necessary contribution from private creditors on terms consistent with a sustainable medium-term payments profile. Such consequences could include the need for a program revision to provide for additional adjustment by the country concerned or the option of reduced official financing, or, conversely, a decision by the IMF to lend into arrears if a country has suspended payments while seeking to work cooperatively and in good faith with its private creditors and is meeting other program requirements.

vi. When all relevant decisions have been taken, the Fund should set out publicly how and what certain policy approaches have been adopted, in line with the Köln framework. (Group of 7 2000a, annex II)

This language was endorsed by the Okinawa Summit in July 2000, which also welcomed the contributions of private creditors, including bondholders, to several recent IMF programs (Group of 7 2000b). Those contributions are discussed in the next part of this chapter.

At its meeting in April 2000, moreover, the Fund's IMFC issued a communiqué containing language nearly identical to that in the first two paragraphs of the G-7 statement, but it replaced the "operational guidelines" with a single paragraph that assigned fewer responsibilities to the IMF and made no explicit mention of the Paris Club. Instead of stating that the IMF and the country should agree on a financing plan and that the Paris Club should oversee compliance with the principle of comparability, it said that IMF-supported programs should strongly emphasize medium-term sustainability and strike an appropriate balance between the contributions of private and official creditors. It also replaced item (v) in the operational guidelines with this brief statement:

> The Committee agrees that the IMF should consider whether private sector involvement is appropriate in programs supported by the Fund. In this regard, the Committee also agrees on the need to provide greater clarity to countries about the terms and conditions of their programs. (IMF 2000a, para. 16)

At its next meeting, the managing director reported that members of the Executive Board were not yet agreed on some of the issues raised by the Köln framework. Some favored a rule-based approach under which the extent of a member's access to IMF resources would depend on the member's pursuit of "concerted" private-sector involvement.[22] Others had reservations. Further research was needed, moreover, before the IMF could assume all of the tasks assigned to it under the operational guidelines endorsed by the Okinawa Summit (IMF 2000e).[23]

Achieving the Objectives of the Architecture Exercise

We turn now to the implementation of recommendations made in the course of the architecture exercise, stressing recent developments bearing on crisis prevention and crisis resolution. We focus first on two strategies aimed at crisis prevention: efforts to identify vulnerable countries before they succumb to crises, and efforts to foster compliance with international standards and codes in order to strengthen the infrastructure of emerging-market countries. We then examine two strategies aimed at crisis resolution: efforts to reform the policies and practices of the IMF, and efforts to involve private-sector creditors in resolving the debt-related problems of emerging-market countries.

Detecting Vulnerability

Many attempts have been made to develop early warning systems in order to identify vulnerable countries before they succumb to currency crises.[24] Such efforts involve four steps: (1) quantifying the definition of a crisis, (2) selecting indicators of potential vulnerability, (3) testing the

---

22. The term *concerted* is the current euphemism for "coercive" or anything not purely voluntary.

23. Unfortunately, the next IMFC communiqué referred to "the framework agreed in April 2000," by which it presumably meant the one presented in its own communiqué, not the Köln framework or the operational guidelines issued at the April G-7 meeting. In his long discussion of these texts, Roubini (2000) fails to mention the IMFC communiqués and thus leaves the misleading impression that the G-7 texts represent the view of the entire official community.

24. Goldstein, Kaminsky, and Reinhart (2000) survey and extend those efforts, and the following discussion draws on their work. The discussion here is narrower, however, because they also cover banking crises and the track record of the rating agencies. On the latter, see also Reisen and von Maltzan (1999) and Reinhart (2001), who find that downgrades of sovereign debt ratings have tended to reflect currency and banking crises rather than predict them.

explanatory power of those indicators, and (4) asking how often the most useful indicators correctly predict *subsequent* crises, how often they fail do so, and how often they issue false alarms.[25]

Currency crises are usually defined for this purpose as instances of abnormally large depreciations, large reserve losses, or combinations of the two, and most studies have found that the following variables are good leading indicators of those crises: appreciation of the real exchange rate, low growth rates of output and exports, a high or rising ratio of the money supply to reserves, and large amounts of short-term foreign borrowing or short-term debt.[26] Morris Goldstein, Graciela Kaminsky, and Carmen Reinhart (2000) find, in addition, that rapidly rising equity prices, a large current account deficit, and the onset of a banking crisis raise a country's vulnerability to a currency crisis.[27] Contradicting the conventional wisdom, however, their study and most others find that big budget deficits have little crisis-predicting power.[28]

---

25. One can evaluate models of this sort without making out-of-sample forecasts, by asking how often the models fail to identify crises that actually occurred within the sample period and how often they falsely identify crises that did not occur. But out-of-sample tests are more rigorous. Therefore, Goldstein, Kaminsky, and Reinhart (2000) base their early warning model on the crises that occurred in 1970-95 and ask how well it predicts crises that occurred in 1996-97. Similarly, Berg and Pattillo (1999) reestimate models devised by Frankel and Rose (1996), Sachs, Tornell, and Velasco (1996a), and Kaminsky (1998) and subject them to out-of-sample tests. They find that the first two models do poorly in predicting the Asian crisis and that the reestimation of those models also alters the statistical significance of certain explanatory variables. Kaminsky's model is more stable and successful, and it is the precursor of the Goldstein-Kaminsky-Reinhart model. For an interesting variant of the Goldstein-Kaminsky-Reinhart strategy, see Osband and Van Rijckeghem (2000), who search for country characteristics (and sets of characteristics) that enable them to define crisis-free zones and ask which countries lie within them.

26. As various studies use different ways to disaggregate capital flows and debt, their findings are hard to compare. When Berg and Pattillo (1999) reestimate the model employed by Frankel and Rose (1996), they find that vulnerability is reduced when capital inflows consist largely of concessional borrowing and foreign direct investment and is raised by large public-sector borrowing, but they find that vulnerability is unaffected by the ratio of short-term debt to total debt. Yet Goldstein, Kaminsky, and Reinhart (2000) find that vulnerability is raised when short-term capital inflows are large relative to GDP; see also Radelet and Sachs (1998). Rodrik and Velasco (1999) find that a high ratio of short-term debt to reserves helps predict reversals of capital inflows, but their result may merely indicate that reversals can more readily occur when foreign creditors hold large short-term claims that they can liquidate quickly.

27. Most of the earlier studies, by contrast, attached little explanatory power to the current account deficit. For a list of explanatory variables used in various studies and the numbers of studies in which they were shown to be statistically significant, see Kaminsky, Lizondo, and Reinhart (1998, table A4).

28. Studies that focus mainly on the timing of crises, rather than potential vulnerability to them, also attach importance to world interest rates and to the growth rate of output in the industrial countries; see, e.g., Meese and Rose (1998) and Milesi-Ferretti and Razin (2000).

Most studies of this sort use standard econometric methods (e.g., probit regressions) to test the explanatory power of the country characteristics chosen as promising candidates. But Goldstein, Kaminsky, and Reinhart (2000) attack the problem differently. They use a two-step strategy proposed initially by Kaminsky and Reinhart (1999). First, they compute a threshold for each crisis indicator, making it flash a danger signal whenever it crosses that threshold. The threshold for each indicator is obtained by minimizing the noise-to-signal ratio for that indicator taken by itself. (The noise-to-signal ratio is the number of times that an indicator wrongly warns of a crisis divided by the number of times that it rightly warns of a crisis.) Second, they use a weighted sum of the number of flashing indicators to estimate the probability that a particular country will suffer a crisis within two years. The weights used in adding the flashing indicators are the reciprocals of their noise-to-signal ratios, a device that gives the heaviest weights to the most reliable indicators. When they used their strategy to make out-of-sample forecasts for the Asian countries, it assigned a high probability to the Thai, Malaysian, and Philippine crises but a low probability to the Indonesian crisis.[29]

What use might be made of these results? First, they draw attention to sources of vulnerability, indicating the need for remedial action. If a high ratio of money to reserves raises vulnerability, then hold more reserves. If a rising ratio does so too, then hold down the growth of the money stock or raise the stock of reserves apace with the money stock. If large short-term borrowing or large short-term debt raises vulnerability, then take steps to reduce short-term capital inflows. Goldstein, Kaminsky, and Reinhart (2000) note that these remedial actions would deprive their indicators of predictive power. But that result, they say, would be highly desirable.

Second, the publication of reliable leading indicators might induce more prudent behavior by the private sector. Unlike a fire alarm, which goes off suddenly and demands the immediate evacuation of a building, the signals sent by leading indicators tend to grow loud gradually and thus call for a measured response by investors, not for capital flight. (In the Thai case, however, they grew loud quite rapidly; the probability of a Thai crisis rose from under 30 percent in mid-1996 to more than 90 percent before the end of the year. But other loud alarms were also ringing, and the Thai authorities were almost alone in refusing to heed them.)

If a highly respected private-sector institution, such as the Institute of International Finance, began to publish on its Web site a set of leading indicators for emerging-market countries, together with summary mea-

---

29. When used to predict currency crises in the 12 months starting with June 1996, their strategy put South Africa, the Czech Republic, Thailand, Korea, and the Philippines at the head of the list, and four of them suffered currency crises in 1997-98 (South Africa did not); but it put Indonesia in the middle of the list.

sures of their previous track record, no one could object. But what about the IMF? Should it also do that?

Clearly, the IMF and other public-sector institutions should make similar calculations and use them to focus their attention on potentially serious problems. If a fairly reliable set of early warning signals shows that a country is courting a crisis, the staff of the Fund should look closely at the country without waiting until the next Article IV consultation. And if the signal is loud enough, the Fund should enter promptly into consultations with the country. But to take the next step—to issue a public warning whenever leading indicators and other information suggest that a country is courting a crisis—would be risky for the Fund because of the prominent role it plays.

The Birmingham Summit (Group of 7 1998) suggested that the IMF might issue public warnings, and others have said so too. William Cline (2000a), for example, has argued that the IMF should have warned private investors about Thailand's problems before the Thai crisis erupted. It had, after all, warned the Thai government that it faced serious trouble. But there are compelling objections to public warnings by the Fund. If it fails to issue a warning, private investors may blame the Fund for the losses they suffer after a crisis erupts. That is the risk emphasized by Alexandre Lamfalussy (2000). Conversely, if it issues a warning, it may be accused of provoking a crisis that would not have erupted had the Fund not done so. That is the risk emphasized by Barry Eichengreen (1999b). Hence, the Fund may be damned whatever it does, and there may be no way to decide whether it was in fact culpable. Early warning indicators can detect vulnerability. A vulnerable country, however, may not succumb to a crisis unless it suffers a run of bad luck of the sort suffered by Mexico in 1994, and no econometric model can predict assassinations, insurrections, or political crises.

The *threat* to issue a public warning could perhaps be useful. Such a threat might have made the Thai authorities sit up and take notice. But the Fund cannot threaten to "go public" unless it is ready to do so when its warnings are ignored, and its Executive Board would be reluctant to do that or to let the managing director do it.[30]

---

30. In an earlier paper (Kenen 2000d), I suggested that the Fund threaten to go public when its confidential warnings are ignored, and a similar suggestion was made by the French finance minister, Dominique Strauss-Kahn ("A Fix, Not a Fudge," *Financial Times*, 16 April 1998). I now believe that my suggestion was unrealistic politically. There may be some merit in an alternative proposal made by an IIF working group:

> In some cases, countries may not respond effectively to warning signals coming from an IMF surveillance report, or private sector warnings such as an IIF country assessment or a rating agency action. In such circumstances, senior representatives of the private sector . . . could visit the country to explain to the authorities why the country's policies appear unsustainable, and could recommend that the country initiate intensive consultations with key financial firms and, in most cases, with the IMF. (IIF 1999, 34)

Strengthening the Infrastructure in Emerging-Market Countries

The international financial institutions have been engaged for many years in efforts to strengthen the institutional infrastructure and policymaking processes of their member countries. The most comprehensive efforts were those undertaken in the countries of Central and Eastern Europe, to help them move from planned to market economies. They included advice, technical assistance, and the use of IMF conditionality. And the use of conditionality to foster reform was not new: the Fund had used it even earlier to accelerate structural reform in developing countries—especially those that qualified for drawings under the Extended Fund Facility (EFF), which had been designed in the 1970s for countries with balance of payments problems that could not readily be resolved unless the countries made fundamental changes in their institutional arrangements and policies.

With the advent of the Asian crisis in 1997, the Fund sought once again to use conditionality as a way to promote fundamental reform. It did not confine itself to the subset of reforms deemed essential for resolving the crisis. Recall the long list of conditions attached to Fund programs for Thailand, Indonesia, and Korea. Those countries were asked to dismantle domestic monopolies, end the preferential treatment of certain industries, liberalize trade in goods and financial services, privatize state enterprises, strengthen corporate governance and combat corruption, introduce bankruptcy regimes, and overhaul the financial sector. Little attention was paid to priorities—what must be done immediately to solve the countries' acute problems and what might be done later on to reduce the risk and severity of future crises.

There is a more basic objection, however, to using conditionality to promote fundamental reform, especially crisis-preventing reform. The Fund can attach conditions to Fund-financed programs for countries already beset by crises, but that is like locking the barn door after the horse is stolen. Conditionality cannot be used to impose reforms on countries that are not in crisis and do not need help from the Fund. Further-

---

Furthermore, Goldstein (1998) has suggested that the Fund can issue public warnings rather routinely and undramatically in Article IV reports, in the *World Economic Outlook*, and in speeches by the managing director. The same suggestion was made obliquely by the group of outside experts appointed to assess the effectiveness of IMF surveillance; they urged the Fund to sharpen its surveillance by focusing on the sustainability of countries' policies, debt profiles, and exchange rates and by paying less attention to other policy issues (IMF 1999c). But some of the Fund's executive directors politely rejected that advice because it "ran counter to the demands of the membership and international community for increasing emphasis on the interactions between macroeconomic, structural, and social policies" (IMF 1999c, 4). (The executive directors agreed, however, on the need for the Fund to pay more attention to vulnerability—that it should enhance its analysis of the capital account, the financial sector, and the treatment of contagion.)

more, conditionality does not last long enough to foster reforms that require much time to complete, and this objection will hold with more force now that the Fund has moved to reduce the number of multiyear programs by limiting access to the EFF (IMF 2001b). The objection is particularly applicable to financial-sector reform:

> [R]eal reform in the banking system takes years to accomplish because it entails new ways of measuring and managing risk, new regulations, and new supervisory procedures. These changes are both politically difficult (because the politically powerful must forgo subsidies) and technically challenging. The time horizon necessary to implement successful reform is at least five years (judging from the successful examples of Argentina and Chile, which did so very aggressively and voluntarily). Building effective financial institutions, and reforming the legal and regulatory environment in which they operate, is a protracted and difficult learning process, even when countries have the political will to do so. The horizon of IMF crisis assistance and conditionality . . . is simply not suited to achieve true reform in the banking sector. (Calomiris 1998b, 280)

Many have made the same point.[31]

In the course of the architecture exercise, however, a different approach gradually developed. As various bodies, including the Fund, began to promulgate standards and codes by which to judge the quality of bank supervision, securities-market supervision, bankruptcy regimes, corporate governance, and other institutional arrangements, the official community began to devise ways of using the standards and codes to assess the quality of those arrangements in individual countries.

In 1999, the IMF and World Bank introduced the Financial Sector Assessment Program (FSAP). Under that program, a team from the Fund and Bank, augmented by other experts, undertakes an intensive examination of a country's adherence to certain key standards and codes—the Fund's data dissemination standards, the code on transparency in monetary and financial policies, and the codes on banking supervision, securities-market supervision, insurance supervision, and payments systems.[32] Participation in the FSAP is voluntary, and the assessments are not published. The Fund uses the results to prepare a Financial Sector Stability Assessment (FSSA) for the participating country. This assessment is then used to help Fund missions identify problems that call for attention in subsequent Article IV consultations, as well as in program design and the Fund's technical assistance programs. The World Bank uses the results to prepare a Financial Sector Assessment (FSA), which is used for analogous pur-

---

31. See, e.g., Ahluwalia (2000), Lamfalussy (2000), and Minton Beddoes (1999); on the analogous problems of gearing up to make effective use of a new bankruptcy regime, see Eichengreen (1999b).

32. Self-assessments have sometimes been used in lieu of external assessments, but they have not always been very reliable; some participants in self-assessments readily concede that they were not sufficiently critical of their own countries' regimes.

poses within the Bank. Twelve countries agreed to participate in the first experimental round of assessments under the FSAP, and the Fund has since decided to continue the program. But participation will still be voluntary, and the assessments will remain confidential. (The Fund did decide, however, that an FSSA could be published with the consent of the country concerned.)

The Fund has also begun another voluntary program—the preparation of Reports on the Observance of Standards and Codes (ROSCs). These are developed on a "modular" basis and may contain as many as 11 modules—one for each standard or code covered by the FSAP and others covering fiscal transparency, corporate governance, accounting and auditing standards, and insolvency regimes.[33] Once again, publication requires the consent of the country concerned, but most of the countries involved thus far have agreed to publication, and ROSCs have begun to appear on the Fund's Web site. More than 110 modules had been completed by the end of March 2001, and 73 had been published; but the Fund and Bank have warned that seven to eight more years might be needed to produce as many as four ROSC modules for each member of the Fund (IMF and World Bank 2001).

The publication of the assessments produced by the FSAP and of the ROSCs themselves can perhaps encourage compliance with international standards and codes if the private sector is willing and able to use them when forming its judgments about credit risk and related matters. In fact, the official community appears to count heavily on market discipline to foster compliance with these standards and codes (see Crockett 2000; FSF 2000b; Fischer 1999; IMF and World Bank 2001). Thus far, however, the private sector seems to know little about the various standards and codes or the Fund's efforts to publicize its findings concerning compliance with them (see FSF 2000a; IMF 2000c). For this and other reasons discussed in chapter 5, it may be imprudent to rely mainly on market discipline. Other carrots and sticks may be needed.

Limiting Reliance on IMF Financing

Throughout the architecture exercise, the official community has insisted that large-scale official financing has been and should be "exceptional" rather than ordinary practice. But words and deeds do not always match. Although the numbers usually quoted often overstate the amounts of official financing actually available to crisis-stricken countries, the amounts obtained by Thailand, Indonesia, Korea, and Brazil and, more recently, Argentina and Turkey were abnormally large. Furthermore, the

---

33. All these key standards and codes are included in the list of 12 produced by the FSF (reproduced in n. 5, above), but the FSF also lists the Forty Recommendations of the FATF.

Fund has institutionalized large-scale financing by creating the SRF; it is designed to provide larger amounts of official financing than a country can obtain under a standby arrangement (i.e., an ordinary quota-based drawing).

The Risks and Costs of Large-Scale Financing

Some participants in the debate about the international financial architecture have favored large-scale financing. Recall the recommendation of the Meltzer Report (IFIAC 2000), which called on the IMF to serve as the lender of last resort to a limited group of countries with sound banking systems. Yet most participants in the debate have taken the opposite view, that the Fund's normal quota-based limits should be applied more strictly. They give several reasons for their view.

First, large-scale financing runs the risk of encouraging governments to follow imprudent policies and encouraging private-sector lenders to make imprudent loans—the familiar versions of the moral hazard argument. These risks are often overstated, but they are not negligible.

No sensible government will knowingly court the risk of a currency crisis in the belief that it will obtain large-scale official financing. The economic and social costs of the Asian crisis were enormous, despite the amounts of financing provided. And few governments rush to the Fund when they see trouble ahead. In fact, some governments wait too long, believing that they can solve their problems without having to pay the political costs of submitting to conditionality. Nevertheless, the prospect of large-scale financing can have two worrisome effects. It can encourage governments to cling too long to pegged exchange rates, and it can tempt them to rely excessively on foreign currency borrowing when running budget deficits and managing their debts.

The official community sought to discourage governments from clinging too long to pegged rates when it warned that large-scale financing might not be forthcoming for countries that intervene heavily to defend pegged rates. David Lipton (2000) argues, however, that governments may ignore that warning unless the amount of official financing is limited ex ante rather than denied ex post. Thus far, moreover, the official community has not done enough to dispel the belief that governments facing debt problems can count on large-scale financing to resolve them. It has warned private creditors repeatedly that the official community will not provide large-scale financing to keep them from suffering losses should a debt crisis occur. But it has not addressed the same warning explicitly to debtor governments, and there has been a striking disjuncture between its words and deeds.

The problem of creditor moral hazard has likewise been overstated. No one has adduced compelling evidence that the scale of financing in the late 1990s raised the volume of new lending to emerging-market countries—apart from the Russian case.[34] Nevertheless, routine recourse to large-scale financing may eventually have that effect, especially if the official community declines to adopt a more forceful approach to private-sector involvement. When large-scale financing is used to buy time for a crisis-stricken country to reach a voluntary agreement with its private-sector creditors, one should not expect the terms of the agreement to treat the creditors harshly. Voluntary agreements cannot be reached without offering them "sweeteners." The record shows that clearly.[35] Therefore, they are not an adequate antidote to creditor moral hazard.

One more consideration is relevant here. Michael Mussa et al. (2000) argue quite rightly that the denial of large-scale financing in the Mexican case would have imposed huge losses on the innocent victims of the crisis in order to impose rather moderate losses on imprudent investors. But repeated resort to large-scale financing may tip the balance of benefits and costs by raising the likelihood of future crises and thus raising the number of innocent victims.

There is another objection to large-scale official financing. The privatization of international capital flows calls for the privatization of crisis management—the participation of private-sector creditors in the resolution of financial crises—but the availability of large-scale financing masks the need for that involvement. This "burden-sharing" argument is logically distinct from the moral hazard argument. The latter is concerned with the future behavior of private investors and lenders; the former is concerned with their previous behavior. If investors and lenders come to believe that they were unduly optimistic about the outlook for a particular country, and thus halt capital inflows suddenly, they should have to help the country cope with the consequences. Sometimes, of course, the change in investors' views is the result of worrisome changes in a country's policies. Too often, however, foreign investors change their views abruptly. Rather than tap the brake pedal at the first sign of danger, they wait until they must hit it hard because they have no other way to avoid an accident. Financial markets may not be "unstable" but they are very

---

34. See, however, the paper by Dell' Ariccia, Godde, and Zettelmeyer (2000), cited in chapter 2, which raises doubts about the validity of previous research on this issue.

35. When "haircuts" on bond exchanges are computed using the initial prices of the old bonds, the calculations show that investors have taken large losses. But when they are computed using the market prices of the bonds just before the terms of the exchanges are announced, the calculations show that investors have come out ahead, and that is a sensible way to measure impact on a mark-to-market investor; see IMF (2000e) and Roubini (2000). But see also Cline (2000b, 26), who argues that "the fulfillment of an obligation should be judged against its original value, not the level to which it has fallen under distress." (It should also be noted that the market price of a bond just before an exchange may be unduly depressed by uncertainty about the terms of the forthcoming exchange, and use of the market price may thus overstate the net gain to the investor.)

volatile, and the inhabitants of those markets have an obligation to mitigate the consequences of that volatility.[36]

Finally, official financing in excess of normal quota-based limits cannot be provided routinely without imparting more elasticity to the financial resources of the IMF. The NAB and GAB are the only reliable source of additional financing, and they are not easily activated. The Fund can create Special Drawing Rights (SDRs), but only to meet a global need for additional reserve assets, not to finance its own operations.

Reconfiguring the Fund

Those who favor a return to the normal quota-based limits on access to IMF credit do not necessarily rule out large-scale financing in truly exceptional circumstances. The task force convened by the Council on Foreign Relations proposed that the Fund's facilities be reorganized to draw a sharp distinction between "country crises" and "systemic crises" and to treat them differently.[37] Most country crises would be handled by ordinary quota-based drawings. But truly exceptional country cases, requiring unusually large amounts of financing, would be handled by activating the NAB and would therefore require the consent of the countries participating in the NAB.[38] The task force defined systemic crises as multicountry crises requiring large-scale official financing because they threaten to impair the performance of the world economy or the ability of financial markets to judge the creditworthiness of individual borrowers. Those crises, it said, should be treated differently. A new "contagion

---

36. Lamfalussy (2000) offers a similar "ethical" argument for burden sharing; see also Geithner (2000). Cline (2000b) argues, however, that there is no "burden" to be shared when a crisis reflects a pure creditor panic. Official financing will restore confidence all by itself and thus induce a resumption of capital inflows that will permit repayment of the official financing. Therefore, the official sector will bear no burden unless it provides financing on concessional terms. And the crisis-stricken country will bear no burden, because it will not have to make any painful policy changes. Roubini (2000) makes a similar point. If action is taken promptly, at the first sign of a creditor panic, a full bailout of private creditors is formally equivalent to a full "bail-in." They are equally able to keep a pure creditor panic from affecting the capital account of the crisis-stricken country, obviating the need for the country to modify its policies. If, indeed, the official community can commit itself credibly to a full bailout, the country will not have to ask for it, as the panic will end right away. But this formal equivalence holds only under strong assumptions about private-sector behavior. Roubini concedes, moreover, that pure creditor panics are rare and that policy changes are usually needed to bring about a restoration of investor confidence. That, he says, is the justification for the current approach to crisis resolution, which relies on a combination of policy adjustment, official financing, and voluntary private-sector involvement.

37. Task Force on the Future International Financial Architecture (1999), cited hereafter as CFR Task Force (1999).

38. Furthermore, the credit risk would be borne by those countries rather than the IMF.

facility" should be created and financed by a onetime issuance of SDRs.[39] It would replace the SRF and CCL and would provide unconditional assistance to countries adversely affected by temporary shocks largely beyond their control—a fall in commodity prices, a contraction of capital flows to emerging-market countries, or an increase of interest rate spreads. Disbursements from the contagion facility would be made swiftly and would be front-loaded, but activation would require the consent of a supermajority of the countries providing the SDRs. (This last proposal has much merit and could be adopted without adopting the other reforms and the new financial arrangements proposed by the task force. A super-majority could be required to approve a drawing on the present SRF. That in itself might diminish the frequency with which the Fund provides large-scale financing.)

Others have also proposed the reconfiguration of IMF facilities.[40] But the details matter less than the basic issue raised by the task force and others. They have sought to distinguish between systemically important countries and systemic crises. Admittedly, the two are not unrelated. A country is systemically important if its problems are likely to impair the functioning of international financial markets, and that is most likely to be true if the country itself is large or a large participant in those markets. But the size of the country is less important than the nature of its problem. Thailand is not a large country, and the Thai crisis of 1997 was not deemed initially to have systemic implications. Nevertheless, it drew attention to serious vulnerabilities in other Asian countries.

Consider another example. If Argentina's current problems were due to a large current account deficit resulting from the appreciation of the US dollar and the depreciation of the Brazilian real, they would not be systemic. The policy changes required to reduce a current account deficit rarely have calamitous effects on other countries or international financial markets. But Argentina's problems are due largely to the belief that it will not be able to service its large foreign currency debt. Therefore, they have a systemic dimension, not because Argentina is large but because its bonded debt is large compared to the total of emerging-market debt traded on international markets. Yet two more requirements must be met before one can make a compelling case for large-scale official financing to resolve this sort of problem. First, there must be reason to believe that large-scale financing will avert—not merely delay—the need to restruc-

---

39. To meet the requirements of the Fund's Articles of Agreement, the SDRs would be issued to all of the Fund's members, but they would then transfer them to the Fund to finance the contagion facility. (As in the case of financing via the NAB, the credit risk attached to lending by the contagion facility would thus be borne by the Fund's members providing the SDRs, not by the Fund itself.)

40. See, for example, the plans proposed by Knight, Schembri, and Powell (2000) and Williamson (2000b), discussed in chapter 3.

ture the country's debt. Second, there must be reason to believe that the restructuring of that debt would have ramifications that could not be contained without extending large-scale assistance to other countries.[41]

The architecture exercise has not confronted this issue squarely. Late in the course of the exercise, several changes were made in the terms and conditions attached to the use of IMF credit. But most of the changes were aimed at reducing the demand for IMF credit, not at reducing the supply.

Speaking at the London Business School in December 1999, soon after his appointment as secretary of the treasury, Lawrence Summers called for a "streamlining" of the Fund's facilities (Summers 1999a).[42] The Fund, he said, should phase out long-term lending and rely primarily on three "core" facilities: short-term standby arrangements for countries with non-systemic balance of payments problems, the SRF for countries suffering systemic capital account crises, and the CCL for countries seeking to ward off contagion. "We also believe," he said, "that the pricing of these facilities needs careful consideration" (1999a). Higher charges should be attached to normal standby arrangements, and the terms of access to the CCL should be made more attractive than those of the SRF, as countries will then be encouraged to make the policy changes needed to protect them from contagion. Summers went on to say what he and others had said before—that the IMF must be capable of providing "very large-scale financing" in the event of a "truly exceptional systemic threat," but that normal quota-based limits should apply "to all but a fraction of cases" (1999a). But he made no attempt to explain how to define a systemic threat.

Shortly thereafter, the Fund's Executive Board began an exhaustive review of all Fund facilities. It abolished three special-purpose facilities that were no longer being used. It liberalized the terms of access to the CCL, which was not attracting applicants. It shortened the time periods

---

41. If the first condition is not met and the country has then to restructure its debt, large-scale assistance for others may still be required. This was, of course, the rationale for assisting Brazil in August 2001, even before a decision was made about further help for Argentina. The subsequent decision to provide $5 billion of additional Fund credit for Argentina was not meant to resolve its debt problem but rather to combat a credit crunch caused by large withdrawals from Argentine banks. An additional $3 billion was earmarked for future use but could be made available earlier to support a "voluntary and market-based operation to increase the viability of Argentina's debt profile" (IMF *News Brief*, 21 August 2001). But the nature of that operation was not disclosed immediately, and it is far from clear that the $3 billion will suffice to catalyze a major restructuring of Argentina's debt, even if Argentina uses the money to buy zero-coupon dollar bonds, uses them to collateralize new long-term bonds of its own, and then swaps its new bonds for existing debt, as was done in the case of the Brady bonds.

42. Delong and Eichengreen (2001) suggest that some of the proposals made in that speech were designed to demonstrate that the US Treasury did not reject out of hand all of the recommendations in the Meltzer Report.

within which countries are "expected" to repay conventional IMF drawings—those made under standby arrangements and those from the EFF. And it agreed to impose higher charges on large balances outstanding as a result of conventional drawings.[43]

To make the CCL more attractive, the Executive Board decided that a country will not have to provide as much supporting documentation as was previously required when submitting a quantified framework describing its future policies. Furthermore, the country must be making good progress in meeting the requirements of the SDDS and a "critical mass" of other standards, rather than each one separately. Finally, it will not have to undergo a detailed review of its policies when it seeks to activate its CCL. There will be an expeditious review at the time of activation, in which the country will be given "the strong benefit of the doubt" (but there will be a postactivation review, in which the Fund and the country will reach understandings regarding the country's future policies). Finally, the Executive Board reduced the commitment fee for a CCL and the surcharge for a drawing on a CCL. Previously, the surcharge was the same as the one for a drawing from the SRF, which starts at 300 basis points above the charge for a conventional drawing but rises to 500 basis points with the passage of time. Now, the CCL surcharge will start at 150 basis points and rise to 350 basis points.

To speed up the repayment of conventional drawings, the Board adopted "time-based expectations" that will hold ahead of the mandatory deadlines. Under a standby arrangement, for example, a country must start to repay a drawing 3¼ years after the drawing and repay it completely 5 years after the drawing. Hereafter, it will be "expected" to start making repayments 2¼ years after a drawing and repay it completely 4 years after the drawing. The board did not adopt the suggestion, made by Secretary Summers, that higher charges be imposed on all conventional IMF drawings. Instead, it imposed a surcharge on conventional drawings in excess of certain cumulative limits; hereafter, a country must pay an additional 100 basis points when its drawings exceed 200 percent of quota and 200 basis points when they exceed 300 percent of quota.

Applying the Köln Framework

The history of the architecture exercise outlined in the first part of this chapter focused on the evolution of official views about private-sector involvement in crisis resolution. It paid little attention to the ways in which the official community was trying to achieve private-sector involvement, apart from describing the initial effort to restructure interbank claims on

---

43. For more on these changes, as well as those described below, see IMF (2000b) or Goldstein (2001).

Korea. But several efforts were made to restructure sovereign debt in and after 1999, using some of the "tools" listed in the Köln framework. It has indeed been suggested that the Köln framework did little more than codify the strategies devised to deal with those cases.[44] Three cases deserve particular attention, because of the issues they raised and the precedents they set.[45]

Ukraine and Debt Sustainability

The first case involved Ukraine. In September 1998, just after the Russian crisis, Ukraine faced the need to redeem a tranche of treasury bills denominated in domestic currency. To prevent the Ukrainian government from using official funds to repay private creditors, the IMF imposed a reserve floor—one of the tools subsequently listed in the Köln framework. Therefore, Ukraine offered to exchange the maturing bills for zero-coupon eurobonds. The offer was quite successful, because the maturing bills were held by a small number of institutional investors and the terms of the exchange were very attractive. Ukraine made up-front cash payments, and the new eurobond carried a high interest rate. Furthermore, the holders of the maturing bills had no satisfactory alternative. They had little chance of winning a lawsuit, because the treasury bills had been issued under Ukrainian law; those who did not swap their bills for new eurobonds would be paid off in Ukrainian currency and could not convert it into foreign currency.

The 1998 exchange, however, stored up problems for the future, because the new eurobond had a short maturity. Those problems were compounded in 1999 when a bond held mainly by one foreign investor came due for repayment. At first, Ukraine refused to repay it, citing the reserve floor imposed by the IMF. But when the bondholder refused to consider restructuring and threatened to invoke cross-default and acceleration clauses, Ukraine was obliged to redeem it by issuing a new tranche of an existing eurobond, which was due for redemption in 2001. Hence,

---

44. See IMF (2000c), where this view is ascribed to private-sector critics.

45. Comprehensive accounts of those cases are provided by the IMF (2000c, 2001a); see also Cline (2000b), Eichengreen (2000a, 2000b), Eichengreen and Rühl (2000), and Roubini (2000). Two more cases are often cited. In 1999, the IMF required Romania to roll over 80 percent of its maturing debt. As Romania could not do that, the IMF told it to issue new debt in order to redeem its maturing debt. Before its new IMF program came into effect, however, Romania drew down its reserves to repay its maturing debt. This action did not cause the IMF to cancel the new program. Instead, the Fund required Romania to issue new debt in an amount sufficient to rebuild its reserves. And when Romania did not do that either, the IMF backed off. The other case involved commercial-bank claims on Russia, representing old Soviet-era debt. Russia had defaulted on those claims in August 1998, along with its other debt. In early 2000, however, it reached a debt-restructuring agreement with its London Club creditors, although the debt involved had been restructured previously, in 1997.

Ukraine faced an "insurmountable repayment peak" (Eichengreen and Rühl 2000) and sought therefore to flatten that peak by making another debt exchange.

In February 2000, Ukraine offered to exchange four maturing eurobonds and two so-called Gasprom bonds for two new eurobonds with seven-year maturities. Once again, the offer was attractive; it did not involve debt forgiveness, there would be no interest-free grace period, and the accrued interest on the old bonds would be paid in cash. Furthermore, Ukraine made clever use of the collective action clauses embedded in three of the old eurobonds.[46] It declined to convene a bondholders' meeting until it had collected binding proxies from investors favoring the bond exchange and thus had the votes required to bind in all of the bondholders.

Pakistan and Paris Club Comparability

The second case involved Pakistan. In 1999, as a condition for restructuring Pakistan's debt to its official creditors, the Paris Club required Pakistan to seek comparable treatment from the private holders of its eurobonds. (The Paris Club has always insisted that debtor countries obtain compara-ble treatment from their private creditors. In previous cases, however, it applied that principle to bank loans, not bonds, because the debtors with which it was dealing did not have significant amounts of bonded debt.) Pakistan demurred at first; but when a military government seized power, Pakistan was unable to raise new money by issuing new bonds. Therefore, it offered to exchange three maturing eurobonds for a six-year eurobond, and the offer was accepted by holders accounting for 99 percent of the maturing eurobonds. (Those bonds were held mainly by investors in the Middle East, which may help explain the success of the bond exchange.)

As all of the old eurobonds had been issued under UK law, they had collective action clauses. But Pakistan did not invoke them, because of concerns about the possible outcome of a bondholders' meeting. Bond-holders had been angered by the Paris Club's demand for comparable treatment and might have expressed that anger by rejecting Pakistan's offer. Once the exchange was completed, moreover, the only remaining holders were those who had rejected it, and they could not be expected to show approval at a bondholders' meeting. Fortunately, the handful of dissident creditors never initiated legal action.

Ecuador and Exit Consents

The third case involved Ecuador, and it raised a number of controversial issues. Because Ecuador faced serious economic problems in 1999, its

---

46. Because the three bonds had been issued under Luxembourg law, which resembles UK law, they had collective action clauses. The fourth bond did not have them, but it was held

president announced in August that the government had decided to withhold the interest payment due on one of its Brady bonds. According to Barry Eichengreen (2000a), the government and its foreign advisers believed that this announcement would force the bondholders to agree to a restructuring. To buy time for that to happen and to avoid an immediate default, Ecuador asked the bondholders to let it pay the interest due by using the collateral earmarked for that purpose. Instead, the requisite number of bondholders, 25 percent, voted to accelerate repayment.[47]

Just before that vote, however, the IMF announced that it would not require Ecuador to reach agreement with its bondholders before approving Ecuador's request for an IMF program. This statement did little more than reaffirm the Fund's existing policy: it was prepared to lend into arrears when a country was making a good faith effort to reach agreement with its creditors. But Eichengreen and Christof Rühl (2000) suggest that Ecuador's creditors saw it to be something more—an endorsement of Ecuador's default on its Brady bonds. William Cline (2000b), likewise accuses the Fund of making Ecuador a "guinea pig" for a new, more aggressive policy toward private-sector creditors and notes that Ecuador's program, approved later by the Fund, was based on cash-flow projections that implied the restructuring of Ecuador's whole foreign currency debt— its eurobonds as well as its Brady bonds.

Eight months after it defaulted on its Brady bonds, Ecuador made an exchange offer. It would swap all of its defaulted foreign bonds, eurobonds and Brady bonds, for a new 30-year eurobond. The offer was successful, even though Ecuador's foreign bonds were more widely held than those of Pakistan or Ukraine—and by a more heterogeneous group of investors. In addition, the defaulted bonds lacked collective action clauses, having been issued under US law, and there was thus no way for Ecuador to bind in dissident creditors. But one of its advisers hit on a novel device for dealing with dissident creditors: the use of exit consents. Under US law, the payment terms of an existing bond cannot be altered without the unanimous consent of the bondholders. It is nevertheless possible to make other changes with the consent of a simple majority, and that is the route that Ecuador took. Every bondholder accepting Ecuador's offer had to endorse several changes in the terms of the defaulted bonds (so-called disfiguring amendments) that made it harder for dissident creditors to reject Ecuador's offer and initiate litigation.[48]

---

by small investors, and Ukraine's investment bankers succeeded in persuading them to accept the exchange offer.

47. Although Ecuador's bondholders did not actually meet, this episode is often cited as proof that bondholders' meetings can lead to "strange and exotic" outcomes (IMF 2000c).

48. The disfiguring amendments deleted the following provisions: the requirement that all defaults be cured before an acceleration can be rescinded, the prohibition of Brady bond purchases by Ecuador during a default and of any further Brady bond restructuring, the

Precedents and Problems

These recent attempts to secure private-sector involvement have been strongly criticized. Eichengreen and Rühl (2000) raise three objections. First, the countries involved are comparatively small, and bondholders may therefore conclude that they should shun small countries' bonds in favor of large countries' bonds. Small countries could then lose market access, and the concentration of bondholders' exposure on a few large countries could raise systemic risk. Second, Ecuador's attempt to single out its Brady bonds had unforeseen consequences. Ecuador's aim was to preserve its ability to issue additional eurobonds.[49] But this selective strategy failed when Ecuador's eurobonds and domestic debt were contaminated by the activation of the cross-default clauses in its Brady bonds. Furthermore, Ecuador's strategy undermined the prevailing seniority structure—the supposition that Brady bonds were senior to eurobonds and foreign debt was senior to domestic debt. Finally, Eichengreen and Rühl criticize the official community for failing to exploit the opportunity afforded by these episodes to promote the inclusion of collective action clauses in new bond issues. Until those clauses are widely used, they argue, there will be no way to drive bondholders to the bargaining table, because there won't be a bargaining table. Restructuring will be too costly for debtor countries, and the IMF will be unable to stand aside when restructuring efforts fail. Investors, moreover, will anticipate intervention by the Fund, so they will have no incentive to restructure their claims.

This assessment is too pessimistic. It was written before Ecuador had worked its way back from default with the aid of exit consents. It can indeed be argued that exit consents represent a viable substitute for collective action clauses. They can be used to modify the terms of bonds already issued, whereas collective action clauses can be included only in newly issued bonds. There is, however, an obvious objection to relying on exit consents. If debtors employ them frequently, investors may start to insist that new bond covenants be written in ways that preclude their future use. It would take several years, of course, to complete that process—as much time as it would take to add collective action clauses to all bond covenants. But the process could start quite soon if debtors begin to rely routinely on the use of exit consents.

---

cross-default and negative pledge clauses, and the requirement that Ecuador maintain the listing of the old bonds on the Luxembourg stock exchange (IMF 2001a). Buchheit and Gulati (2000) discuss in detail the legislative and case-law basis for the exit consent strategy.

49. Recall that Brady bonds embody commercial-bank claims that were reduced and restructured in order to close out the debt crisis of the 1980s. Because they represent previously restructured debt, they were commonly regarded as being senior to eurobonds. As no one can issue new ones, however, Ecuador and its advisers saw no obvious reason to take that view; for more on the issues involved, see Petas and Rahman (1999) and Roubini (2000).

Furthermore, Eichengreen and Rühl may attach too much importance to collective action clauses. Cline (2000b) and others maintain that they had little to do with the success of recent bond exchanges. Pakistan did not invoke them, although they were available; Ukraine did make use of them, but only after the fact, soliciting proxies from bondholders who had already accepted its offer. And Ecuador could not use them, because its bonds were issued under US law. Nouriel Roubini (2000) goes so far as to say that collective action clauses are an "empty shell," though he concedes that their absence may help explain why some bond exchanges have been generous to investors.

The truth may lie between the polar positions taken by Eichengreen and Rühl (2000) on the one hand and Roubini (2000) on the other. The mere existence of collective action clauses cannot be expected to influence decisively the behavior of any bondholder, unless the bondholders are few in number and can play strategic games. Nor can collective action clauses bind in dissident creditors, unless the terms of a bond exchange are sufficiently generous to attract the support of the many bondholders whose votes are needed to invoke the clauses—usually those who hold 75 percent of the bond issue being retired. Once those bondholders are satisfied by the terms of an offer, they should be willing to join with the debtor in seeking to forestall harassment by the remaining bondholders. Absent those clauses, however, a country trying to restructure its debt may indeed be obliged to make an extravagant offer—one designed to elicit support from virtually all of the bondholders, especially those whose holdings are sufficiently large to make it worthwhile for them to initiate litigation.[50]

Overly generous offers can have two worrisome consequences. First, they can get in the way of combating creditor moral hazard. Second, and more important, they can produce destabilizing debt dynamics. The risk of that outcome was foreseen by the G-22 (Group of 22 1998a), and it was the problem facing Ukraine following the debt exchanges of 1998 and 1999.

Pakistan's experience posed an additional difficult problem—how to interpret and apply Paris Club comparability. Cline (2000b) and others assert that the concept itself is flawed. Official creditors, they say, are motivated partly by political concerns when they make loans to developing countries and when they reschedule debt. Private creditors are differently motivated and should not be forced to mimic the offers made by Paris Club creditors. There are practical problems, too. The interest rates on official loans are lower than those on private loans, and official and private creditors use those different interest rates when computing the net present values of the concessions they make to their debtors. As a

---

50. Although there was no litigation in the cases considered here, there was successful litigation in an earlier case, Elliott Associates vs. Republic of Peru; see IMF (2001a).

result, a dollar of debt rescheduled for one year by an official creditor has a higher net present value than a dollar of debt rescheduled for one year by a private creditor, and the two are hard to compare. Finally, private creditors believe that the Paris Club should be bound by the same strict principle of comparability. This argument was made when Russia restructured its debts to commercial banks and arose again when Ecuador restructured its foreign bonds. In both cases, the debtor country asked the Paris Club for "reverse comparability," and its private creditors were happy to chime in.[51]

Note, in conclusion, that none of the cases considered here involved a large emerging-market country—a fact that led Daniel Tarullo (2001, 37) to write, "I know of no official at the Fund or in a G-7 country who would argue with a straight face that an economically or strategically significant country would be treated similarly." Furthermore, those cases involved the restructuring of sovereign debt, not private-sector debt. In fact, recent discussions of private-sector involvement have focused almost exclusively on sovereign debt. The problems posed by the volatility of short-term private debt—especially interbank debt, which Alan Greenspan (1998) described as being potentially the Achilles' heel of the international financial system—ceased to attract attention as soon as the Asian crisis ended. They could crop up again, however, and we will return to them in the next chapter.

---

51. The complex issues raised in this paragraph are discussed at length in IIF (2001), IMF (2000e), and Roubini (2000).

5

The Architecture Exercise: What's Missing?

The architecture exercise is not over. Work continues at the IMF on the development of early warning indicators, ways of detecting risks residing in national balance sheets, and macroprudential indicators for the financial sector. The Fund has created a Capital Markets Consultative Group and an International Capital Markets Department, and it has begun to employ a more parsimonious approach to conditionality.[1] Furthermore, the Fund has continued to work on developing operational guidelines for private-sector involvement, something it was asked to do after the G-7 governments set out their own guidelines at the 2000 Okinawa Summit. At the 2001 Genoa Summit, moreover, the G-7 finance ministers discussed the roles of the multilateral development banks, and they are apt to receive close attention during the next phase of the architecture exercise.[2]

---

1. Henceforth, structural conditions will be included in Fund programs only when they are critical for achieving those programs' macroeconomic objectives. Those that are relevant though not critical *may* be included in Fund programs if they fall within the Fund's core areas of responsibility, but not as the subject of separate performance criteria or structural benchmarks; instead, they should be monitored as part of the overall assessment of a country's progress under its Fund program (IMF 2001c).

2. In his first public statements on the international financial institutions, Paul O'Neill, the US secretary of the treasury, urged the IMF to work harder at crisis prevention, but he paid more attention to the World Bank. Its scope, he declared, has been too diffuse. It should focus more sharply on the core objective of raising income per capita and on countries that lack capital-market access. He also endorsed a proposal made by the Meltzer Commission—substituting grants for loans that are unlikely to be repaid. "If it is a grant," he said, "we should call it a grant and not a loan" (O'Neill 2001). The United States made that same proposal at the Genoa Summit in 2001, but it was not adopted.

Old tasks, however, remain unfinished. There are now a great many standards and codes but very few carrots and sticks with which to foster compliance, and the official community is relying too heavily on market discipline. It is also unduly optimistic about the speed with which emerging-market countries can upgrade their financial systems. Hence, they should be strongly encouraged to adopt interim measures aimed at insulating their financial systems from the intrinsic volatility of international capital flows. There are principles, tools, and guidelines to foster private-sector involvement in crisis resolution, but they rely too heavily on the ability of crisis-stricken countries to elicit cooperation from the private sector—from domestic debtors as well as foreign creditors. Stronger and speedier methods are needed to cope with creditor panics, as well as debt-related problems such as those of Pakistan, Ukraine, and Ecuador, discussed in the previous chapter. There are, in short, some big pieces missing from the new international financial architecture.

This chapter starts with crisis prevention. What more can be done to encourage compliance with international standards and codes, so as to strengthen the financial systems of emerging-market countries? What might be done in the interim to reduce their vulnerability to fluctuations in capital flows? The chapter then turns to crisis resolution. What can be done to stem capital outflows from crisis-stricken countries and to manage debt problems more deftly without inviting the introduction of comprehensive capital controls or giving the IMF the quasi-judicial power to stay creditor litigation?

Promoting Compliance with Standards and Codes

Many carrots and sticks might be used to promote compliance with international standards and codes. In 1999, the Financial Stability Forum established a task force on the implementation of standards, which compiled a long list of strategies (FSF 2000a). A few examples follow.[3]

- Include specific financial-sector reforms in IMF conditionality with the aim of achieving compliance during the course of an IMF-supported program.

- Condition access to certain IMF facilities, such as the Supplemental Reserve Facility (SRF) and Contingent Credit Line (CCL), on a country's progress in complying with key standards, or impose more onerous terms, such as higher charges, on countries failing to make progress.

---

3. This list is my own; it draws on Kenen (2000b). The FSF task force made no mention of the first strategy, using conditionality, and it couched some of its other suggestions in more guarded terms. It also listed objections to each strategy.

- Impose higher capital requirements on cross-border bank loans to countries that have not complied with the relevant standards, such as the Basel Core Principles.

- Refuse to grant entry to foreign banks that come from countries that have not complied with those standards, and supervise more intensively the existing affiliates of banks that come from those countries.

Some of these strategies could be adopted unilaterally by individual governments, although they would be more effective if they were adopted collectively. Others would require concerted action by the official community. Objections have been raised to all of them, however, and most have quietly been rejected or discarded.

The Retreat from Official Incentives

There are persuasive objections to the first strategy, using conditionality to foster financial-sector reform. The Fund adopted that approach during the Asian crisis, when Thailand, Indonesia, and Korea were made to include far-reaching financial-sector reforms in their Fund-supported programs. This strategy, however, has several serious defects discussed in chapter 4. It cannot be applied preemptively or uniformly; it does not work well for reforms that take much time to implement, such as the upgrading of bank supervision; and it was partly to blame for the overloading of conditionality in the 1990s.[4]

Other objections apply to the next strategy, using compliance with standards—or progress in achieving such compliance—to govern access to IMF credit or to set the terms of access to a particular IMF facility. It can be used rather easily to govern access to a single Fund facility, such as the CCL, but it would be hard to use comprehensively. It would be hard politically, because it could deprive a country of the financing vitally needed to cope with a serious crisis. And it would therefore be risky, because a country cut off completely from Fund credit might be tempted to adopt other, systemically harmful ways of combating a crisis. Hence, the threat to deny future financing might not be credible. It would be equally hard for the Fund to impose more onerous terms of access, such as higher charges, on countries that had not made adequate progress in

---

4. The Fund, however, should not forswear the use of conditionality if it adopts the contractual approach proposed in the next section of this chapter. A country that does not enter into a long-term contract with the Bank and Fund after being urged to do so should be warned to expect that it will be asked to undertake major financial-sector reforms whenever it seeks Fund financing—including financing under an ordinary standby arrangement.

complying with key standards.[5] The Fund imposes different charges for drawings on different facilities, such as the Supplemental Reserve Facility (SRF), the Contingent Credit Line (CCL), and the Poverty Reduction and Growth Facility (PRGF), but has never, to my knowledge, imposed different charges on different countries that seek to draw on the same facility. Furthermore, the prospect of having to pay higher charges may not do much to foster compliance with the relevant standards: the immediate political cost of adopting reforms to stave off higher charges may be seen as exceeding the future financial cost of paying higher charges.

Introducing carrots and sticks into the Basel capital-adequacy framework looked to be a more promising strategy, and it was considered initially by the Basel Committee on Banking Supervision. Bank claims on a sovereign, it suggested, should not obtain a reduced risk weighting unless the borrowing country subscribes to the Special Data Dissemination Standard (SDDS); claims on a foreign bank should not obtain a reduced risk weighting unless the foreign bank's supervisor is implementing the Basel Committee's Core Principles (BCBS 1997); and claims on a foreign securities firm should not obtain a reduced risk weighting unless the foreign firm's supervisor is implementing IOSCO's Objectives and Principles of Securities Regulation (FSF 2000a). But in a subsequent paper, the Basel Committee abandoned this strategy. As judgments about compliance with standards will tend to be qualitative, it said, the committee did not wish to create a regime in which compliance would be assessed in a "mechanical fashion" (BCBS 2001). This concern is legitimate but not very persuasive. Supervisors of banks making cross-border loans will still have to make judgments about the risk characteristics of those loans, and their judgments may not be very different from those they would have made had they taken explicit account of the borrowing countries' compliance with the relevant standards. Furthermore, the IMF and other official bodies will still have to make judgments about compliance by individual countries. Excising compliance with standards from the capital-adequacy regime will deprive the official community of a powerful way to foster financial-sector reform.

The fourth strategy listed above is, therefore, the only survivor, a result confirmed when the Financial Stability Forum received a report from its follow-up group on the implementation of standards (FSF 2000b). The report stated clearly that official incentives are needed, because market discipline not may be sufficient. Many market participants do not currently take account of a country's adherence to standards when making risk assessments; weak domestic financial systems can impose negative externalities on the international financial system; and markets, focused on end results, may fail to recognize progress in the implementation of

---

5. This was the strategy recommended by the CFR Task Force (1999).

standards. Furthermore, it would be inconsistent for the official sector to ask that the private sector take account of implementation without also doing so in its own decisions. But in its recommendations, the follow-up group confined itself to the fourth strategy:

> National authorities should be encouraged to give greater consideration to a foreign jurisdiction's observance of relevant standards as one of the factors in making market access decisions.
>
> National authorities should give greater consideration to a foreign jurisdiction's observance of relevant standards as one of the factors in supervision and regulation of (a) subsidiaries or branches of foreign institutions from that jurisdiction; or (b) domestic institutions dealing with counterparties in that jurisdiction. (FSF 2000b, 13-14)

It said nothing whatsoever about the use of carrots and sticks by the international financial institutions.

We are thus left with market discipline, which is not very well suited to the purpose at hand. The reason was mentioned in both of the FSF reports (2000a, 2000b): insofar as market participants pay any attention to the quality of prudential supervision in a counterparty's country, they are concerned with the absolute quality of that supervision. They do not—and should not—care very much about a country's progress.[6] This difficulty is compounded by another. Most of the relevant standards aim at defining "best practice" rather than minimally acceptable practice,[7] and those who drafted the standards defined best practice by contemplating the sophisticated financial systems of the industrial countries. That is why developing countries insist that compliance must be voluntary and why they insist on being assessed in terms of their progress, not their absolute compliance. Some of them also worry about the goodness of fit between their own institutions and practices and those of the developed countries—and some are deeply suspicious of the entire exercise, seeing it as an insidious attempt to replace their indigenous institutions with those of the developed countries, thereby paving the way for foreign dominance of their financial systems.

---

6. In the same vein, the IMF and World Bank (2001) noted that market participants would like to have simple quantified ratings rather than nuanced assessments.

7. The codes concerned with transparency constitute an exception. The requirements of the SDDS are defined operationally, not as goals that governments must strive everlastingly to reach, and the codes concerned with transparency in fiscal, monetary, and financial policies define "good" practices rather than best practice. Goldstein (2001) seems to regard all of the key standards as minimum requirements, but most others describe them explicitly as statements about best practice; see, e.g., Eichengreen (1999b), Evans (2000), Folkerts-Landau and Lindgren (1998), and White (1999). It should nonetheless be noted that the Basel Committee has issued a manual for use in assessing compliance with the Core Principles, in which it distinguishes between essential criteria and additional desirable criteria, and similar efforts are being made by other standard-setting bodies (Evans 2000).

Even those countries that are not hostile to the whole exercise frequently express concerns about institutional incongruities—whether international standards can be applied to their indigenous institutions and whether those institutions can be reformed without disrupting practices that have served them rather well. Andrew Crockett (2000) acknowledges that international standards must be designed for adoption by countries with widely different histories and institutional structures (see also Köhler 2000). Barry Eichengreen (1999b, 27) makes the same point bluntly: "Given how economic, social, and political circumstances differ across countries, there should be a strong presumption that the same arrangements are not suitable for all of them." Furthermore, he notes, the international financial institutions do not possess the expertise and personnel required to give each country detailed advice in all of the relevant areas, even if that were desirable.[8]

A Contractual Approach

These legitimate concerns must not be allowed stand in the way of reform. No emerging-market country should be expected to import the laws, regulations, and modes of corporate governance used in the industrial countries. There are, after all, significant differences among the industrial countries' regimes. Yet emerging-market countries must acknowledge the need for some international standardization. Governments, financial institutions, and corporations that seek to participate in international capital markets must adopt the rules, conventions, and practices commonly used by those markets. In the last few years, moreover, the international financial institutions have been acquiring the expertise required to make them useful partners in the design and implementation of financial-sector reform.

What form should that partnership take? There may be a need for a new regime to foster financial-sector reform—one that can meet three requirements. The regime must allow for the fact that financial-sector reform is a time-consuming process; it involves the recruitment and training of bankers, traders, accountants, lawyers, and regulators, not merely the making of laws and regulations. The regime must also allow for the fact that many reforms are bound to elicit strong political opposition and must therefore be homegrown. They should be designed not by the IMF or an ad hoc team of foreign advisers who arrive with their minds and baggage full of standard blueprints, but by those most familiar with the domestic environment—political, juridical, and institutional. They should

---

8. The IMF and World Bank (2001) cite these concerns in their report on the implementation of standards. Thus far, however, they have found that ROSCs "appropriately allow for consideration of cross-country differences in stages of development and administrative capacity, as well as different cultural and legal traditions" (2001, 13).

be disseminated and debated before they take final form. Otherwise, they are bound to engender objections from those directly affected by them and could eventually fall victim to the law of unintended consequences. Finally, enforceable deadlines are needed, along with carrots and sticks, which is why the international financial institutions have an important role to play.

These requirements might be met by a new regime based on formal contracts between a government, on the one hand, and the IMF and World Bank, on the other. Each contract would describe in detail the financial-sector reforms that the government pledges to complete during the life of the contract (which might typically last five to seven years). The preparation of the contract would involve four steps: (1) A list of needs would be defined by the Financial Sector Assessment Program (FSAP). (2) The reforms themselves would be designed by a group of experts chosen by the government, who would include civil servants, private-sector participants, and advisers from other countries—emerging-market as well as developed. (3) After being approved by the country's government, the experts' proposals would be published, debated, and revised before being submitted formally to the Fund and Bank. (4) The proposals would be translated into contractual obligations, with a deadline for each step in the reform process—adopting the necessary legislation, introducing the relevant regulations, and, when appropriate, establishing and staffing the new institutions required for implementation. The Fund and Bank would then monitor the country's progress, year by year, over the life of the contract.

What might a government gain from entering into this sort of contract? First, the reforms could be designed and adapted carefully to the country's needs and institutional setting—something that cannot readily be done under crisis conditions. Having made such a contract, moreover, the country would be protected against an abrupt demand for financial-sector reform should a future crisis erupt. Suppose that a country having a financial-sector contract sought to draw on the Fund during the life of the contract. It might have to modify its macroeconomic policies but would not be told to undertake further financial-sector reform, except insofar as required to cope with its immediate problem. By slimming the scope of conditionality, moreover, the contract by its very existence would reduce the time required to reach agreement with the Fund and would thus grant faster access to IMF financing. Finally, a country with a financial-sector contract, or one that had been told that it did not need one, could be promised easier access to the IMF, with more funding or front-loading, if it was meeting its obligations.[9]

---

9. Knight, Schembri, and Powell (2000) make a similar suggestion.

The provisions of a long-term contract would also give operational meaning to the notion of progress in the implementation of international standards. By publishing the terms of a country's contract and assessing its subsequent adherence to that contract, the Bank and Fund could convey to market participants information they could not easily extract from the snapshot provided by a Report on the Observance of Standards and Codes (ROSC) or from an Article IV report updating developments after a ROSC. A country's progress would be measured against its contractual obligations, not against the abstract goals set out in the various standards and codes. Once it had met its contractual obligations, moreover, the country itself and its private-sector borrowers would move automatically into a safer risk class.

Interim Measures

One financial-sector contract might suffice to put in place the set of reforms most urgently needed in a particular country. Other countries might have to make two or three such contracts in order to complete the many reforms required to strengthen their financial systems. In the meantime, however, countries having serious financial-sector problems should be strongly encouraged to adopt interim measures aimed at reducing their vulnerability to financial crises. In fact, a country's contract with the Bank and Fund might commit it to adopt one or more of the measures listed by the Working Group on Capital Flows set up by the Financial Stability Forum (FSF 2000c).

The working group introduced the subject with this general observation: "Especially when the supervisory regime is not adequate, or supervisory resources are scarce, national authorities might consider a set of more explicit recommendations dealing notably with liquidity and foreign exchange exposures" (FSF 2000c, 32). It then listed several measures: imposing limits on banks' open foreign currency positions, reducing reserve or liquidity requirements on long-term foreign currency debt relative to those on short-term debt, imposing special reserve requirements on foreign currency funding, and requiring banks to hedge their foreign currency exposures and to insist their borrowers also do so as a condition for obtaining loans.[10] The working group went on to note that

10. The need to ensure that borrowers cover their own foreign currency exposures was obviously meant to rule out the imprudent practice of many Asian banks in the 1990s. They hedged their foreign currency exposures by making foreign currency loans to domestic firms that had no foreign currency revenues or claims. It may indeed be wise to insist that banks hedge their foreign currency exposures by making forward contracts with foreign banks or domestic counterparties approved by the central bank, rather than trying to hedge them by making foreign currency loans. Similar restrictions could be imposed on the use of complex derivative instruments that can likewise be employed to offset or incur foreign currency exposure; see the discussion in Garber (1996) and Garber and Lall (1998).

such explicit regulations can be only a partial and transitory substitute for adequate banking supervision. Regulatory requirements generally are less effective when banks are utilizing sophisticated risk management systems for foreign currency exposure.... However, such measures may be effective when banks are using less sophisticated risk management systems. They have the advantage that they can be implemented quickly by bank supervisors with resource limitations. (FSF 2000c, 32)

Other official bodies have made similar statements, including the finance ministers of the G-7 countries in their report to the Köln Summit:

The use of controls on capital inflows may be justified for a transitional period as countries strengthen the institutional and regulatory environment in their domestic financial systems. Where financial sectors and supervisory regimes are weak, safeguards may be appropriate to limit foreign currency exposure of the banking system. (Group of 7 1999b, para. 30e)

Many others recommend safeguards of this sort.[11] Even the IMF, which had wanted its members to move to capital account convertibility, has come around to endorsing their use as a way to "moderate the pace of short-term inflows" (Fischer 1999, F564).

What do we know about the effectiveness of these interim measures? Several countries have used taxes or tax-equivalent measures to limit capital inflows, including Brazil, Chile, Colombia, and Malaysia, and the Chilean experience has been widely studied.[12]

In 1991, Chile imposed a reserve requirement on foreign borrowing. A sum equal to 20 percent of the amount borrowed had to be deposited with the central bank, where it would earn no interest, and it had to be held there for a minimum of 90 days and a maximum of one year. In 1992, the reserve requirement was raised to 30 percent and extended to one year regardless of the initial maturity of the external credit; and the regime was later broadened to outflank circumvention. It was made to cover all forms of foreign financial investment in Chile, including foreign purchases of Chilean equities.[13] Five questions have been asked about the Chilean regime: Did it confer more autonomy on Chilean monetary policy?

---

11. See, e.g., Blinder (1999), Caprio and Honohan (1999), Feldstein (1999), Goldstein and Calvo (1996), Lamfalussy (2000), CFR Task Force (1999), and IIF (2001). But see Eichengreen et al. (1998a), who warn that interim measures targeted at banks cannot adequately substitute for prudential supervision, even temporarily. Such measures cannot prevent other forms of imprudent behavior by banks or protect the banks from imprudent behavior by others. Their point is well taken, although they carry it too far.

12. On the Colombian and Brazilian cases, see Agosin and Ffrench-Davis (1995); on the Malaysian case, see Rodrik and Velasco (1999).

13. Agosin and Ffrench-Davis (1997) describe the evolution and principal features of the Chilean regime. The 30 percent reserve requirement was suspended in 1998, but the regime was not dismantled until 2001.

Did it insulate Chile from other countries' crises? Did it reduce the volume of capital inflows? Did it reduce the volume of short-term inflows relative to long-term inflows? And could it be readily emulated by other countries?

Sebastian Edwards (2000) concludes that the Chilean regime did confer more autonomy on domestic monetary policy, but that the effect was small and transitory. He also finds, however, that it did not protect Chile from other countries' crises. The tequila effect of 1995 did not hit Chile nearly as hard as it hit Argentina, but Chile was strongly affected by the Asian crisis (Edwards 1998, 1999a). Few studies find that the regime had any significant impact on the overall volume of capital inflows,[14] but most find that it shifted the composition of inflows in the desired direction: short-term inflows fell relative to long-term inflows.[15]

The Chilean regime was leaky, as everyone agrees.[16] And other, larger countries would find it harder to monitor capital inflows and minimize evasion. But it is not especially hard to monitor bank borrowing and thus use tax-equivalent measures to hold down the banks' foreign debts pending the further development of prudential supervision. Eichengreen (1999b) and Guillermo Calvo and Carmen Reinhart (2000c) warn that attempts to reduce bank-related inflows would probably lead to larger amounts of short-term corporate borrowing. That would not matter much, however, if the attempt to reduce bank-related inflows was meant to diminish the vulnerability of the banking system, not to reduce short-term borrowing per se.[17]

Martin Wolf ("Caging the Bankers," *Financial Times*, 20 January 1998) sums it up succinctly. There is, he says, an overwhelming case for the regulation of foreign currency borrowing by commercial banks:

> Prudential control over short-term foreign currency borrowing by institutions underpinned by the state is inescapable. The [Asian] crisis shows, once again, that banks fall into this category—that they are part of the public sector. Unregu-

---

14. But see Reinhart and Smith (1998), who find that it did reduce total inflows.

15. See Edwards (2000) and the studies cited there. Edwards notes that the effect on short-term inflows shows up most clearly when inflows are classified by original maturity rather than remaining maturity. But that is what one would expect; long-term inflows are reclassified automatically as short-term inflows when they approach maturity, and this reclassification necessarily raises the share of short-term inflows among the total. Edwards argues that remaining maturities are more relevant than original maturities for assessing vulnerability. Original maturities are more relevant, however, for assessing the effectiveness of the regime.

16. Garber (1998) notes, however, that the Chilean regime withstood efforts to evade it via financial engineering.

17. Eichengreen (1999b) also warns that corporations might be induced to engage in arbitrage by taking on external debt and depositing the foreign currency proceeds with domestic banks. That would not be problematic, however, if a reserve requirement or outright tax were levied on the banks' short-term foreign currency debt, including foreign currency deposits owed to domestic entities.

lated flows of short-term international capital are a license to rack up losses at the expense of taxpayers. If banks are not to be reformed, they must be more securely caged.

Banks, of course, must be reformed. That is the principal aim of the effort to strengthen prudential supervision in emerging-market countries by fostering compliance with the Basel Core Principles. Until that is achieved, however, the banks *should* be caged. Asian banks have reduced their dependence on foreign currency funding, but other countries' banks have not, and a contraction of interbank lending played a prominent role in the recent Turkish crisis.

Short Notes on Other Shortcuts

Before we turn from crisis prevention to crisis resolution, two more questions need attention. Can emerging-market countries strengthen their financial systems by admitting foreign banks? And what can we learn from Malaysia's attempt to cope with the Asian crisis by restricting capital outflows rather than trying preemptively to regulate capital inflows?

Those who answer "yes" to the first question adduce several arguments. Foreign banks, they say, will diversify the asset base of a country's banking system, reducing its vulnerability to domestic shocks. They will provide and impart scarce managerial skills, which will enhance the quality of bank lending, as well as loan-loss provisioning and overall risk management. Finally, foreign banks can count on financial support from their parent banks, including foreign currency credit that is not available locally when it is urgently needed.[18] Others warn, however, that competition from strong foreign banks may threaten the survival of domestic banks and may therefore induce them to "gamble for redemption."[19]

Unfortunately, participants in this debate rarely distinguish between two strategies—letting foreign banks set up local affiliates, and letting foreign banks buy into domestic banks.[20] The two strategies have different consequences for a country's banking system and for its domestic banks.

The entry of foreign banks as separate entities, competing with domestic banks, can strengthen a country's banking system, taken as a whole, but it may not do much to strengthen the domestic banks themselves. Foreign banks will impart much-needed skills to their local employees, who will, in turn, transfer them to domestic banks whenever they change jobs.

18. For these and other arguments favoring foreign bank entry, see Calomiris (1998a), Caprio and Honohan (1999, 2001), Eichengreen (1999b), Fischer (1999), and Meltzer (1999).

19. See Chang and Velasco (1999) and Williamson (2000a); Eichengreen (1999b) also mentions this possibility.

20. See, however, Calomiris (1998a), who focuses explicitly on the second strategy.

Foreign banks will diversify the asset base of a country's banking system but may not have any first-order effect on the asset base of the domestic banks. Foreign banks may be able to borrow from their parent banks, but that will not be helpful to domestic banks. Finally, foreign banks may tend to concentrate on wholesale banking, which will not raise the quality of the banking services available to firms and households. There are thus reasons to question the efficacy of this first strategy.

The case for the second strategy is stronger. When a foreign bank acquires a domestic bank, totally or partially, it strengthens that bank directly. It may not diversify the asset base of the domestic bank, but it will indirectly add that asset base into its own asset base, by pooling its global gains and losses. It will also want to upgrade the staff and internal controls of the domestic bank. If foreign banks acquire the strongest domestic banks, other domestic banks may be more strongly tempted to gamble for redemption. Therefore, this strategy is not a substitute for tight prudential supervision; the two must go together. But it may be a powerful way to strengthen a country's banking system.

What about capital-outflow controls? Economists never tire of saying that controls on capital outflows are more costly and less effective than controls on capital inflows. They are more costly, it is said, because they discourage capital inflows as well as capital outflows, and because they are harder to enforce. A foreign investor is free to choose among many destinations and can readily bypass a country that uses capital-import controls rather than trying to evade them. Residents and foreigners confined to a single country by capital-outflow controls will try very hard to evade them whenever they come to distrust the country's prospects or policies. For that same reason, moreover, capital-outflow controls tend to spawn corruption. Finally, capital-outflow controls have often been used to delay the making of policy changes that are inevitable and become more painful when they are deferred. Imbalances build up until they are rectified. They rarely go away.[21]

When, therefore, Malaysia imposed controls on capital outflows in September 1998, it was roundly criticized. It was told that it should take the same unpleasant medicine that Thailand, Korea, and others were taking and that it would be unable to borrow on international capital markets and thus would suffer grave damage.[22] But Malaysia fared rather well after imposing controls: interest rates fell, output rose, and Malaysia built up its reserves while pegging the ringgit firmly to the dollar. In fact, the Malaysian economy recovered in much the same way as the Thai

---

21. For a concise survey of supporting evidence, see, e.g., Edwards (1999a).

22. See the comments collected in Kaplan and Rodrik (2001).

economy, though more slowly than the Korean economy.[23] And Malaysia was able to borrow again in 1999, when it floated a $1 billion bond issue at a 330 basis-point premium (Kaplan and Rodrik 2001).

There are two interpretations of this seemingly odd result. Edwards (1999a) concludes that Malaysia's controls did not do much harm—but did not do much good, either. Others say that the controls were redundant because the pressure on the ringgit had subsided before they were imposed (see, e.g., Dornbusch 2001; Mussa et al. 2000). But Ethan Kaplan and Dani Rodrik disagree:

> Far from being out of the woods, the Malaysian economy in late August 1998 was still mired in a financial quagmire. Whether this was partly its own doing is irrelevant from our current perspective. The crucial point is that Malaysia's policy framework in September 1998 looked as fragile as Thailand's had been in July 1997 or Korea's in November 1997. (Kaplan and Rodrik 2001, 21)

The ringgit, they say, was under great pressure, and the foreign financial press was predicting that Malaysia would have to seek help from the IMF.

Therefore, Kaplan and Rodrik conduct a "time-shifted" comparison in which they contrast Malaysia's performance in 1998-99, after it imposed capital controls, pegged its exchange rate, and reduced its interest rates, with the performance of the Thai and Korean economies in 1997-98, when they were swallowing the medicine prescribed by the IMF. This is their main conclusion:

> Previous comparisons have asked how Malaysia did relative to Korea or Thailand after September 1998. We have asked instead how Malaysia did compared to Korea or Thailand when the latter were undergoing their IMF programs (while making allowance for changes in the external environment). We have shown that the first approach yields answers that on balance make the capital controls look bad. The second approach yields answers that make the controls look very good. (Kaplan and Rodrik 2001, 32)

Which approach is right? Kaplan and Rodrik invite the reader to decide—and that is not easy. One paper on one episode is rarely decisive. Kaplan and Rodrik rightly note that Malaysia's situation was more precarious in September 1998 than others have inferred from the behavior of the ringgit during the previous months—and it would become more precarious in the ensuing months, after Prime Minister Mahathir dismissed his deputy, Anwar Ibrahim. But one must also point out that Malaysia's banking system was somewhat less fragile than those of Thailand and Korea, which helps explain why Malaysia was not hit as hard at the beginning of the Asian crisis.

---

23. See Edison and Reinhart (2000), who also find that Malaysia's capital controls were more effective than those used by Thailand in early 1997 before the acute phase of its currency crisis.

Finally, consider another time-shifted comparison. What would have happened to Malaysia in 1997-98 if, at the start of the Asian crisis, foreign investors had expected that Malaysia would impose capital-outflow controls? The anticipation might have done great damage. That indeed is the strongest reason for taking the conventional view. Whatever one's judgment about the outcome of the Malaysian episode, it would be wrong to conclude that capital-outflow controls are a first-best remedy for a currency crisis.

Rethinking Private-Sector Involvement

We come now to the biggest bit of unfinished architecture—finding viable ways to involve the private sector in the resolution of debt-related crises. In his recent paper on the architecture exercise, Morris Goldstein (2001) quotes statements by G-7 and IMF officials in which they praise the progress made in fostering private-sector involvement.[24] But others are less comfortable. Mervyn King (1999) says that "much remains obscure," and an IMF report concedes that "the international community does not have at its disposal the full range of tools that would be needed to ensure a reasonably orderly—and timely—involvement of the private sector" (IMF 2000d, 12). The critics, however, are too polite. The current approach is deeply flawed, because it relies much too heavily on voluntary cooperation by the private sector.

The Limits to Voluntary Cooperation

The premium placed on voluntary cooperation leads to undue delay, forcing crisis-stricken countries to adopt excessively harsh policies in order to restore investor confidence and, in too many cases, forcing the official community to provide large-scale financing. It also forces debtor countries to offer exceedingly generous settlements that sow the seeds of future crises. Such settlements threaten the debtor countries with unstable debt dynamics, and they reward imprudent lenders, who should be made to understand that a country unable to service its debt on the original terms cannot be expected to service its debt on more onerous terms.

The private sector has warned repeatedly that any departure from the voluntary approach will undermine the discipline that sustains international lending—the so-called bonding role of debt. If the official commu-

---

24. See also Köhler (2000), Geithner (2000), and the survey by Roubini (2000), who describes the Köln framework as a set of "clear principles and tools" for striking the right balance between the private sector's need for guidelines and the official sector's need for flexibility in addressing specific cases. But Roubini admits that there is still a need to clarify the terms of the trade-off between official financing and reliance on voluntary private-sector involvement.

nity adopts a coercive approach, debtors will find it too easy to default. Thus, Gerald Corrigan (2000) warns that the use of involuntary standstills, especially officially sanctioned, would pose a clear and present danger to the "culture of credit" in international capital markets, and an IIF working group has similarly cautioned against any form of official pressure or coercion:

> Some of the public discussion of crisis resolution has stressed the need to "bind" creditors into support programs. Any shift toward involuntary mechanisms for private sector participation, however, would tend to defeat a key purpose of the 1990s approach, namely the emphasis on prompt restoration of market access. The most tangible binding mechanism is IMF "lending into arrears." ... The September 1998 decision by the IMF Executive Board to widen the 1989 policy permitting such lending, to encompass bonds and other nonbank credits, seems counterproductive, especially at a time of retrenchment in capital flows to emerging markets. (IIF 1999)

The IIF has also objected obliquely to the imposition of a reserve floor to keep a debtor country from using reserves or IMF credit to repay private creditors (one of the "tools" listed in the Köln framework), because "meeting financial obligations is a legitimate and essential use of reserves and balance-of-payments financing." (IIF 2001, 6)[25]

Yet these objections elide two issues: the effects of coercion on the balance of bargaining power between debtor countries and their private creditors and thus on the terms of debt restructurings, and the effects of coercion on the ability of debtor countries to shirk their contractual obligations without being punished. The two overlap to some extent. The terms of a restructuring enter into the cost paid by the debtor when it refuses to honor its contractual obligations. But the analytical literature on the bonding role of debt looks in a different direction by stressing two other forms of punishment.

The first form of punishment is emphasized by Michael Dooley (2000a). It is the immediate adverse effect of a protracted negotiation between a debtor country and its foreign creditors. By disrupting financial intermediation in the debtor country, a protracted negotiation impairs the productivity of the capital stock and leads to a larger output loss, and it is the size of the output loss that deters a debtor from defaulting. On this view, which goes back to Jeremy Bulow and Kenneth Rogoff (1989), an effort to coordinate creditor behavior can be counterproductive. By shortening the time it takes to reach agreement on a debt restructuring, it reduces the amount of domestic disruption, diminishes the output loss, and thus makes it less costly for a debtor to default.

---

25. William Rhodes ("Don't Press-Gang the Private Sector," *Financial Times,* 13 October 1999) expresses concern about two other "troublesome" proposals: the mandatory inclusion of collective action clauses in debt contracts, and the amendment of Article VIII.2(b) of the Fund's Articles of Agreement to make the enforcement of loan contracts subject to the foreign exchange regulations of the debtor country—a matter to which we will return later.

The second form of punishment is emphasized by William Cline (2000b). It is the effect of a default on the debtor's reputation and its ability to borrow again. If it can no longer borrow, it cannot engage in consumption smoothing on behalf of its citizens.[26] On this view, which goes back to Jonathan Eaton and Mark Gersovitz (1981), the welfare loss resulting from more volatile consumption is the main deterrent to default.[27] This reputational argument is more plausible than the one advanced by Dooley, and it may help explain why emerging-market countries have agreed to expensive debt exchanges. A government that defaults today on its maturing debt is apt to have trouble tomorrow rolling over the rest of its debt, may have to default again, and will then suffer additional damage to its reputation. But access to new borrowing for consumption smoothing is not the only reason for wanting to preserve a reputation for repaying debt on time—access to new borrowing for investment may be a more important motive.

If reputational considerations are paramount, however, then the concerns of the private sector are overblown. Coercive behavior by the official sector may lead to debt restructurings that are less attractive from the creditors' standpoint, and they cannot be blamed for objecting to that prospect. But coercion today in respect of debt restructuring cannot be deemed to imply coercion tomorrow in respect of new private-sector lending. Lenders can still refuse to lend if they see fit to punish a debtor for a "strategic" default or for mismanaging its economic policies in ways that impair its ability to repay its debts.[28]

The undue emphasis on voluntary cooperation is compounded by another, more serious defect of the official approach to private-sector involvement. It emerged most clearly in a statement by the G-7 finance ministers and central bank governors issued in September 1999, between the Köln and Okinawa Summits:

> When a country's underlying capacity to pay is strong and prospects for the spontaneous restoration of market access on viable terms are good, the combination of official financing and policy adjustment should allow the country to regain full market access with voluntary approaches. In other cases, the early restoration of full market access on terms consistent with medium term external sustainability

---

26. Eichengreen (1999b) also emphasizes the "collateral damage" to a debtor's reputation but does not explicitly invoke the consumption-smoothing argument.

27. Dooley (2000a) takes note of this argument but says (rather elliptically) that it seems very weak relative to the amount of debt actually observed.

28. The IIF working group quoted above makes this same point obliquely: "The central issue is the borrowing government's assessment of the relative value of early return to private capital markets. The greater the weight placed on this objective, the more the government tends to understand the need for temporary high prices. The less the weight, the more borrowing governments tend to allow outcomes to slide toward reschedulings and restructurings" (IIF 1999, 51).

may not be realistic, and the use of a broader spectrum of tools may be warranted to provide for an adequately financed program and a sustainable medium term payments profile. In these cases, responsibility lies with debtors and creditors to work cooperatively to find a solution to the country's debt problems within the context of an IMF program that addresses the country's immediate financing gap, provides an appropriate balance between official and private financing, . . . and is sustainable over the medium term. (Group of 7 1999a, Annex, para. 5)

In effect, voluntary approaches should always be used *except* in the case of a country with an unsustainable debt burden, where the "broader spectrum of tools" may be needed, including those that the G-7 countries are fond of describing euphemistically as "concerted" approaches. Horst Köhler used the same dichotomous formulation:

There is broad agreement that the operational framework for private sector involvement should rely as much as possible on market-oriented solutions and on voluntary approaches. It is also undisputed that there may be exceptionally difficult cases that call for more concerted approaches to involve the private sector, *including the possibility of standstills as a truly last resort.* (Köhler 2000; emphasis added)

In a recent Fund document, however, we find an anomaly. It cites Korea, Pakistan, and Ukraine as examples of the concerted approach (IMF 2000d). Yet those are the very same cases that officials and others commonly cite as successful examples of the voluntary approach.

There was, of course, coercion in the case of Pakistan, which was told by the Paris Club that it had to seek comparable treatment from its private creditors, and there was likewise coercion in the case of Ukraine, which was prevented from using its reserves to redeem maturing debt. In both instances, however, coercion was applied to the debtor, not its private creditors. In the Korean case, by contrast, the country's commercial-bank creditors were subjected to strong pressure. They were told, in effect, to roll over their claims on Korean banks; otherwise, they would doom the whole effort to stave off a default—from which the banks themselves would suffer. Many terms have been used to describe this episode. Michael Mussa et al. (2000) say that the foreign banks undertook a "voluntary" rescheduling; Barry Eichengreen (2000b) speaks of "moral suasion" applied by the banks' regulators; Steven Radelet and Jeffrey Sachs (1998) assert that the rollover was "enforced" by the IMF as a condition for further disbursements of official funds. Those who classify it differently, however, tend nevertheless to agree that it was unique and cannot be readily replicated. They give four reasons.

First, the number of foreign banks was relatively small, and they dealt directly with the Korean government, not the Korean banks, because the government had guaranteed the debts of the Korean banks.[29] Second, the

29. For that same reason, moreover, the subsequent conversion of the foreign banks' claims into bonds had the effect of substituting sovereign debt for private debt, and this had the

asymmetric liberalization of Korea's capital account regime had restricted corporate borrowing from foreign banks, so there was little risk that foreign banks would run down their claims on Korean firms when asked to roll over their claims on Korean banks. Third, Korea was deemed to be a systemically important country, and the official community had invested its reputation, as well as its money, in the attempt to resolve the Korean crisis; had that not been the case, the major industrial countries might have been more reluctant to put pressure on their banks. Finally, and most important for what lies ahead, the provision of large-scale official financing had allowed foreign banks to run down their claims on Korean banks. Those least willing to roll over their claims were able to exit totally; others were able to reduce their exposure to acceptable levels.[30]

There was a stabilization of interbank claims and trade credits during the Brazilian crisis. The Brazilian authorities were reluctant to request it. They were said to be concerned about causing other investors, foreign and domestic, to run down their holdings of Brazilian government debt (see Cline 2000b; IMF 2000c). But they were also worried about another possibility. Banks reluctant to agree to a freeze might run down their claims very fast, before the freeze could take effect (see IMF 1999e). In the end, however, Brazilian officials convened meetings with the banks, persuaded them to stabilize their interbank claims and trade credits, and helped them devise a reporting system to monitor compliance. In the Korean case, arm-twisting by the official sector had been used to achieve a stabilization of interbank credits; in the Brazilian case, peer pressure was used instead.

Clearly, the best way to prevent a huge and disruptive contraction of a country's short-term debt is to keep the debt from growing to levels as high as it did before the Asian crisis. That is why so much attention has been paid to strengthening prudential supervision and why other measures should be used in the interim to limit interbank borrowing. When creditor panics occur, however, it is manifestly imprudent to rely on voluntary or quasi-voluntary measures to contain them unless the official community is willing and able to throw much money at the problem. Stronger measures are required to halt the liquidation of short-term

---

further effect of reducing to zero the risk weighting of the foreign banks' claims; under the existing version of the Basel capital-adequacy accord, banks did not hold any capital against claims on an OECD government (IMF 2000c). On the other unique features listed in the text, see Eichengreen (1999b, 2000a, 2000b) and IMF (1999e).

30. Eichengreen (2000a), Giannini (1999), and the IMF (2000d) all stress this point. Boorman and Allen (2000) wonder whether the Fund should have tried to achieve a concerted rollover at an earlier stage, not only in Korea but also in Thailand, and Roubini (2000) asks the same question. The IIF working group (IIF 1999) says that there should have been an earlier signal of the official community's interest in involving Korea's private creditors. But if a large run-down of claims had to occur before the foreign banks would agree to a rollover, stronger pressure might have been needed to obtain an earlier rollover.

foreign currency claims and to halt it promptly. This brings us to the case for standstills.

Suspensions, Stays, and Standstills

Three sorts of debt-related problems can be addressed by a mandatory standstill—a brief suspension of debt payments combined with a stay of litigation. The first is the one just considered, in which a creditor panic threatens to cause a sharp depreciation of a country's currency—whether the currency was pegged or floating before the onset of the panic. The second is the case of a country that is temporarily unable to make all of its debt service payments—because a large lump of debt is about to mature and cannot be refinanced on sustainable terms, or because the country has suffered a temporary fall in its export earnings or rise in its import payments. The third is the case of a country that faces an unsustainable debt burden over the long run because of its own past errors or because of an adverse shock, such as a seemingly permanent worsening of its terms of trade.

In the first case, the country needs immediate cash-flow relief, as well as time to quell the panic by making the policy changes required to reassure panicky creditors or to let the panic subside by itself as creditors come to their senses. In the second case, official financing can resolve the problem and may be the best remedy, but if it is unavailable or inadequate, the country will have to reschedule its debt. In the third case, of course, the country must reduce its debt; there is no other way to deal with an unsustainable debt burden. In the first case, then, a standstill should suffice. In the second and third cases, it cannot suffice but can be helpful; it can buy time for the debtor country to convince its creditors that longer-lasting relief is required—debt rescheduling in the second case and debt reduction in the third.

This taxonomy is quite different from the one imbedded implicitly in the current official approach to private-sector involvement. It reverses the usual pairing of problems and solutions. A mandatory standstill may well be a first-best remedy for a creditor panic, but that is the case in which the current official approach recommends a combination of policy changes to restore investor confidence, modest amounts of official financing, and voluntary private-sector involvement. A standstill would be helpful in the second case as well, but it will not be necessary if official financing is forthcoming promptly. A standstill would be helpful in the third case, too, but it is not a substitute for outright debt reduction. The current official approach, however, pays little attention to the second case and recommends a concerted approach only in the third case.[31]

---

31. The G-22 working group on international financial crises touched obliquely on the second case when it discussed the coverage of a debt suspension. A suspension, it said,

The weakness of the current official approach can be highlighted differently. In chapter 2, the Fund's Asian strategy was described as being precariously balanced, because its success in combating a creditor panic depended on the amount of financing supplied and the amount of adjustment required. Yet the converse was also true. The amounts of financing supplied and adjustment required depended on how successful the strategy was in combating creditor panic. In other words, the size of the "financing gap" was thoroughly endogenous. That is always true in crises of this sort, and there is a temptation to do what the Fund did. It put up large amounts of money in the hope of restoring confidence but doled out too little money to fill the whole financing gap, with the result that the gap grew larger.[32] In the other two cases considered above, the size of the financing gap is more easily measured, along with the size of the contribution that should come from the private sector via debt rescheduling or debt reduction. In those cases, however, the Fund should do more than measure the financing gap. It should also assess how any proposed agreement between a debtor country and its foreign creditors will affect the sustainability of the debtor's situation. It should not hesitate to warn that it will not provide further financing if the agreement is defective from that crucial standpoint.[33]

The Problems Posed by Standstills

If mandatory standstills are to be used more frequently, however, four difficult issues must be addressed. (1) Would they have the counterproductive effect of making investors flee faster? (2) Are comprehensive exchange controls required to enforce a standstill? (3) Who should impose a standstill—and how? (4) Can debtors be protected from litigation when they suspend debt payments?

---

should cover only those types of debt that are contributing "substantially" to a country's payments problem (Group of 22 1998a).

32. Boorman and Allen (2000) also stress the endogeneity of the financing gap in the case of a creditor panic, while Miller and Zhang (2000) argue that standstills can relieve the IMF of the need to furnish large-scale financing to cope with a creditor panic. See also Williamson (2000b), who frames the issue starkly. A creditor who fears that debt restructuring is a possibility will want to exit immediately. Hence, limited official financing is an unsatisfactory remedy, as some will be able to exit but others will not. The official community must therefore choose between unlimited financing and a standstill, and the former is apt to create moral hazard if it is used routinely. When faced with a country beset by a creditor panic, Williamson says, the Fund should require the country to impose a standstill while it negotiates with the Fund for limited bridge financing. (Williamson's point echoes one made abstractly by Roubini 2000, that a full "bailout" is formally equivalent to a full "bail-in"; see n. 36 of chapter 4, above.)

33. If the Fund is to take this strong stand, however, it should also convey to the private sector as early as possible its views about the nature of a country's problems and the role that the private sector should play in resolving those problems.

The risk that standstills will serve merely to accelerate a rush for the exit and, perhaps, produce contagion is the most common objection to them.[34] Mervyn King (1999) suggests, by contrast, that once standstills are part of the furniture, they will cease to be viewed as ad hoc responses and may no longer have those effects; and others have argued that the threat—or promise—of a standstill can actually quell a creditor panic by convincing creditors that they don't have to beat the rest to the exit. But these arguments are not very persuasive. They assume implicitly that creditors know what will happen after a standstill expires and can therefore be absolutely sure that they will not have to provide longer-term relief in the form of debt rescheduling or outright debt reduction. Yet the objection itself is not really germane to the choice at issue. The choice is not between a standstill and prompt, large-scale official financing, but between a mandatory standstill and an attempt to organize a voluntary rollover. Experience to date suggests that a rollover cannot be achieved until reluctant creditors have already left or run down their claims to levels at which they are willing to roll them over. Hence, there is no way to know a priori which will provoke the larger reduction in the creditors' claims—the threat of a mandatory standstill or the rundown of claims that has to occur before creditors will agree to a voluntary rollover.[35]

Critics often argue that standstills cannot be enforced without exchange controls and that many countries can no longer use them because they have dismantled the apparatus required to enforce them (see, e.g., Geithner 2000; IMF 2000d; Roubini 2000). That is not necessarily so. The G-22 working group on international financial crises provides a response:

> A selective suspension, even if mandatory, may not require the use of comprehensive capital and exchange controls. A government can suspend its own debt payments, and it may be possible to suspend payments on some types of private sector debt, such as the foreign currency debts of banks, without imposing comprehensive capital controls. An announcement by the government without any binding enforcement mechanism may suffice to induce substantial compliance by most of the main private sector debtors. (Group of 22 1998a, 31)

The working group noted, however, that a selective suspension could give rise to fears that it will be widened or that comprehensive controls may be coming. Furthermore, one must concede that a suspension of

---

34. See, e.g., Fischer (1999), Geithner (2000), and Lipton (2000). An IMF paper on private-sector involvement goes so far as to call this the test by which all such proposals must be judged (IMF 1999e). Roubini (2000) asserts that the run-down of interbank claims on Brazil in the second half of 1998 was triggered in part by the Korean episode and the fear that a similar "coercive" solution might be adopted in the Brazilian case. See also IMF (2000d), which lists several reasons for fearing that a standstill is apt to exacerbate contagion.

35. One Fund study raises another possibility: the credible threat of a suspension may lead private creditors to agree to a voluntary rollover sooner than they would in the absence of that threat (IMF 2000d).

debt payments not backed by exchange controls cannot prevent domestic debtors with large foreign currency obligations from purchasing foreign exchange as a precaution against the resumption of creditor flight when the suspension expires. Without controls, then, there may not be a one-to-one correspondence between the coverage of a suspension and the balance of payments relief it provides.

There are two answers to the third question: Who should impose a standstill? Some proponents of standstills want the IMF to do that. Curzio Giannini (1999) and John Williamson (2000b) suggest, for example, that a country seeking support from the Fund and having a debt-related problem should be required by the Fund to impose a temporary standstill. But Morris Goldstein (2001), David Lipton (2000), and others believe that the decision should reside with the country itself, as it must bear the reputational cost of imposing a standstill.[36] Others acknowledge the force of that argument, but they believe that governments may be inclined to act precipitously. Therefore, they say that a government should not impose a standstill without the consent of the Fund or some similar entity (see, e.g., Martin 1998, 1999).[37] But they should not be worried about the risk of precipitous action. Most governments are keenly aware of the reputational cost that they will incur if they resort to standstills and the cost they will impose on their private-sector debtors. Furthermore, Fund approval would not confer immunity from disruptive litigation—the fourth and final problem that must be addressed.

In an influential paper written right after the Mexican crisis, Jeffrey Sachs (1995) sought to design the equivalent of a bankruptcy regime for sovereign debtors. To provide protection against litigation, he looked to Article VIII.2(b) of the Fund's Articles of Agreement. That provision says in part,

> Exchange contracts which involve the currency of any member and which are contrary to the exchange control regulations of that member maintained or imposed consistently with this Agreement shall be unenforceable in the territories of any member.

There are, however, two huge obstacles to using this provision in the manner proposed by Sachs. First, it cannot be used to shield a sovereign debtor; no government can claim to have its hands tied by its own exchange controls. Second, Article VIII.2(b) has been construed quite narrowly by US and UK courts; they have interpreted "exchange contracts"

---

36. Eichengreen (2000a) points out, moreover, that the IMF may be seen to be unduly disposed to endorse suspensions because of its need to protect its own preferred-creditor status.

37. Eichengreen (2000a) makes a similar suggestion but for a different reason: a country may opt for a standstill in order to defer painful policy changes.

to be contracts involving an exchange of currencies rather than debt contracts.[38] It would, of course, be possible for the Fund's Executive Board to issue its own interpretation of Article VIII.2(b) in an attempt to protect private-sector debtors from the risk of litigation when they are barred from making debt payments by a mandatory standstill; but national courts might choose not to be bound by the board's interpretation. Debtors cannot be protected from the risk of litigation without changing the actual language of Article VIII.2(b), and any amendment to the Fund's Articles of Agreement has to be ratified by three-fifths of the Fund's membership having at least 85 percent of the total voting power. This means, in turn, that an amendment to Article VIII.2(b) would require the approval of the US Congress, which is unlikely to grant it.[39]

To bypass this obstacle, others suggest that the Fund "endorse" a standstill (see, e.g., Miller and Zhang 2000; Radelet and Sachs 1998). But this suggestion is weaker than the one mentioned before—that standstills should not be imposed without the consent of the Fund—and does not resolve the problem. No endorsement by the Fund, whether strong or weak, can protect a debtor country against litigation.

Solving the Problems Posed by Standstills

There is another, more promising approach—adding a standstill provision to every debt contract or to the subset of contracts involving foreign currency debt. This approach was suggested by Paul Martin (1998) and by Willem Buiter and Anne Sibert (1999), and it was also mentioned by the G-22 working group on international financial crises:

> It is also worth considering the addition of options to sovereign bonds and interbank credit lines that would allow a debtor government or debtor banks to extend the maturity of a bond or credit line for a specified period of time at a predetermined spread. Such options could be exercised to ease pressure on the government and the banking system in the event of a liquidity crisis. Such provisions could have an effect opposite to the effect of the put options that have been exercised in certain recent crises. These put options have reduced the maturity of various credits and thus exacerbated market pressures. (Group of 22 1998a, 12)

Under the scheme devised by Buiter and Sibert (1999), each government, on its own, would require the inclusion of a rollover option in *all* foreign

---

38. See IMF (2000d) and the more extensive treatment by Tarullo (2001), who also deals with the next point covered in the text.

39. Eichengreen (1998) is undoubtedly right in saying that any such amendment would be widely regarded as taking one step too many toward an international bankruptcy regime and tipping the balance too strongly in favor of debtors. In fact, the US Treasury appears to take that view—or believes that the Congress would take it; see Geithner (2000).

currency debt contracts, including the government's own obligations.[40] They call it the Universal Debt Rollover Option with a Penalty (UDROP). The rollover option would allow the individual borrower, at his or her sole discretion, to extend the maturing debt for a fixed period, say 90 days, by paying a penalty. The option could be exercised only if the debt had been serviced in full, apart from the pending final payment, and it would not be renewable. Buiter and Sibert suggest that the penalty be defined as a "hefty" addition to the spread over LIBOR that the debtor would normally pay (and that the normal spread might be defined by a long-run moving average of the actual market spread).

The size of the penalty and other features of the rollover option applicable to a particular debt contract would be set by the parties concerned, not by the government or by any international body. There would, of course, be no need to provide any explicit protection against litigation. A creditor cannot object to a fixed-term debt suspension when it is built into the debt contract to which the creditor has assented. This, indeed, is the most attractive feature of the scheme, compared to other ways of imposing a standstill.[41]

As debtors would have to pay heavily to exercise the option, the rollover option would not be exercised under orderly market conditions. Buiter and Sibert believe, however, that it would be exercised widely under crisis conditions, with the result that all foreign currency creditors—public and private, foreign and domestic—would be bailed in automatically. Korea and Brazil, they say, would have benefited from their scheme. Buiter and Sibert acknowledge that individual debtors might be tempted to exercise the rollover option under normal market conditions if they cannot pay their own debts. They would therefore entertain a variant of their scheme in which a country's central bank would have to declare that a "crunch" had arrived before individual debtors could exercise their options. But they decline to entertain another variant in which that task would be assigned to the IMF.[42] More important, they do not even deign

---

40. They would therefore include rollover options in foreign currency contracts between domestic residents, as well as contracts involving contingent claims (where the amount to be rolled over would be the value of the liability if and when the contingency materialized). But they would *not* include them in debt contracts like the Mexican *tesobonos*, with foreign currency indexing. Yet indexed contracts should in fact contain such options; they create what amounts to a foreign currency claim when, as in the Mexican case, foreigners run down their holdings and swap the domestic currency proceeds for foreign currency, depleting the country's currency reserves or causing the domestic currency to depreciate hugely.

41. It is mainly for this reason that rollover clauses should be written into the government's own obligations even under the modified version of the Buiter-Sibert scheme proposed below. They would serve in effect to nullify the usual waiver of sovereign immunity by protecting the government against litigation.

42. Their reason, however, is not the one given by others, that it is the responsibility of a country's own government to bear the onus and cost of suspending the country's debt

to mention a more radical departure from their basic scheme—an arrangement under which a central bank declaring a crunch would automatically activate all of the rollover options, including those of private debtors.[43]

In its present form, the Buiter-Sibert scheme can lead to a ragged response instead of a prompt, comprehensive standstill. Consider a country with two groups of banks that have large foreign currency debts. One group has weak balance sheets; the other has strong balance sheets. The central bank can distinguish between them and will not lend heavily to the weak banks, but foreigners cannot distinguish between them. Suppose that the banks' foreign creditors begin to run down their claims. All of the banks will buy foreign currency to repay their debts. The weak banks, however, will soon find it impossible to borrow enough domestic currency to buy the foreign currency they need, because the central bank will not supply it, and they will therefore exercise their rollover options. But the strong banks can continue to repay their debts for as long as they can buy foreign currency at a price that does not impair their solvency.

If the country's exchange rate is fixed, its reserves will continue to fall (albeit at a slower pace) after the weak banks exercise their UDROPs, and it could exhaust its reserves if the strong banks do not exercise their UDROPs because of the interest penalty they would incur. And when the country runs out of reserves, it must let its currency depreciate. If the country's exchange rate was floating initially, it will begin to depreciate immediately, before the weak banks exercise their UDROPs, and it will continue to depreciate (albeit at a slower pace) after they have done so. But the depreciation of the country's currency will not force the strong banks to exercise their UDROPs until they can no longer afford to buy the foreign currency needed to pay off their debts. Hence, the banks' response to the crisis will not halt the depreciation of the domestic currency until it has done very serious damage to all of the banks' balance sheets.

This story resembles the actual outcome in the Korean case, where foreign currency creditors were not bailed in until the creditor panic turned into a currency crisis. If the penalty rate is high enough to discourage some debtors from exercising their rollover options quickly, it may be too high to produce a rapid, coordinated response by a country's debtors. It would therefore be better to employ a modified version of the Buiter-Sibert scheme—one that would *require* all debtors to exercise their rollover options simultaneously.

---

payments. They are instead concerned that the IMF would be influenced by extraneous considerations, including a country's compliance with IMF standards of good conduct, and they believe that the IMF does not have the expertise or political independence to be an effective arbiter.

43. Although he does not say so explicitly, Martin (1998) appears to favor this sort of arrangement.

This change would require two modifications in the Buiter-Sibert scheme. If the government or central bank were given the right to activate all of the rollover options, the necessary legislation would have to define the conditions under which it could do so.[44] If private-sector debtors could be forced to exercise their rollover options, they should be compensated for part of the penalty they will then have to pay. The fiscal cost of doing that, however, may be much smaller than the fiscal cost of an interest rate defense, which is what a country might have to adopt if it had no way to impose a standstill.

To be sure, it would take a great deal of time to write rollover clauses into the whole stock of foreign currency debt. They could not be inserted into existing debt contracts. The problem is much like the one involved in writing collective action clauses into the whole stock of debt. But there is also an important difference between them. In the case of collective action clauses, borrowers fear that their inclusion will raise the cost of issuing new debt, although that fear may be unfounded.[45] In the present case, by contrast, the interest penalty compensates the creditor, and the size of the penalty could still be set by the parties directly involved, as proposed by Buiter and Sibert, even if the central bank were given the power to activate all of the rollover clauses.

Like other measures discussed above, the inclusion of rollover clauses in debt contracts could raise the risk of triggering anticipatory flight. For reasons already given, however, that risk is often exaggerated. The number of creditors rushing for the exits to avoid a temporary standstill may be no larger than the number who must exit or reduce their claims before an agreement can be reached to roll over foreigners' claims voluntarily. The inclusion of rollover clauses could contribute to contagion but could perhaps have the opposite effect by preventing a creditor panic from causing a full-fledged currency crisis, with its inevitable spillover effects on other countries. But a standstill may be the most sensible way to avoid the need for large-scale official financing; and because rollover clauses preclude litigation, their inclusion in sovereign and private debt contracts may be the best way to impose a standstill.

Summing Up

The architecture exercise has been reform on the run. The swift succession of crises in the 1990s forced the official community to move quickly, but

---

44. The same thing would have to be done, however, under the variant of the Buiter-Sibert scheme in which the central bank would have to declare when a crunch had arrived before individual debtors could exercise their UDROPs.

45. See the findings of Eichengreen and Mody (2000a, 2000b). Note also that bondholders may have less reason to be wary of rollover clauses. Unlike collective action clauses, which may affect their bargaining power in a future negotiation involving a reduction in the value of their claims, the activation of a rollover clause would only delay for, say, 90 days the contractual payments they are supposed to receive. (But it would be wise to make sure that

each crisis differed from the one before, and the official community was required repeatedly to integrate new tactics into its overall strategy—a sort of galloping incrementalism. It was at the same time constrained by an imperfect political consensus across the G-7 governments themselves as well as across the much larger membership of the International Monetary Fund. There have been disagreements about the causes of crises, ways to prevent them, and ways to resolve them.

This book has devoted much attention to those disagreements and their implications for the form and functioning of the international financial system. Along the way, it has drawn some broad conclusions and made some specific recommendations. Taken together, they provide the context and agenda for the next phase of the architecture exercise.

The Framework

Let us return to the starting point of the architecture exercise—the decision to provide massive official financing when Mexico's currency crisis became a debt crisis as *tesobono* holders declined to roll over their holdings. Whatever one's views about the causes of the currency crisis—whether it was due to bad luck, bad policy, or the two together—one cannot deny that the *tesobono* crisis represented a creditor panic. The decision to resolve it by providing massive official financing may have been the right response, given the risk that a standstill or default could have had very grave consequences for Mexico and for other countries. Creditor panic played a role in the Asian crisis, too, and the official community would have been wrong to adhere rigidly to the conventional quota-based limits on the supply of IMF credit.

IMF quotas have been revised periodically, but they have not been adjusted systemically to meet the needs of countries with open capital markets. Under the Bretton Woods system, access to Fund credit was meant to provide short-term financing for countries that lacked sufficient reserves to cope with transitory shocks adversely affecting their current account balances or that needed to buy time to adjust to longer-lasting shocks. It was not meant to cope with reductions in capital inflows or with debt-related problems. During the debt crisis of the 1980s, Fund credit was used extensively to help countries deal with debt problems and, in the process, catalyze private-sector involvement in the resolution of those problems. During the 1990s, however, capital account liberalization greatly heightened the need for official financing to deal with sudden shifts in capital flows.

Routine recourse to large-scale financing is apt to encourage imprudent behavior by private-sector lenders and by governments as well. Lenders will make risky bets, expecting to be bailed out. Governments will pursue unsustainable policies, incurring excessive external debt and clinging tenaciously to unsustainable exchange rates despite stern warnings from

---

the terms of the rollover clauses posed no obstacle to secondary trading in the affected instruments during the 90-day period of a debt suspension.)

the official community that it will not provide large-scale financing to countries that persist in defending those exchange rates. It has therefore been suggested that the IMF refuse to provide large-scale financing—that it should adhere hereafter to its conventional quota-based limits. But this recommendation is unrealistic. The quota-based limits are too small and cannot readily be revised to reflect the needs of countries exposed to huge shifts in capital flows. Quotas determine voting power in the IMF, as well as access to Fund credit, and governments strongly resist any redistribution of quotas that will reduce their influence over the Fund's policies.

There is thus need for flexibility, but it must be rule-based flexibility. Governments must know what to expect when they seek help from the Fund, and the Fund itself must be able to justify any and all departures from its adherence to its usual quota-based limits on access to Fund credit. It cannot allow its members' appetite for debt to govern its own policies.

The Fund sought to obtain this sort of flexibility when it established the SRF and CCL. But the criteria for access to the SRF are not very well defined, and the CCL has not attracted applicants despite the Fund's recent attempt to make it more attractive. For reasons described earlier, governments seeking assurance of access to Fund credit seem to prefer to make precautionary drawings of the conventional sort rather than expose themselves to the risks adhering to a CCL—the risk that they may have to make major policy changes when they seek to activate a CCL, and the risk that they may be told by the Fund that they no longer qualify for a CCL. The attempt to straddle prequalification and conditionality has had little success.

Four more observations deserve repetition. They pertain to the problem of contagion, the role and scope of conditionality, the case for mandatory standstills, and the grain of truth residing in the two-corner approach to choosing exchange rate arrangements.

The premise that led to the creation of the CCL, that countries with open capital markets risk being the innocent victims of contagion and need special protection, is contradicted by the nature of contagion. There have been innocent victims, but not very many. Countries that suffer contagion are, for the most part, those that are seen to display worrisome similarities to a crisis-stricken country. Furthermore, truly innocent victims may have to make policy changes when they succumb to contagion. No country can avoid the need to alter its policies when capital inflows fall abruptly or give way to outflows. Even in the rare case of an irrational creditor panic—one that is driven by fear, not fact—the restoration of rationality does not guarantee a speedy return to the status quo ante. Although capital outflows will cease, capital inflows may not revive quickly, and the affected country has then to adjust to smaller inflows. Financing is not a substitute for adjustment, and prequalifaction is not a substitute for conditionality.

Nevertheless, conditionality must be aimed narrowly at adjustment, not at far-reaching reform of a country's infrastructure. Some reforms may be required to rehabilitate a country's banking system when, as is often the case, a currency crisis is caused or compounded by a banking crisis. But reforms that can be postponed should be deferred or, better yet, made in advance of the crisis. That is the rationale for the contractual scheme outlined earlier in this chapter.

The use of mandatory standstills, also recommended here, will not obviate the need for official financing—not even large-scale financing. Critics of standstills are right to warn that they can have damaging side effects. The threat of a standstill can cause foreign creditors to exit while they can, although the resulting rundown of claims may be no larger than the reduction that is likely to occur before foreign creditors are ready to roll over their claims voluntarily. A standstill cannot prevent a country's residents from rushing for the exit, nor can it prevent them from purchasing foreign currency while it is in place, so as to resume their debt payments after it expires. Therefore, a country confronting a creditor panic or one faced with the need to restructure its external debt may need official financing to prevent a precipitous depreciation of the country's currency and avoid dysfunctional adjustment of the sort that occurred during the Asian crisis.

Finally, the Fund must wean countries away from pegged exchange rates and should not hesitate to caution them against the use of a currency board regime to stave off future crises. In fact, the Fund should be rather skeptical of a request for Fund credit to resolve the banking problems that occur endogenously when countries with currency boards suffer big capital outflows. A currency board is supposed to induce a sharp contraction of bank credit whenever it pays out reserves to buy up its own country's currency. And a currency board by itself does not necessarily afford relief from debt-related problems. It can prevent the monetization of debt but cannot prevent the creation of debt. Few countries, moreover, can afford to fix their exchange rates forever, and those that can risk doing so may be better served by opting for formal dollarization. All others should move toward the opposite corner—managed flexibility.

The Agenda

How can the official community plot and follow a sensible course, without relying on rigid rules or pursuing a case-by-case approach that has no readily defensible rationale? It should rely on what can be called *presumptive* prequalification.

Countries that follow prudent policies and meet certain other tests should be entitled to expect that they will obtain large-scale financing when they truly need it. No other country should obtain large-scale financing unless the Fund's Executive Board decides, by a large supermajority, that the country's problems are apt to do serious damage to other countries, whether because of the country's size relative to others tightly linked to it or because its problems threaten to impair the functioning of international financial markets.

How should the Fund decide that a country is following prudent policies? How should it communicate its findings?

The Fund's regular Article IV consultations offer a natural starting point. Suppose that the Fund's staff concludes that a country is accumulating too much short-term foreign debt relative to its reserves, that its debt burden will be unsustainable over the long run given the country's fiscal stance, or that the country may soon face the need to refinance a large dollop of debt under difficult market conditions. The managing director should advise the country *confidentially* that he or she will refuse to recommend that the country receive large-scale financing if it seeks to draw on the Fund during the next year. And the managing director should convey the same sort of warning if, in the judgment of the staff, the country's exchange rate is unsustainable and it is defending its exchange rate stubbornly by drawing down its reserves or incurring large reserve-related liabilities. Such a warning would not bar the country from making an ordinary quota-based drawing. Furthermore, it could be overridden by the Executive Board and would, of course, be rescinded as soon as the country had taken steps to rectify the situation.

What preconditions should govern a country's eligibility for unusually large amounts of Fund credit? They should be chosen with the aim of encouraging countries to adopt the measures proposed elsewhere in this book:

- The country should have subscribed to the SDDS and be meeting its main requirements, particularly those pertaining to the reporting of reserves, reserve-related liabilities, and the external position of the country's private sector, especially its banking sector.

- It should have invited the Fund and Bank to conduct a financial-sector assessment and, if advised to do so, should have entered into a financial-sector contract of the type proposed in this chapter and be meeting the deadlines set out in that contract.

- It should have introduced collective action clauses into its government's foreign currency bonds.

- It should have adopted legislation requiring the inclusion of 90-day rollover options in all of its foreign currency obligations, public and private, and should have put in place the procedures required to trigger the exercise of those options.

A country failing to meet these preconditions might nevertheless receive large-scale financing if the Fund's Executive Board concludes that refusing its request would put other countries at serious risk or impair the functioning of international financial markets. A suitable supermajority could waive one or more of the preconditions.

This is an ambitious agenda and one that may not appeal to the G-7 governments or the larger membership of the IMF. A less ambitious agenda, however, will not afford sufficient protection in the event of future crises. It is utterly unrealistic to count entirely on crisis prevention. Mistakes will be made. Accidents will happen. Better, then, to be safer than sorry.

References

Agénor, Pierre-Richard. 1995. Credibility, Reputation, and the Mexican Peso Crisis. International Monetary Fund, Washington. Photocopy.

Agénor, P.-R., J. Aizenman, and A. Hoffmaister. 2000. *The Credit Crunch in East Asia: What Can Bank Excess Liquid Assets Tell Us?* NBER Working Paper 7951. Cambridge, MA: National Bureau of Economic Research.

Agosin, Manuel R., and Ricardo Ffrench-Davis. 1995. Managing Capital Inflows in Latin America. University of Chile and Economic Commission for Latin America, Santiago de Chile. Photocopy.

Agosin, Manuel R., and Ricardo Ffrench-Davis. 1997. Managing Capital Inflows in Chile. *Estudios de Economía* 24: 297-321.

Ahluwalia, Montek S. 2000. *Reforming the Global Financial Architecture.* London: Commonwealth Secretariat.

Alba, Pedro, Amar Bhattacharya, Stijn Clasessens, Swati Ghosh, and Leonardo Hernandez. 1999. The Role of Macroeconomic and Financial Sector Linkages in East Asia's Financial Crisis. In *The Asian Financial Crisis: Causes, Contagion, and Consequences,* eds. Pierre-Richard Agénor, Marcus Miller, David Vines, and Axel Weber. Cambridge: Cambridge University Press.

Alesina, Alberto, and Robert J. Barro. 2000. *Currency Unions.* NBER Working Paper 7927. Cambridge, MA: National Bureau of Economic Research.

Alston, Lee J., and Andrés A. Gallo. 2000. *Evolution and Revolution in the Argentine Banking System under Convertibility: The Roles of Crises and Path Dependence.* NBER Working Paper 8008. Cambridge, MA: National Bureau of Economic Research.

Bacchetta, Philippe, and Eric van Wincoop. 1998. *Capital Flows to Emerging Markets: Liberalization, Overshooting, and Volatility.* NBER Working Paper 6530. Cambridge, MA: National Bureau of Economic Research.

Bagehot, Walter. 1873. *Lombard Street.* London: Kegan Paul.

Baig, Taimur, and Ilan Goldfajn. 1999. Financial Market Contagion in the Asian Crisis. *IMF Staff Papers* 46: 167-95.

Bank for International Settlements (BIS). 1998. *Annual Report.* Basel: Bank for International Settlements.

Barth, Marvin, and Trevor Dinmore. 1999. *Trade Prices and Volumes in East Asia through the Crisis*. International Finance Discussion Paper 643. Washington: Board of Governors of the Federal Reserve System.

Basel Committee on Banking Supervision (BCBS). 1997. *Core Principles for Effective Banking Supervision*. Basel: Basel Committee on Banking Supervision.

Basel Committee on Banking Supervision (BCBS). 2001. *Overview of the New Basel Capital Accord: Consultative Document*. Basel: Basel Committee on Banking Supervision.

Bénassy-Quéré, Agnès, and Benoît Coeuré. 2000. *Big and Small Currencies: The Regional Connection*. CEPII Working Paper 2000-10. Paris: Centre d'Études Prospectives et d'Information Internationale.

Berg, Andrew, and Catherine Pattillo. 1999. Are Currency Crises Predictable: A Test. *IMF Staff Papers* 46: 107-37.

Bernanke, Ben, and Mark Gertler. 1995. Inside the Black Box—The Credit Channel of Monetary Policy Transmission. *Journal of Economic Perspectives* 9: 27-48.

Bernard, Henri, and Joseph Bisignano. 1999. Information, Liquidity, and Risk in the International Interbank Market: Implicit Guarantees and Private Credit Market Failure. Bank for International Settlements, Basel. Photocopy.

Bhagwati, Jagdish. 1999. The Capital Myth: The Difference between Trade in Widgets and Trade in Dollars. *Foreign Affairs* 77: 7-12.

Blinder, Alan S. 1999. Eight Steps to a New Financial Order. *Foreign Affairs* 78: 50-63.

Boorman, Jack, and Mark Allen. 2000. A New Framework for Private Sector Involvement in Crisis Prevention and Crisis Management. In *Reforming the International Financial System: Crisis Prevention and Response*, ed. Jan Joost Teunissen. The Hague: Forum on Debt and Development.

Bordo, Michael D., and Harold James. 1999. *The International Monetary Fund: Its Present Role in Historical Perspective*. NBER Working Paper 7724. Cambridge, MA: National Bureau of Economic Research.

Bordo, Michael D., and Anna J. Schwartz. 1998. *Under What Circumstances, Past and Present, Have International Rescues of Countries in Financial Distress Been Successful?* NBER Working Paper 6824. Cambridge, MA: National Bureau of Economic Research.

Bosworth, Barry. 1998. The Asian Crisis in Context. *International Finance* 1: 289-310.

Bosworth, Barry P., and Susan M. Collins. 1999. Capital Flows to Developing Economies: Implications for Saving and Investment. *Brookings Papers on Economic Activity* 1: 143-79.

Boughton, James M. 2000. From Suez to Tequila: The IMF as Crisis Manager. *Economic Journal* 110: 273-91.

Brealey, Richard. 1999. The Asian Crisis: Lessons for Crisis Management and Crisis Prevention. *International Finance* 2: 249-72.

Buch, Claudia M., and Ralph P. Heinrich. 1999. Twin Crises and the Intermediary Role of Banks. *International Journal of Finance & Economics* 4: 313-23.

Buchheit, Lee C., and G. Mitu Gulati. 2000. Exit Consents in Sovereign Bond Exchanges. *UCLA Law Review* 48: 59-84.

Buiter, Willem H. 1999. *The EMU and the NAMU: What Is the Case for a North American Monetary Union?* CEPR Discussion Paper 2181. London: Centre for Economic Policy Research.

Buiter, Willem H., and Anne C. Sibert. 1999. UDROP: A Contribution to the New International Financial Architecture. *International Finance* 2: 227-47.

Bulow, Jeremy I., and Kenneth Rogoff. 1989. A Constant Recontracting Model of Sovereign Debt. *Journal of Political Economy* 97: 155-78.

Burnside, Craig, Martin Eichenbaum, and Sergio Rebelo. 1998. *Prospective Deficits and the Asian Currency Crisis*. NBER Working Paper 6758. Cambridge, MA: National Bureau of Economic Research.

Calomiris, Charles W. 1998a. Blueprints for a New Global Financial Architecture. Columbia University, New York. Photocopy.

Calomiris, Charles W. 1998b. The IMF's Imprudent Role as Lender of Last Resort. *Cato Journal* 17: 275-94.

Calvo, Guillermo A. 1998. Understanding the Russian Virus. Paper presented to the Deutsche Bank Conference on Emerging Markets, Washington (3 October).

Calvo, Guillermo A., Leonardo Leiderman, and Carmen M. Reinhart. 1993. Capital Inflows and Real Exchange Rate Appreciation in Latin America. *IMF Staff Papers* 40: 108-51.

Calvo, Guillermo A., and Enrique G. Mendoza. 1996. Mexico's Balance-of-Payments Crisis: A Chronicle of a Death Foretold. *Journal of International Economics* 41: 235-64.

Calvo, Guillermo A., and Enrique G. Mendoza. 2000. Rational Contagion and the Globalization of Securities Markets. *Journal of International Economics* 51: 79-113.

Calvo, Guillermo A., and Carmen M. Reinhart. 2000a. *Fear of Floating.* NBER Working Paper 7993. Cambridge, MA: National Bureau of Economic Research.

Calvo, Guillermo A., and Carmen M. Reinhart. 2000b. *Fixing for Your Life.* NBER Working Paper 8006. Cambridge, MA: National Bureau of Economic Research.

Calvo, Guillermo A., and Carmen Reinhart. 2000c. When Capital Inflows Suddenly Stop. In *Reforming the International Monetary and Financial System*, eds. Peter B. Kenen and Alexander K. Swoboda. Washington: International Monetary Fund.

Calvo, Sara, and Carmen M. Reinhart. 1996. Capital Flows to Latin America: Is There Evidence of Contagion Effects? In *Private Capital Flows to Emerging Markets after the Mexican Crisis*, eds. Guillermo A. Calvo, Morris Goldstein, and Eduard Hochreiter. Washington: Institute for International Economics.

Capie, Forrest. 1998. Can There Be an International Lender of Last Resort? *International Finance* 1: 311-25.

Caprio, Gerard, Michael Dooley, Danny Leipziger, and Carl Walsh. 1996. The Lender of Last Resort Function under a Currency Board: The Case of Argentina. *Open Economies Review* 7: 625-50.

Caprio, Gerard, and Patrick Honohan. 1999. Restoring Banking Stability: Beyond Supervised Capital Requirements. *Journal of Economic Perspectives* 13: 43-64.

Caprio, Gerard, and Patrick Honohan. 2001. *Finance and Growth: Policy Choices in a Volatile World.* Oxford: Oxford University Press for the World Bank.

Céspedes, Luis Felipe, Roberto Chang, and Andrés Velasco. 2000. *Balance Sheets and Exchange Rate Policy.* NBER Working Paper 7840. Cambridge, MA: National Bureau of Economic Research.

CFR Task Force. *See* Task Force on the Future International Financial Architecture.

Chang, Roberto, and Andrés Velasco. 1999. *Liquidity Crises in Emerging Markets: Theory and Policy.* NBER Working Paper 7272. Cambridge, MA: National Bureau of Economic Research.

Chinn, Menzie D. 1998. *Before the Fall: Were East Asian Currencies Overvalued?* NBER Working Paper 6491. Cambridge, MA: National Bureau of Economic Research.

Chinn, Menzie D., Michael P. Dooley, and Sona Shrestha. 1999. *Latin America and East Asia in the Context of an Insurance Model of Currency Crises.* NBER Working Paper 7091. Cambridge, MA: National Bureau of Economic Research.

Chote, Robert, et al. 1998. *Financial Crises and Asia.* CEPR Conference Report 6. London: Centre for Economic Policy Research.

Claessens, Stijn, Simeon Djankov, and Giovanni Ferri. 1998. Corporate Distress in East Asia: Assessing the Impact of Interest and Exchange Rate Shocks. World Bank, Washington. Photocopy.

Cline, William R. 2000a. Improving the International Monetary Fund. Paper prepared for the US International Financial Institution Advisory Commission. Photocopy.

Cline, William R. 2000b. The Role of the Private Sector in Resolving Financial Crises in Emerging Markets. Paper presented to the NBER Conference on Economic and Financial Crises in Emerging Market Economies, Woodstock, VT (19-21 October).

Coeuré, Benoît, and Jean Pisani Ferry. 2000. *An Intellectual and Institutional Retrospective on the Reform of the International Financial Architecture.* Paris: Conseil d'Analyse Économique.

Cohen, Benjamin Jerry. 1998. *The Geography of International Money.* Ithaca, NY: Cornell University Press.

Cole, Harold L., and Timothy J. Kehoe. 1996. A Self-fulfilling Model of Mexico's 1994-1995 Debt Crisis. *Journal of International Economics* 41: 309-30.

Cooper, Richard N. 1998. Should Capital Account Convertibility Be a World Objective? In *Should the IMF Pursue Capital Account Convertibility?* by Stanley Fischer et al. Essays in International Finance 207. Princeton, NJ: International Finance Section, Princeton University.

Cooper, Richard N. 1999. Should Capital Controls Be Banished? *Brookings Papers on Economic Activity* 1: 89-125.

Corbett, Jenny, and David Vines. 1999. The Asian Crisis: Lessons from the Collapse of Financial Systems, Exchange Rates and Macroeconomic Policy. In *The Asian Financial Crisis: Causes, Contagion, and Consequences,* eds. Pierre-Richard Agénor, Marcus Miller, David Vines, and Axel Weber. Cambridge: Cambridge University Press.

Corrigan, Gerald. 2000. Resolving Financial Crises: A Shared Responsibility. *Goldman Sachs Economic Weekly* (May).

Corsetti, Giancarlo, Paolo Pesenti, and Nouriel Roubini. 1998a. *Paper Tigers? A Model of the Asian Crisis.* NBER Working Paper 6783. Cambridge, MA: National Bureau of Economic Research.

Corsetti, Giancarlo, Paolo Pesenti, and Nouriel Roubini. 1998b. *What Caused the Asian Currency and Financial Crisis? Part I: A Macroeconomic Overview.* NBER Working Paper 6833. Cambridge, MA: National Bureau of Economic Research.

Corsetti, Giancarlo, Paolo Pesenti, and Nouriel Roubini. 1998c. *What Caused the Asian Currency and Financial Crisis? Part II: The Policy Debate.* NBER Working Paper 6834. Cambridge, MA: National Bureau of Economic Research.

Crockett, Andrew. 2000. Progress toward Greater International Financial Stability. Paper presented to the Conference on Reforming the Architecture of Global Economic Institutions, Bank of England, London (5-6 May).

De Bonis, Riccardo, Alessandro Giustiniani, and Giorgio Gomel. 1999. Crises and Bail-Outs of Banks and Countries: Linkages, Analogies, and Differences. *The World Economy* 22: 55-86.

De Brouwer, Gorden. 2001. *Hedge Funds in Emerging Markets.* Cambridge: Cambridge University Press.

De Gregorio, José, Barry Eichengreen, Takatoshi Ito, and Charles Wyplosz. 1999. *An Independent and Accountable IMF.* Geneva: International Center for Monetary and Banking Studies.

Dekle, Robert, and Kenneth M. Kletzer. 2001. *Domestic Bank Regulation and Financial Crises: Theory and Empirical Evidence from East Asia.* NBER Working Paper 8322. Cambridge, MA: National Bureau of Economic Research.

Dell' Ariccia, Giovanni, Isabel Godde, and Jeromin Zettelmeyer. 2000. Moral Hazard and International Crisis Lending: A Test. International Monetary Fund, Washington. Photocopy.

Delong, J. Bradford, and Barry Eichengreen. 2001. Between Meltdown and Moral Hazard: The International Monetary and Financial Policies of the Clinton Administration. Paper presented to the Kennedy School Conference on the Economic Policies of the Clinton Administration, Harvard University, Cambridge, MA (26-29 June).

Demirgüç-Kunt, Asli, and Enrica Detragiache. 1998. The Determinants of Banking Crises in Developing and Developed Countries. *IMF Staff Papers* 45: 81-109.

Diamond, Douglas, and Philip Dybvig. 1983. Bank Runs, Deposit Insurance, and Liquidity. *Journal of Political Economy* 91: 401-19.

Diwan, Ishac, and Bernard Hoekman. 1999. Competition, Complementarity, and Contagion in East Asia. In *The Asian Financial Crisis: Causes, Contagion, and Consequences*, eds. Pierre-Richard Agénor, Marcus Miller, David Vines, and Axel Weber. Cambridge: Cambridge University Press.

Dooley, Michael P. 1999. Are Capital Inflows to Developing Countries a Vote for or Against Economic Policy Reforms? In *The Asian Financial Crisis: Causes, Contagion, and Consequences*, eds. Pierre-Richard Agénor, Marcus Miller, David Vines, and Axel Weber. Cambridge: Cambridge University Press.

Dooley, Michael P. 2000a. *Can Output Losses Following International Financial Crises Be Avoided?* NBER Working Paper 7531. Cambridge, MA: National Bureau of Economic Research.

Dooley, Michael P. 2000b. A Model of Crises in Emerging Markets. *Economic Journal* 110: 256-72.

Dooley, Michael P., and Inseok Shin. 2000. *Private Inflows When Crises Are Anticipated: A Study of Korea.* NBER Working Paper 7992. Cambridge, MA: National Bureau of Economic Research.

Dooley, Michael P., and Carl E. Walsh. 1999. Academic Views of Capital Flows: An Expanding Universe. In *Capital Flows and the International Financial System*, eds. David W. R. Gruen and Luke Gower. Sydney: Reserve Bank of Australia.

Dornbusch, Rudi. 2001. *Malaysia: Was It Different?* NBER Working Paper 8325. Cambridge, MA: National Bureau of Economic Research.

Dornbusch, Rudiger, Ilan Goldfajn, and Rodrigo Valdés. 1995. Currency Crises and Collapses. *Brookings Papers on Economic Activity* 2: 219-69.

Eaton, Jonathan, and Mark Gersovitz. 1981. *Poor-Country Borrowing in Private Financial Markets and the Repudiation Issue.* Princeton Studies in International Finance 47. Princeton, NJ: International Finance Section, Princeton University.

Eatwell, John, and Lance Taylor. 1998. *International Capital Markets and the Future of Economic Policy.* Working Paper III-9. New York: Center for Economic Policy Analysis, New School for Social Research.

Edison, Hali J., Pongsak Luangaram, and Marcus Miller. 2000. Asset Bubbles, Domino Effects, and "Lifeboats": Elements of the East Asian Crisis. *Economic Journal* 110: 309-34.

Edison, Hali J., and Carmen M. Reinhart. 2000. *Capital Controls During Financial Crises: The Case of Malaysia and Thailand.* International Finance Discussion Paper 662. Washington: Board of Governors of the Federal Reserve System.

Edwards, Sebastian. 1997. *The Mexican Peso Crisis: How Much Did We Know? When Did We Know It?* NBER Working Paper 6334. Cambridge, MA: National Bureau of Economic Research.

Edwards, Sebastian. 1998. *Interest Rate Volatility, Capital Controls and Contagion.* NBER Working Paper 6756. Cambridge, MA: National Bureau of Economic Research.

Edwards, Sebastian. 1999a. How Effective Are Capital Controls? *Journal of Economic Perspectives* 13: 65-84.

Edwards, Sebastian. 1999b. *On Crisis Prevention: Lessons from Mexico and East Asia.* NBER Working Paper 7233. Cambridge, MA: National Bureau of Economic Research.

Edwards, Sebastian. 2000. Exchange Rate Regimes, Capital Flows and Crisis Prevention. Paper presented to the NBER Conference on Economic and Financial Crises in Emerging Market Economies, Woodstock, VT (19-21 October).

Eichengreen, Barry. 1995. *International Monetary Arrangements for the 21st Century.* Washington: Brookings Institution.

Eichengreen, Barry. 1997. *Exchange Rate Stability and Financial Stability.* Working Paper C97-092. Berkeley: Center for International and Development Economics Research, University of California.

Eichengreen, Barry. 1998. *International Economic Policy in the Wake of the Asian Crisis.* Working Paper C98-102. Berkeley: Center for International and Development Economics Research, University of California.

Eichengreen, Barry. 1999a. Kicking the Habit: Moving from Pegged Rates to Greater Exchange Rate Flexibility. *Economic Journal* 109: C1-C14.

Eichengreen, Barry. 1999b. *Toward a New International Financial Architecture.* Washington: Institute for International Economics.

Eichengreen, Barry. 2000a. *Can the Moral Hazard Caused by IMF Bailouts Be Reduced?* Geneva: International Center for Monetary and Banking Studies.

Eichengreen, Barry. 2000b. Is Greater Private Sector Burden Sharing Impossible? In *Reforming the International Monetary and Financial System,* eds. Peter B. Kenen and Alexander K. Swoboda. Washington: International Monetary Fund.

Eichengreen, Barry, and Ricardo Hausmann. 1999. *Exchange Rates and Financial Fragility.* NBER Working Paper 7418. Cambridge, MA: National Bureau of Economic Research.

Eichengreen, Barry, and Ashoka Mody. 2000a. *Would Collective Action Clauses Raise Borrowing Costs?* NBER Working Paper 7458. Cambridge, MA: National Bureau of Economic Research.

Eichengreen, Barry, and Ashoka Mody. 2000b. *Would Collective Action Clauses Raise Borrowing Costs? An Update and Additional Results.* Working Paper C00-114. Berkeley: Center for International and Development Economics Research, University of California.

Eichengreen, Barry, and Richard Portes. 1995. *Crisis? What Crisis? Orderly Workouts for Sovereign Debtors.* London: Centre for Economic Policy Research.

Eichengreen, Barry, and Andrew K. Rose. 1998. *Staying Afloat when the Wind Shifts: External Factors and Emerging-Market Banking Crises.* NBER Working Paper 6370. Cambridge, MA: National Bureau of Economic Research.

Eichengreen, Barry, and Andrew K. Rose. 1999. Contagious Currency Crises: Channels of Conveyance. In *Changes in Exchange Rates in Rapidly Developing Countries,* eds. Takatoshi Ito and Anne O. Krueger. Chicago: University of Chicago Press.

Eichengreen, Barry, and Andrew Rose. 2001. To Defend or Not to Defend? That Is the Question. Paper presented to the NBER Conference on Management of Currency Crises, Monterey, CA (28-31 March).

Eichengreen, Barry, Andrew K. Rose, and Charles Wyplosz. 1996. *Contagious Currency Crises.* NBER Working Paper 5681. Cambridge, MA: National Bureau of Economic Research.

Eichengreen, Barry, and Christof Rühl. 2000. *The Bail-In Problem: Systematic Goals, Ad Hoc Means.* NBER Working Paper 7653. Cambridge, MA: National Bureau of Economic Research.

Eichengreen, Barry, et al. 1998a. *Capital Account Liberalization: Theoretical and Practical Aspects.* IMF Occasional Paper 172. Washington: International Monetary Fund.

Eichengreen, Barry, et al. 1998b. *Hedge Funds and Financial Market Dynamics.* IMF Occasional Paper 166. Washington: International Monetary Fund.

Eichengreen, Barry, et al. 1999. *Transition Strategies and Nominal Anchors on the Road to Greater Exchange-Rate Flexibility.* Essays in International Finance 213. Princeton, NJ: International Finance Section, Princeton University.

Evans, Huw. 2000. *Plumbers and Architects: A Supervisory Perspective on International Financial Architecture.* Occasional Paper 4. London: Financial Services Authority.

Feldstein, Martin. 1998. Refocusing the IMF. *Foreign Affairs* 77: 20-33.

Feldstein, Martin. 1999. A Self-Help Guide for Emerging Markets. *Foreign Affairs* 78: 93-109.

Fernandez-Arias, Eduardo, and Peter J. Montiel. 1996. The Surge in Capital Inflows to Developing Countries: An Analytical Overview. *World Bank Economic Review* 10: 51-77.

Financial Stability Forum (FSF). 2000a. *Issue Paper of the Task Force on Implementation of Standards.* Basel: Financial Stability Forum.

Financial Stability Forum (FSF). 2000b. *Report of the Follow-Up Group on Incentives to Foster Implementation of Standards.* Basel: Financial Stability Forum.

Financial Stability Forum (FSF). 2000c. *Report of the Working Group on Capital Flows.* Basel: Financial Stability Forum.

Financial Stability Forum (FSF). 2000d. *Report of the Working Group on Highly Leveraged Institutions*. Basel: Financial Stability Forum.

Financial Stability Forum (FSF). 2000e. *Report of the Working Group on Offshore Centres*. Basel: Financial Stability Forum.

Financial Stability Forum (FSF). 2001. *Compendium of Standards*. http://www.fsforum.org/Standards/Home.html (20 June).

Fischer, Stanley. 1996. Summing Up. In *Private Capital Flows to Emerging Markets after the Mexican Crisis*, eds. Guillermo A. Calvo, Morris Goldstein, and Eduard Hochreiter. Washington: Institute for International Economics.

Fischer, Stanley. 1997. *Capital Account Liberalization and the Role of the IMF*. Washington: International Monetary Fund.

Fischer, Stanley. 1999. Reforming the International Financial System. *Economic Journal* 109: F557-76.

Fischer, Stanley. 2000. *On the Need for an International Lender of Last Resort*. Essays in International Economics 220. Princeton, NJ: International Economics Section, Princeton University.

Fischer, Stanley. 2001a. Exchange Rate Regimes: Is the Bipolar View Correct? *Journal of Economic Perspectives* 15: 3-24.

Fischer, Stanley. 2001b. *Reducing Vulnerabilities: The Role of the Contingent Credit Line*. Washington: International Monetary Fund.

Fischer, Stanley, et al. 1998. *Should the IMF Pursue Capital Account Convertibility?* Essays in International Finance 207. Princeton: International Finance Section, Princeton University.

Flood, Robert P., and Olivier Jeanne. 2000. *An Interest Rate Defense of a Fixed Exchange Rate*. CEPR Discussion Paper 2507. London: Centre for Economic Policy Research.

Folkerts-Landau, David, and Carl-Johan Lindgren. 1998. *Toward a Framework for Financial Stability*. Washington: International Monetary Fund.

Forbes, Kristin. 2001. *Are Trade Linkages Important Determinants of Country Vulnerability to Crises?* NBER Working Paper 8194. Cambridge, MA: National Bureau of Economic Research.

Forbes, Kristin, and Roberto Rigobon. 1999. *No Contagion, Only Interdependence: Measuring Stock Market Co-movements*. NBER Working Paper 7267. Cambridge, MA: National Bureau of Economic Research.

Frankel, Jeffrey A. 1997. Sterilization of Money Inflows: Difficult (Calvo) or Easy (Reisen)? *Estudio de Economía* 24: 263-85.

Frankel, Jeffrey A. 1999. *No Single Currency Regime Is Right for All Countries or at All Times*. Essays in International Finance 215. Princeton, NJ: International Finance Section, Princeton University.

Frankel, Jeffrey A., and Andrew K. Rose. 1996. Currency Crashes in Emerging Markets: An Empirical Treatment. *Journal of International Economics* 41: 351-66.

Frankel, Jeffrey A., and Sergio L. Schmukler. 1996. Country Fund Discounts and the Mexican Crisis of December 1994: Did Local Residents Turn Pessimistic Before International Investors? *Open Economies Review* 7: 511-34.

Frankel, Jeffrey A., and Sergio L. Schmukler. 1998. Crisis, Contagion, and Country Funds: Effects on East Asia and Latin America. In *Managing Capital Flows and Exchange Rates*, ed. Reuven Glick. Cambridge: Cambridge University Press.

Frankel, Jeffrey, Sergio Schmukler, and Luis Servén. 2000. *Variability and the Vanishing Intermediate Exchange Rate Regime*. NBER Working Paper 7901. Cambridge, MA: National Bureau of Economic Research.

Frankel, Jeffrey A., and Shang-Jim Wei. 1994. Yen Bloc or Dollar Bloc? Exchange Rate Policies of the East Asian Economies. In *Macroeconomic Linkage: Savings, Exchange Rates, and Capital Flows*, eds. Takatoshi Ito and Anne O. Krueger. Chicago: University of Chicago Press.

Furman, Jason, and Joseph P. Stiglitz. 1998. Economic Crises: Evidence and Insights from Asia. *Brookings Papers on Economic Activity* 2: 1-113.

Garber, Peter M. 1996. Managing Risks to Financial Markets from Volatile Capital Flows: The Role of Prudential Regulation. *International Journal of Finance & Economics* 1: 183-95.

Garber, Peter M. 1998. *Derivatives in International Capital Flows.* NBER Working Paper 6623. Cambridge, MA: National Bureau of Economic Research.

Garber, Peter M., and Subir Lall. 1998. Derivative Products in Exchange Rate Crises. In *Managing Capital Flows and Exchange Rates: Perspectives from the Pacific Basin,* ed. Reuven Glick. Cambridge: Cambridge University Press.

Geithner, Timothy F. 2000. *Resolving Financial Crises in Emerging Market Economies: Remarks before the Securities Industry Association and Emerging Market Traders Association.* Washington: US Treasury (23 October).

Ghosh, Atish R., Anne-Marie Gulde, and Holger C. Wolf. 2000. Currency Boards: More than a Quick Fix? *Economic Policy* 31: 207-335.

Giannini, Curzio. 1999. *Enemy of None but a Common Friend of All? An International Perspective on the Lender-of-Last-Resort Function.* Essays in International Finance 214, Princeton, NJ: International Finance Section, Princeton University.

Glick, Reuven, and Andrew K. Rose. 1999. Contagion and Trade: Why Are Currency Crises Regional? In *The Asian Financial Crisis: Causes, Contagion, and Consequences,* eds. Pierre-Richard Agénor, Marcus Miller, David Vines, and Axel Weber. Cambridge: Cambridge University Press.

Goldfajn, Ilan, and Taimur Baig. 1998. Monetary Policy in the Aftermath of Currency Crises: The Case of Asia. International Monetary Fund, Washington. Photocopy.

Goldfajn, Ilan, and Poonam Gupta. 1999. Does Tight Monetary Policy Stabilize the Exchange Rate? International Monetary Fund, Washington. Photocopy.

Goldstein, Morris. 1997. *The Case for an International Banking Standard.* Washington: Institute for International Economics.

Goldstein, Morris. 1998. *The Asian Financial Crisis: Causes, Cures, and Systemic Implications.* Washington: Institute for International Economics.

Goldstein, Morris. 2000. IMF Structural Policies. Paper presented to the NBER Conference on Economic and Financial Crises in Emerging-market Economies, Woodstock, VT (19-21 October).

Goldstein, Morris. 2001. An Evaluation of Proposals to Reform the International Financial Architecture. Paper presented to the NBER Conference on Management of Currency Crises, Monterey, CA (28-31 March).

Goldstein, Morris, and Guillermo A. Calvo. 1996. What Role for the Official Sector? In *Private Capital Flows to Emerging Markets after the Mexican Crisis,* eds. Guillermo A. Calvo, Morris Goldstein, and Eduard Hochreiter. Washington: Institute for International Economics.

Goldstein, Morris, Graciela L. Kaminsky, and Carmen M. Reinhart. 2000. *Assessing Financial Vulnerability: An Early Warning System for Emerging Markets.* Washington: Institute for International Economics.

Goldstein, Morris, and Phillip Turner. 1996. *Banking Crises in Emerging Economies: Origins and Policy Options.* BIS Economic Papers 46. Basel: Bank for International Settlements.

Goodhart, Charles. 1999. Myths about the Lender of Last Resort. *International Finance* 2: 339-60.

Greenspan, Alan. 1998. Remarks before the 34th Annual Conference on Bank Structure and Competition of the Federal Reserve Bank of Chicago. Washington: Federal Reserve Board (7 May).

Grenville, Stephen, and David Gruen. 1999. Capital Flows and Exchange Rates. In *Capital Flows and the International Financial System,* eds. David W. R. Gruen and Luke Gower. Sydney: Reserve Bank of Australia.

Group of 7. 1995. *Communiqué of the Halifax Summit.*

Group of 7. 1996. *Communiqué of the Lyon Summit.*

Group of 7. 1997. *Final Report to the G-7 Heads of State and Government on Promoting Financial Stability.*

Group of 7. 1998. *Strengthening the Architecture of the Global Financial System: Report of G-7 Finance Ministers to G-7 Heads of State or Government for Their Meeting in Birmingham.*

Group of 7. 1999a. *Statement of G-7 Finance Ministers and Central Bank Governors* (25 September).

Group of 7. 1999b. *Strengthening the International Financial Architecture: Report of the G-7 Finance Ministers to the Köln Economic Summit.*

Group of 7. 2000a. *Statement of G-7 Finance Ministers and Central Bank Governors* (15 April).

Group of 7. 2000b. *Strengthening the International Financial Architecture: Report from the G-7 Finance Ministers to the Heads of State and Government.*

Group of 10. 1996. *The Resolution of Sovereign Liquidity Crises: A Report to the Ministers and Governors.* Washington: International Monetary Fund.

Group of 22. 1998a. *Report of the Working Group on International Financial Crises.* Washington: Group of 22 [Willard Group].

Group of 22. 1998b. *Report of the Working Group on Strengthening Financial Systems.* Washington: Group of 22 [Willard Group].

Group of 22. 1998c. *Report of the Working Group on Transparency and Accountability.* Washington: Group of 22 [Willard Group].

Haggard, Stephan. 2000. *The Political Economy of the Asian Financial Crisis.* Washington: Institute for International Economics.

Hahm, Joon-Ho, and Frederic S. Mishkin. 2000. *Causes of the Korean Financial Crisis.* NBER Working Paper 7483. Cambridge, MA: National Bureau of Economic Research.

Hanke, Steve H., and Kurt Schuler. 1994. *Currency Boards for Developing Countries.* San Francisco: International Center for Economic Growth.

Hausmann, Ricardo, Michael Gavin, Carmen Pages-Serra, and Ernesto Stein. 1999. *Financial Turmoil and the Choice of Exchange Rate Regime.* Working Paper 400. Washington: Inter-American Development Bank.

Henning, C. Randall. 1999. *The Exchange Stabilization Fund: Slush Money or War Chest?* Washington: Institute for International Economics.

Institute of International Finance (IIF). 1996. *Resolving Sovereign Financial Crises.* Washington: Institute of International Finance.

Institute of International Finance (IIF). 1999. *Report of the Working Group on Financial Crises in Emerging Markets.* Washington: Institute of International Finance.

Institute of International Finance (IIF). 2001. *Principles for Private Sector Involvement in Crisis Prevention and Resolution.* Washington: Institute of International Finance.

International Financial Institution Advisory Commission (IFIAC). 2000. *Report.* Washington: United States Congress.

International Monetary Fund (IMF). 1995. *International Capital Markets.* Washington: International Monetary Fund.

International Monetary Fund (IMF). 1997a. *Communiqué of the Interim Committee of the Board of Governors.* Washington: International Monetary Fund.

International Monetary Fund (IMF). 1997b. *World Economic Outlook: Interim Assessment, December 1997.* Washington: International Monetary Fund.

International Monetary Fund (IMF). 1998a. *Communiqués of the Interim Committee of the Board of Governors.* Washington: International Monetary Fund (16 April).

International Monetary Fund (IMF). 1998b. *International Capital Markets.* Washington: International Monetary Fund.

International Monetary Fund (IMF). 1998c. *World Economic Outlook and International Capital Markets: Interim Assessment, December 1998.* Washington: International Monetary Fund.

International Monetary Fund (IMF). 1998d. *World Economic Outlook, October 1998.* Washington: International Monetary Fund.

International Monetary Fund (IMF). 1999a. *Communiqué of the Interim Committee of the Board of Governors.* Washington: International Monetary Fund (26 September).

International Monetary Fund (IMF). 1999b. *Exchange Rate Arrangements and Currency Convertibility: Developments and Issues.* Washington: International Monetary Fund.

International Monetary Fund (IMF). 1999c. *External Evaluation of IMF Surveillance: Report by a Group of Independent Experts.* Washington: International Monetary Fund.

International Monetary Fund (IMF). 1999d. *International Capital Markets.* Washington: International Monetary Fund.

International Monetary Fund (IMF). 1999e. *Involving the Private Sector in Forestalling and Resolving Financial Crises.* Washington: International Monetary Fund.

International Monetary Fund (IMF). 1999f. *Report of the Managing Director to the Interim Committee on Progress in Strengthening the Architecture of the International Financial System.* Washington: International Monetary Fund.

International Monetary Fund (IMF). 1999g. *Selected Decisions and Selected Documents of the International Monetary Fund.* Washington: International Monetary Fund.

International Monetary Fund (IMF). 1999h. *World Economic Outlook, May 1999.* Washington: International Monetary Fund.

International Monetary Fund (IMF). 2000a. *Communiqué of the International Monetary and Financial Committee.* Washington: International Monetary Fund (April 16).

International Monetary Fund (IMF). 2000b. *IMF Board Agrees on Changes to Fund Financial Facilities.* Washington: International Monetary Fund (Public Information Notice no. 00.79).

International Monetary Fund (IMF). 2000c. *International Capital Markets.* Washington: International Monetary Fund.

International Monetary Fund (IMF). 2000d. *Involving the Private Sector in the Resolution of Financial Crises—Standstills—Preliminary Considerations.* Washington: International Monetary Fund.

International Monetary Fund (IMF). 2000e. *Report of the Managing Director to the International Monetary and Financial Committee on Progress in Reforming the IMF and Strengthening the Architecture of the International Financial System.* Washington: International Monetary Fund.

International Monetary Fund (IMF). 2000f. *World Economic Outlook, October 2000.* Washington: International Monetary Fund.

International Monetary Fund (IMF). 2001a. *Involving the Private Sector in the Resolution of Financial Crises—Restructuring International Sovereign Bonds.* Washington: International Monetary Fund.

International Monetary Fund (IMF). 2001b. *Reforming the International Financial Architecture—Progress through 2000.* Washington: International Monetary Fund.

International Monetary Fund (IMF). 2001c. *Streamlining Structural Conditionality in Fund-Supported Programs: Interim Guidance Note.* Washington: International Monetary Fund.

International Monetary Fund and the World Bank. 2001. *Assessing the Implementation of Standards: A Review of Experience and Next Steps:* Washington: International Monetary Fund and the World Bank.

Irwin, Gregor, and David Vines. 1999. *A Krugman-Dooley-Sachs Third Generation Model of the Asian Financial Crisis.* CEPR Discussion Paper 2149. London: Centre for Economic Policy Research.

Ito, Takatoshi. 1999. *Capital Flows in Asia.* NBER Working Paper 7134. Cambridge, MA: National Bureau of Economic Research.

Ito, Takatoshi. 2000. The Role of IMF Advice: A Postcrisis Examination. In *Reforming the International Monetary and Financial System,* eds. Peter B. Kenen and Alexander K. Swoboda. Washington: International Monetary Fund.

Ito, Takatoshi, Eiji Ogawa, and Yuri Nagataki Sasaki. 1998. *How Did the Dollar Peg Fail in Asia?* NBER Working Paper 6729. Cambridge, MA: National Bureau of Economic Research.

Jeanne, Olivier, and Charles Wyplosz. 2001. *The International Lender of Last Resort: How Large Is Large Enough?* NBER Working Paper 8381. Cambridge, MA: National Bureau of Economic Research.

Kaminsky, Graciela L. 1998. *Currency and Banking Crises: The Early Warnings of Distress.* International Finance Discussion Paper 629. Washington: Board of Governors of the Federal Reserve System.

Kaminsky, Graciela, Saul Lizondo, and Carmen M. Reinhart. 1998. Leading Indicators of Currency Crises. *IMF Staff Papers* 45: 1-48.

Kaminsky, Graciela L., and Carmen M. Reinhart. 1999. The Twin Crises: The Causes of Banking and Balance-of-Payments Problems. *American Economic Review* 89: 473-500.

Kaminsky, Graciela L., and Carmen M. Reinhart. 2000. On Crises, Contagion, and Confusion. *Journal of International Economics* 51: 149-68.

Kaminsky, Graciela L., and Sergio L. Schmukler. 1999. *What Triggers Market Jitters: A Chronicle of the Asian Crisis.* International Finance Discussion Paper 634. Washington: Board of Governors of the Federal Reserve System.

Kaplan, Ethan, and Dani Rodrik. 2001. *Did the Malaysian Capital Controls Work?* NBER Working Paper 8142. Cambridge, MA: National Bureau of Economic Research.

Kenen, Peter B. 1981. Effects of Intervention and Sterilization in the Short Run and the Long Run. In *The International Monetary System under Flexible Exchange Rates*, ed. R. N. Cooper, P. B. Kenen, J. Braga de Macedo, and J. van Ypersele. Cambridge: Ballinger.

Kenen, Peter B. 1986. *Financing, Adjustment, and the International Monetary Fund.* Washington: Brookings Institution.

Kenen, Peter B. 1993. Financial Opening and the Exchange Rate Regime. In *Financial Opening in Developing Countries*, eds. Helmut Reisen and Bernhard Fischer. Paris: OECD Development Centre.

Kenen, Peter B., ed. 1996. *From Halifax to Lyons: What Has Been Done About Crisis Management?* Essays in International Finance 200. Princeton, NJ: International Finance Section, Princeton University.

Kenen, Peter B. 2000a. Currency Unions and Policy Domains. Princeton University, Princeton, NJ. Photocopy.

Kenen, Peter B. 2000b. Financial-Sector Reform in Emerging-Market Countries: Getting the Incentives Right. Contribution to the Panel Discussion on Strengthening the Resiliency of Global Financial Markets. Sponsored by the Per Jacobssen Foundation, Lucerne (4 June).

Kenen, Peter B. 2000c. Involving the Private Sector in Crisis Resolution. In *Currency Crises*, ed. Paul Krugman. Chicago: University of Chicago Press.

Kenen, Peter B. 2000d. The New International Financial Architecture: Reconstruction, Renovation, or Minor Repair? *International Journal of Finance and Economics* 5: 1-14.

King, Mervyn. 1999. *Reforming the International Financial System: The Middle Way.* Speech delivered at the Federal Reserve Bank of New York (9 September). London: Bank of England.

Kiyotaki, Nobuhiro, and John Moore. 1997. Credit Cycles. *Journal of Political Economy* 105: 211-48.

Kletzer, Kenneth, and Mark M. Spiegel. 1998. Speculative Capital Inflows and Exchange Rate Targeting in the Pacific Basin: Theory and Evidence. In *Managing Capital Flows and Exchange Rates*, ed. Reuven Glick. Cambridge: Cambridge University Press.

Knight, Malcolm, Lawrence Schembri, and James Powell. 2000. Reforming the Global Financial Architecture: Just Tinkering Around the Edges? Paper presented to the Conference on Reforming the Architecture of Global Economic Institutions, London, Bank of England (5-6 May).

Köhler, Horst. 2000. *Address to the Board of Governors of the Fund* (26 September). Washington: International Monetary Fund.

Kraay, Aardt. 1998. Do High Interest Rates Defend Currencies During Speculative Attacks? Washington, World Bank. Photocopy.

Krugman, Paul. 1979. A Model of Balance of Payments Crises. *Journal of Money, Credit, and Banking* 11: 311-25.

Krugman, Paul. 1991. Target Zones and Exchange Rate Dynamics. *Quarterly Journal of Economics* 106: 669-82.

Krugman, Paul. 1998a. The Confidence Game. *New Republic,* 5 October.

Krugman, Paul. 1998b. What Happened to Asia? Massachusetts Institute of Technology, Cambridge, MA. Photocopy.

Krugman, Paul. 2000. Balance Sheets, the Transfer Problem, and Financial Crises. In *International Finance and Financial Crises: Essays in Honour of Robert P. Flood, Jr.,* eds. Peter Isard, Assaf Razin, and Andrew K. Rose. Boston: Kluwer Academic Publishers.

Lahiri, Amartya, and Carlos A. Vegh. 2000. *Delaying the Inevitable: Interest Rate Policy and BOP Crises.* NBER Working Paper 7734. Cambridge, MA: National Bureau of Economic Research.

Lamfalussy, Alexandre. 2000. *Financial Crises in Emerging Markets: An Essay on Financial Globalization and Fragility.* New Haven: Yale University Press.

Lane, Timothy, et al. 1999. *IMF-Supported Programs in Indonesia, Korea, and Thailand: A Preliminary Assessment.* IMF Occasional Paper 178. Washington: International Monetary Fund.

Larraín, Felipe, and Andrés Velasco. 1999. *Exchange Rate Policy for Emerging Markets: One Size Does Not Fit All.* Group of Thirty Occasional Paper 30. Washington: Group of Thirty.

Leiderman, Leonardo, and Alfredo E. Thorne. 1996. The 1994 Mexican Crisis and Its Aftermath: What Are the Main Lessons? In *Private Capital Flows to Emerging Markets after the Mexican Crisis,* eds. Guillermo A. Calvo, Morris Goldstein, and Eduard Hochreiter. Washington: Institute for International Economics.

Levy-Yedati, Eduardo, and Federico Sturzenegger. 2000. Exchange Rate Regimes and Economic Performance. Photocopy.

Lipton, David. 2000. Refocusing the Role of the International Monetary Fund. In *Reforming the International Monetary and Financial System,* eds. Peter B. Kenen and Alexander K. Swoboda. Washington: International Monetary Fund.

Martin, Paul. 1998. *Remarks to the Commonwealth Business Forum* (29 September). Ottawa: Finance Canada.

Martin, Paul. 1999. *The International Financial Architecture: The Rule of Law.* Remarks at the Conference of the Canadian Institute for Advanced Legal Studies (12 July). Ottawa: Finance Canada.

Massad, Carlos. 1998. The Liberalization of the Capital Account: Chile in the 1990s. In *Should the IMF Pursue Capital Account Convertibility?* by Stanley Fischer et al. Essays in International Finance 207. Princeton: International Finance Section, Princeton University.

Masson, Paul. 1999. Contagion: Monsoonal Effects, Spillovers, and Jumps between Multiple Equilibria. In *The Asian Financial Crisis: Causes, Contagion, and Consequences,* eds. Pierre-Richard Agénor, Marcus Miller, David Vines, and Axel Weber. Cambridge: Cambridge University Press.

McKinnon, Ronald I. 1998. Exchange Rate Coordination for Surmounting the East Asian Currency Crisis. Stanford University, Stanford, CA. Photocopy.

McKinnon, Ronald I. 2000. The East Asian Dollar Standard, Life After Death? *Banca Monte dei Paschi di Siena Economic Notes* 29: 31-82.

McKinnon, Ronald I., and Huw Pill. 1998. The Overborrowing Syndrome: Are East Asian Countries Different? In *Managing Capital Flows and Exchange Rates,* ed. Reuven Glick. Cambridge: Cambridge University Press.

McKinnon, Ronald I., and Huw Pill. 1999. Exchange Rate Regimes for Emerging Markets: Moral Hazard and International Overborrowing. *Oxford Review of Economic Policy* 15: 19-38.

Meese, Richard A., and Andrew K. Rose. 1998. Exchange Rate Instability: Determinants and Predictability. In *Managing Capital Flows and Exchange Rates*, ed. Reuven Glick. Cambridge: Cambridge University Press.

Mei, Jianping. 1999. Political Risk, Financial Crisis, and Market Volatility. Princeton University, Princeton, NJ. Photocopy.

Meltzer, Allan H. 1999. What's Wrong with the IMF? What Would Be Better? In *The Asian Financial Crisis: Origins, Implications, and Solutions*, eds. William C. Hunter, George G. Kaufman, and Thomas H. Krueger. Boston: Kluwer Academic. Publishers.

Milesi-Ferretti, Gian Maria, and Assaf Razin. 1996. Persistent Current Account Deficits: A Warning Signal? *International Journal of Finance & Economics* 1: 161-81.

Milesi-Ferretti, Gian Maria, and Assaf Razin. 2000. Current Account Reversals and Currency Crises: Empirical Regularities. In *Currency Crises*, ed. Paul Krugman. Chicago: University of Chicago Press.

Miller, Marcus, and Lei Zhang. 2000. Sovereign Liquidity Crises: The Strategic Case for a Payments Standstill. *Economic Journal* 110: 335-62.

Minton Beddoes, Zanny. 1999. Global Finance: Time for a Redesign. *The Economist*, 30 January.

Mishkin, Frederic S. 1996. Understanding Financial Crises: A Developing Country Perspective. In *Annual World Bank Conference on Development Economics, 1996*, eds. Michael Bruno and Boris Pleskovic. Washington: World Bank.

Mishkin, Frederic S. 1998. The Dangers of Exchange-Rate Pegging in Emerging-Market Countries. *International Finance* 1: 81-101.

Mishkin, Frederic S. 1999. *Lessons from the Asian Crisis.* NBER Working Paper 7102. Cambridge, MA: National Bureau of Economic Research.

Montiel, Peter J. 1996. Policy Responses to Surges in Capital Inflows: Issues and Lessons. In *Private Capital Flows to Emerging Markets after the Mexican Crisis*, eds. Guillermo A. Calvo, Morris Goldstein, and Eduard Hochreiter. Washington: Institute for International Economics.

Mussa, Michael. 1999. Reforming the International Financial Architecture: Limiting Moral Hazard and Containing Real Hazard. In *International Capital Flows and the Financial System*, eds. David W. R. Gruen and Luke Gower. Sydney: Reserve Bank of Australia.

Mussa, Michael, Alexander Swoboda, Jeromin Zettelmeyer, and Olivier Jeanne. 2000. Moderating Fluctuations in Capital Flows to Emerging Market Economies. In *Reforming the International Monetary and Financial System*, eds. Peter B. Kenen and Alexander K. Swoboda. Washington: International Monetary Fund.

Obstfeld, Maurice. 1998. The Global Capital Market: Benefactor or Menace? *Journal of Economic Perspectives* 12: 81-101.

Obstfeld, Maurice, and Kenneth Rogoff. 1995. The Mirage of Fixed Exchange Rates. *Journal of Economic Perspectives* 9: 73-96.

O'Neill, Paul H. 2001. *Statement Before the House Committee on Financial Services* (22 May). Washington: US Treasury.

Osband, Kent, and Caroline Van Rijckeghem. 2000. Safety from Currency Crises. *IMF Staff Papers* 47: 238-58.

Padoa-Schioppa, Tommaso. 1988. The European Monetary System: A Long-Term View. In *The European Monetary System*, eds. Francesco Giavazzi, Stefano Micossi, and Marcus Miller. Cambridge: Cambridge University Press.

Park, Chul Yung, and Yunjong Wang. 2000. Reforming the International Financial System: Prospects for Regional Financial Cooperation in East Asia. In *Reforming the International Financial System: Crisis Prevention and Response*, ed. Jan Joost Teunissen. The Hague: Forum on Debt and Development.

Petas, Peter, and Rashique Rahman. 1999. Sovereign Bonds—Legal Aspects that Affect Default and Recovery. *Global Emerging Markets* (Deutsche Bank) 2: 59-78.

Polak, Jacques J. 1991. *The Changing Nature of IMF Conditionality.* Essays in International Finance 184. Princeton, NJ: International Finance Section, Princeton University.

Polak, Jacques J. 1998. The Articles of Agreement of the IMF and the Liberalization of Capital Movements. In *Should the IMF Pursue Capital Account Convertibility?* by Stanley Fischer et al. Essays in International Finance 207. Princeton, NJ: International Finance Section, Princeton University.

Radelet, Steven, and Jeffrey D. Sachs. 1998. The East Asian Financial Crisis: Diagnosis, Remedies, Prospects. *Brookings Papers on Economic Activity* 1: 1-74.

Radelet, Steven, and Jeffrey Sachs. 2000. The Onset of the East Asian Financial Crisis. In *Currency Crises*, ed. Paul Krugman. Chicago: University of Chicago Press.

Reinhart, Carmen. 2001. Sovereign Credit Ratings Before and After Financial Crises. Paper presented to the Conference on the Role of Credit Reporting Systems in the International Economy, Washington, World Bank (1-2 March).

Reinhart, Carmen M., and Vincent R. Reinhart. 1999. On the Use of Reserve Requirements in Dealing with Capital Flow Problems. *International Journal of Finance & Economics* 4: 27-54.

Reinhart, Carmen M., and R. Todd Smith. 1998. Too Much of a Good Thing: The Macroeconomic Effects of Taxing Capital Inflows. In *Managing Capital Flows and Exchange Rates*, ed. Reuven Glick. Cambridge: Cambridge University Press.

Reisen, Helmut, and Julia von Maltzan. 1999. Boom and Bust and Sovereign Ratings. *International Finance* 2: 273-93.

Rodrik, Dani. 1998. Who Needs Capital Account Convertibility? In *Should the IMF Pursue Capital Account Convertibility?* by Stanley Fischer et al. Essays in International Finance 207. Princeton, NJ: International Finance Section, Princeton University.

Rodrik, Dani, and Andrés Velasco. 1999. *Short-Term Capital Flows.* NBER Working Paper 7364. Cambridge, MA: National Bureau of Economic Research.

Rogoff, Kenneth. 1999. International Institutions for Reducing Global Financial Instability. *Journal of Economic Perspectives* 13: 21-42.

Roubini, Nouriel. 2000. Bail-In, Burden-Sharing, Private Sector Involvement (PSI) in Crisis Resolution and Constructive Engagement of the Private Sector. A Primer: Evolving Definitions, Doctrine, Practice, and Case Law. New York University, New York. Photocopy.

Rubin, Robert E. 1998. *Strengthening the Architecture of the International Financial System: Remarks at the Brookings Institution* (14 April). Washington: US Treasury.

Rubin, Robert E. 1999. *Remarks on Reform of the International Financial Architecture to the School of Advanced International Studies* (21 April). Washington: US Treasury.

Sachs, Jeffrey. 1995. Do We Need an International Lender of Last Resort? The Frank D. Graham Memorial Lecture, presented at Princeton University (20 April).

Sachs, Jeffrey, Aaron Tornell, and Andrés Velasco. 1996a. Financial Crises in Emerging Markets: The Lessons of 1995. *Brookings Papers on Economic Activity* 1: 147-98.

Sachs, Jeffrey, Aaron Tornell, and Andrés Velasco. 1996b. The Mexican Peso Crisis: Sudden Death or Death Foretold? *Journal of International Economics* 41: 265-83.

Schadler, Susan, et al. 1993. *Recent Experiences with Surges in Capital Inflows.* IMF Occasional Paper 108. Washington: International Monetary Fund.

Schneider, Martin, and Aaron Tornell. 2000. *Balance Sheet Effects, Bailout Guarantees, and Financial Crises.* NBER Working Paper 8060. Cambridge, MA: National Bureau of Economic Research.

Stiglitz, Joseph. 1998. Macroeconomic Dimensions of the East Asian Crisis. In *Financial Crises and Asia*, by Robert Chote et al. CEPR Conference Report 6. London: Centre for Economic Policy Research.

Stiglitz, Joseph. 1999. Must Financial Crises Be This Frequent and This Painful? In *The Asian Financial Crisis: Causes, Contagion and Consequences*, eds. Pierre-Richard Agénor, Marcus Miller, David Vines, and Axel Weber. Cambridge: Cambridge University Press.

Summers, Lawrence H. 1999a. Statement before the Subcommittee on International Trade and Finance of the Senate Banking Committee (22 April). Washington: US Treasury.

Summers, Lawrence H. 1999b. *The Right Kind of IMF for a Stable Global Financial System: Remarks to the London School of Business* (14 December). Washington: US Treasury.

Takagi, Shinji. 1999. The Yen and Its East Asian Neighbors, 1980-1995: Cooperation or Competition? In *Changes in Exchange Rates in Rapidly Developing Countries*, eds. Takatoshi Ito and Anne O. Krueger. Chicago: University of Chicago Press.

Tarullo, Daniel K. 2001. Rules, Discretion, and Authority in International Financial Reform. Georgetown University Law School, Washington. Photocopy.

Task Force on the Future International Financial Architecture. 1999. *Safeguarding Prosperity in a Global Financial System*. Washington: Institute for International Economics. [Cited as CFR Task Force (1999).]

Thornton, Henry. 1802. *An Enquiry into the Nature and Effects of the Paper Credit of Great Britain*. London: Hatchard.

Tornell, Aaron. 1999. *Common Fundamentals in the Tequila and Asian Crises*. NBER Working Paper 7139. Cambridge, MA: National Bureau of Economic Research.

Ul Haque, Nadeem, and Mohsin S. Khan. 1998. *Do IMF-Supported Programs Work? A Survey of the Cross-Country Empirical Evidence*. Working Paper 98/169. Washington: International Monetary Fund.

US Treasury. 2000. *Response to the Report of the International Financial Institution Advisory Committee*. Washington: US Treasury.

Vines, David. 2000. Reforming the Architecture of Global Economic Institutions. Paper presented to the Conference on Reforming the Architecture of Global Economic Institutions, London, Bank of England (5-6 May).

White, William R. 1999. What Have We Learned from Recent Financial Crises and Policy Responses? Paper presented to the Conference on Lessons from Recent Global Financial Crises. Chicago, Federal Reserve Bank of Chicago (30 September-2 October).

Williamson, John. 1995. *What Role for Currency Boards?* Washington: Institute for International Economics.

Williamson, John. 1996. *The Crawling Band as an Exchange Rate Regime: Lessons from Chile, Colombia, and Israel*. Washington: Institute for International Economics.

Williamson, John. 1998. Crawling Bands or Monitoring Bands: How to Manage Exchange Rates in a World of Capital Mobility. *International Finance* 1: 59-79.

Williamson, John. 2000a. *Exchange Rate Regimes for Emerging Markets: Reviving the Intermediate Option*. Washington: Institute for International Economics.

Williamson, John. 2000b. The Role of the IMF: A Guide to the Reports. Paper presented to the Conference on Developing Countries and the Global Financial Architecture organized by the Commonwealth Secretariat and the World Bank. London, Commonwealth Secretariat (22-23 June).

Working Party on Financial Stability in Emerging-Market Economies. 1997. *Financial Stability in Emerging-Market Economies*. Washington: International Monetary Fund.

World Bank. 1997. *Private Capital Flows to Developing Countries*. Oxford: Oxford University Press for the World Bank.

Zhang, Xiaoming Alan. 1999. *Testing for "Moral Hazard" in Emerging-Market Lending*. Research Paper 99-1. Washington: Institute of International Finance.

INDEX

financial-sector reform, 127
guarantees, 27
hedging, 40n-41n
hedging foreign currency exposures,
    132, 132n
how it spread, 31-34
how it started, 28-31
how it went on spreading, 34-35
innovations at IMF, 7-9
monsoonal effects, 37
policy commitments to IMF, 9
political factors, 25n
push and pull factors, 17
short-term debt, 142
Asian "miracle," 14
  faith in, 27
assassinations, political, 1-2
assessments of adherence to standards
    and codes, 110-11
asset-price behavior, 36n

Bagehot, Walter, 58
  Meltzer Report, 64
bailouts, 2-3
  Asian crisis, 7
  Brazil, 46-47
    amount, 46n-47n
  limiting reliance on IMF, 111-17
    reconfiguring the IMF, 114-17
    risks and costs, 112-14
  Mexican crisis, magnitude, 22, 22n
  new standards for, 97
  packages compared, 7n
  reform conditions creating uncertainty,
    53
balance of payments
  deficits and hard pegs, 77
  Mexico, 20t
balance sheet effects, of high interest
    rates, 42-43
Bangkok International Banking Facility
    (BIBF), 28, 28n, 29n
Bank of England, 57
banking
  Asian crisis, countries compared, 42n
  capital inflows, controlling, 134
  carrots and sticks, 128
  competition from strong foreign banks,
    135
  compliance with standards and codes,
    127
  cross-border loan risks, 128
  exchange rate stability, 39, 41
  foreign banks, 135-36

Indonesia, 9, 10, 33, 33n
Korea, 34-35, 35n
lenders of last resort, 57-58
Mexican crisis, 22
output decline blamed, 42
regulation of foreign currency
    borrowing advocated, 134-35
Thailand, 29
banking crises, 62
Mexico, 68
Bank of Korea, 35
short-term interest rates, 54n
Bank of Mexico, 2, 22
additions to domestic assets, 24n
exchange rate stability, 23, 24
bank regulation, 64
bankruptcy regime
  international, 4n
  objections to, 147n
  rejected, 5
  for sovereign debtors, 50n, 146-47
Bank of Thailand
  currency floated, 30
  short-term interest rates, 54n
  sterilization, 29, 29n
Basel Capital Adequacy Accord, 96n
  carrots and sticks, 128
Basel Committee on Banking Supervision
    (BCBS), 5
  carrots and sticks, 128
  compliance with standards and codes,
    128
  Lyon Summit, 91
Basel Core Principles, 69
  assessing criteria, 129n
  banking reform, 135
  carrots and sticks, 128
  higher capital requirements, 127
  usefulness, 70
Baumgartner letter, 61n
"BBC" proposal, 86
best practice, defining, 129, 129n
bilateral financing, 60
bilateral money, Asian crisis, 33, 33n
Birmingham Summit (1998), 95-96
  prudential supervision, 97n
  public warnings of crisis vulnerability,
    108, 108n-09n
bond exchanges, 113n
eurobonds
  Ecuador, 120, 1231
  Pakistan, 119
  Ukraine, 118-19

bonding role of debt, 138-39
forms of punishment, 139-40, 139*n*
bonds
Brady, 120, 120*n*, 121, 121*n*
Gasprom, 119
issues, 6
private-sector involvement, objections, 121
rescheduling, 91
seniority structure, 121
book, structure of this, 11-12
Brady bonds, 23
Ecuador, 120, 120*n*
Brazil
banking crisis, 142
effects of Korean episode, 145*n*
flexible exchange rates, 84
front-loading by IMF, 54
inflation targeting, 41*n*
large-scale official financing, 116*n*
rollover options, 148
soft landing, 46-47
Bretton Woods System, 75
access to IMF credit, 151
Britain
Bank of England, 57
inflation targeting, 41*n*
Buiter-Sibert scheme, 147-50
burden-sharing argument, 113-14, 114*n*

Calomiris, Charles, 63-64
exchange rate policy, 67
IMF restructuring, 67, 67*n*
Canada, collective action clauses, 101*n*
capital accounts, 17-18
liberalization and sudden shifts in capital flows, 151
premature liberalization and crisis, 27
capital flight
Asian crisis, 7
capital outflow controls, 44
debt suspension, 146
dollarization, 79
FSF working group, 11
Malaysia, 44
rollover clauses, 150
capital flows
liberalizing, 92
WTO liberalizing, 92
capital inflows
Asian crisis, 39, 41
assessing how they are used, 18-19
Chile, 134, 134*n*
Mexico, 23

problem of, 14-19
push and pull factors, 17
sustainability question, 18-19
taxes or tax-equivalent measures limiting, 133
whether to bank or spend an inflow, 16-18
Capital Markets Consultative Group, 125
capital mobility, international, 16-19
capital outflow controls
costs of, 136
G-22 report criticizing, 98, 98*n*-99*n*
Malaysia, 44
capital outflows
creditor panic, 52
financing gap, 54, 54*n*
capital requirements, 64
case-by-case approach, 102
Cavallo, Domingo, 83*n*-84*n*
central banks
credit panics, 62-63
as currency boards, 75-76
fixed exchange rates, 81
as lenders of last resort, 62
Central and Eastern Europe, 109
chartering of banks, 64
Chile
capital inflows, 134, 134*n*
domestic currency debt, 83*n*
reserve requirements on foreign borrowing, 133-34, 133*n*
tequila effect, 134
China, competition impact, 29, 29*n*
cluster analysis, 38, 38*n*
coercion, effects of, 139
coercive behavior, debt restructuring, 139, 140, 140*n*
collateralization, Meltzer Report, 67*n*
collective action
Rey Report, 89-90
types of, 89, 89*n*
collective action clauses
concept of, 69*n*
Ecuador, 120, 122
failure to promote, 121
G-22 report recommendations, 99
IIF report, 91, 91*n*
Köln Summit, 101, 101*n*
Pakistan, 119, 122
prequalification recommendations, 69
presumptive prequalification, 154
private sector on, 139*n*
success questioned, 122

Ukraine, 119, 119n-20n, 122
usefulness, 70
Colosio, Luis Donaldo, 1, 19
communiqués, nature of, 74n
Compensatory Financing Facility (CFF),
  69
  compliance with standards and codes,
    126-27, 127-28
conditionality
  Asian crisis, debate, 94
  Calomiris recommendations, 65
  contractual approach, 127n, 130-32
  criticized, 10
  debate over, 43
  eschewed, for collateral requirements,
    65
  financial-sector reform, 126
    compliance with standards and
      codes, 126, 127
  G-22 working group on, 98
  IMF staff study on effectiveness, 66
  large-scale financing in tranches, 60
  narrow aim of adjustment, 153
  overloading of, 127
  parsimonious approach, 125
  prequalification replacing, 69-71
  rationale, 51-52
  structural conditions, criteria changing,
    125n
  sustainability versus culpability, 52
  to foster reform
    Asian crisis, 109
    Eastern Europe, 109
    objections to, 109-10
  See also policy conditions
confidence, investor, 52-53
  availability of IMF credit, 53
  IMF preoccupation, 53n
  impact of IMF programs debated, 54
Congress (US), peso crisis bailout, 3n
"constructive ambiguity," 58
contagion
  Asian crisis, 35-36
  capital outflow controls, 98n
  causes versus effects, 38n
  Contingent Credit Lines, 8-9
  creation of CCL, 152
  expectational effects, 37
  IMF innovations, 8-9
  Indonesia's response, 32
  monsoonal effects, 36
  nature of, 152
  risk of standstills, 145

rollover clauses, 150
spillover effects, 36-37
tequila effect, 25-26, 25n
Thailand bailout, 31
vulnerability to, 70
contagion facility, 114-15, 115n
Contingent Credit Lines (CCLs), 8-9, 43,
  59
  commitment fees and surcharges, 117
  Executive Board on, 117
  lack of attractiveness, 70-71, 71n
  liberalized, 116
  prequalifying for, 8n
  risks perceived, 152
  Russian crisis, 94
  Summers on, 116
contingent liabilities
  government, 26, 27
  Thailand, 27
contractual approach, to standards and
    codes, 130-32
  advantages, 131
  interim measures, 132-35
  measuring progress, 132
Core Principles for Effective Banking
    Supervision, 5, 91
corporate debt problem, Indonesia, 34
corporate sector, government guarantees
    criticized, 98
corruption, 136
Council on Foreign Relations, 114
country crises, 114
country risk, 83
crawling pegs or bands, 75
  emerging markets, 85
credit channel, 42-43
creditor panics, 9
  Asian crisis, 49, 51, 51n
  capital outflows, 52
  IMF resources, 59
  IMF strategy, 144
  large-scale official financing, 114n
  lender of last resort, 57-58
  managing, 52
  Mexican case, 68
  restoration of rationality, 152
  risk of standstills, 145
  rollover clauses, 150
  standstills, 143, 153
  voluntary or quasi-voluntary
    measures, s, 142
credit panics
  Calomiris and Meltzer Report, 67-68

role of central banks, 62-63
credit union, 61
crises
country versus systemic, 114
galloping incrementalism by
institutions, 150-51
predicting, 105-06
models for, 106*n*, 107
timing of, 106*n*
threshold for crisis indicator, 107
vulnerability to
measuring, 107
remedial action, 107
Crisis Facility, 69
crisis management, distinguishing, 87*n*
crisis prevention, 10-11
compliance with standards and codes,
126
distinguishing, 87*n*
financial-sector reform, 91-92
G-22 Reports, 96-98
O'Neill on, 125*n*
crisis resolution
G-22 Reports, 98-101
Köln Summit, 102, 103
crony capitalism, 33, 66
culture of credit, 139
currency baskets
Argentina, 84*n*
recommendation, 86*n*
currency boards, 75-76, 77, 77*n*, 153
Argentina, 83*n*-84*n*
closer look at two corners, 80-84
crawling away from the corners, 84-86
exiting from, 78-79
as LLRs, 78
small economies, 84
currency convertibility, 92, 93
currency crises
balance sheet effects, 22*n*
debates, 49
defined, 106
first generation models, 55*n*
Mexican crisis, 19, 21, 22
models of Mexican crisis, 13
monetary union versus dollarization,
79
predicting, 107*n*
vulnerability, detecting, 106, 106*n*
currency measures, capital inflows, 16*n*-
17*n*
currency risk, 83
current accounts

deficits and crisis vulnerability, 106,
106*n*
depreciations of Asian currencies, 43

debt crises
debt crisis of the 1980s, 2
Brady bonds, 121*n*
IMF credit uses, 151
Meltzer Report on, 66
G-7 recommendations, 4
large-scale official financing, 5-6
debt default, Ecuador, 120
debt exchanges
destabilizing dynamics, 122
Ecuador, 120
Ukraine, 118-19
debt-monitoring system, 35
debt problems, 99
large-scale financing, 112
Romania, 118*n*
standstills, 143
debt reduction
operational guidelines, 103-04
standstills, 143
debt relief, Halifax Summit, 88-89
debt rescheduling, standstills, 143
debt restructuring
coercive behavior, 139, 140, 140*n*
effects of, 139
IIF, 91*n*
large-scale official financing, 115-16
litigation risks, 122
operational guidelines, 103-04
options, 144*n*
risks and costs, 121
Russia, 118*n*
time to agreement, 139
"voluntary" in Korea, 141-42, 141*n*-42*n*
debt suspensions, 88-89, 100, 100*n*
G-22 working group, 143*n*-44*n*, 145
IMF motives, 146*n*
onus and cost, 148*n*-49*n*
private-sector response, 90-91
recommendations of Rey Report, 89-90
selective, 145-46
debt workouts, 99
de facto pegging
attracting attacks, 85
soft peg, 75, 76, 76*n*
Thailand, 72
defaults
deterrents to, 140
effects of, 140
Korea, 7

Russia's unilateral, 44-46
deflationary pressures, 77
Denver Summit (1997), 93, 93n
deposit insurance, 64
deregulation, financial markets, 15
devaluation
    equilibrium models, 43
    Mexican crisis, 19, 19n, 21, 21f, 24
    peso crisis, 2
developing countries
    adopting "best practice," 93n
    private capital flows, 14t
"directed lending," 10
disfiguring amendments, 120, 120n-121n
disinflation, 82
distribution costs, 81
dollarization, 51, 76, 83
    closer look at two corners, 80-84
    crawling away from the corners, 84-86
    dependent monetary policy, 77
    Ecuador, 77n
    effects, 79n
    exiting from, 78
    de facto versus de jure, 83
    fixed exchange rates, 153
    justifications for, 83
    LLRs under, 78
    risks, 78-79, 83
    El Salvador, 77n
    small economies, 84
    United States compensating, 78n
dynamic hedging, 98n

early warning systems, 3, 86
    indicators, 107
    vulnerable economies, 105-06
Eastern Europe, 109
economic indicators, as signals for crisis
    vulnerability, 107
economic shocks
    Compensatory Financing Facility, 69
    prequalification, 69, 70
Ecuador, 47
    Brady bonds, 120, 120n, 121, 121n
    exit consents, 119-20, 121
efficiency-seeking FDI, 15
election effect, 25n
Emergency Financing Mechanism (EFM),
    59, 71
    G-7 recommendations, 3, 4
    Halifax Summit, 88
emerging markets
    adopting "best practice," 93
    banking systems, 68

capital inflows, 17-18
crawling bands, 85
exchange rate regimes, 76-77, 77n
foreign banks, 135
G-22 working group, 97
investment risk, 15
larger countries' treatment, 123
long-term debt in own currencies, 83
rates of return, 15
reputational factors, 140
Russian default, 45
standards and codes, 130
strengthening infrastructure, 109-11
equilibrium models, devaluation, 43
equitable burden sharing, principle of, 5
equity prices, Asian crisis, 31-32
eurobonds, 47
exchange, Ukraine, 118-19
Europe
    exchange rate regimes, 72, 72n
    monetary union, 79
European Monetary System (EMS)
    crisis (1992-93), 26, 27
        lesson from, 50-51, 50n
    target exchange rates, 75
European Union, 80
exchange contracts, 146-47
exchange rate, Mexico, 21f
exchange rate pegging, 72
    See also pegged rates
exchange rate policy, debates, 50-51, 50n
exchange rate regimes
    architecture exercise and, 72-74
    classifying, 74-77
        free float, 75
        hard peg, 75-77
            three forms compared, 77-80
        managed float, 75
        soft peg, 75
    complex environment, 82-83
    IMF taxonomy, 75n
    systemic risk factor, 73-74
exchange rates
    Asian currencies overall, 42
    balance sheet effects, 42-43
    Brazil, 47
    dollar appreciation, 39, 40
    fixed, 81-82
    flexible, 81
    free floating US dollars, 76n
    impact of interest rate policies, 54-57
    Indonesia, 30f, 40n
    intermediate regime, 75n

Korea, 30*f*, 40*n*
Malaysia, 30*f*
Meltzer Report, 67
Mexico, appreciation, 23-25
monetary shocks, 80-81
nominal, 81
purchasing-power-parity calculations,
31*n*-32*n*
real, 81
role of exchange rate regimes, 39-41
five features of Asian crisis, 39-42
links to dollar, 39, 39*n*
Thai baht, 29-30
Thailand, 30*f*, 40*n*
UDROPs, 149
exchange rate targeting, 41*n*
exchange regulations, loan contracts and,
139*n*
Exchange Stabilization Fund (US), peso
crisis, 2, 3*n*
Executive Board
Köln framework, 105
presumptive prequalification, 154, 155
reviewing facilities, 116-17
standstills as unresolved issues, 103
exit consents
Ecuador, 119-20, 121
objections to, 121
expectational effects, 37
Extended Fund Facility (EFF), structural
reform and conditionality, 109
external crises, resolving, 59-60

"fear of floating," 84
Federal Reserve System, as LLR for
dollarized economies, 78*n*
Finance One, 29
Financial Action Task Force (FATF), 88
financial crises, market-based response,
90-91
financial-market links, 38
financial markets, globally integrated, 15
financial panic, 38
Financial Sector Assessment (FSA), 111
Financial Sector Assessment Program
(FSAP), 110-11
financial-sector reform, 131
financial-sector reform
interim measures, 132-35
objections to conditionality, 110
partnership, shape of, 130-32
presumptive prequalification, 154
proposals, 12
three requirements, 130-31

Financial Sector Stability Assessment
(FSSA), 110, 111
Financial Stability Forum (FSF), 11, 92*n*
report on standards, 128
Working Group on Capital Flows, 132-
33
financing gap, 54, 54*n*
endogeneity of, 144, 144*n*
size of, 144
fixed exchange rates
advantages, 81
exiting from, 82
G-22 working group, 98*n*
over long term, 84
flexible exchange rates, 81
G-22 working group, 98*n*
floating, 71-72
classifying exchange rate regimes, 74-
77
closer look at two corners, 80-83
crawling away from corners, 84-86
exchange rates and architecture
exercises, 72-74
fear of, 83
hard pegging, three forms, 77-80
two-corner approach, 83
See also free floating exchange rates
foreign banks
in emerging markets, 135
strategies for entry, 135-36
foreign direct investment (FDI)
efficiency-seeking, 15
private capital flows to developing
countries, 14*t*
foreign investment, capital inflows, 16-17
formal dollarization, 76, 153
free floating exchange rates, 75
cautions, 85
US dollar, 76*n*
free-rider problem, 6
front-loading, 54, 60

G-7 nations
crisis prevention, 10-11
endorsement of the two-corner
approach, 82*n*
exchange rate regimes, 72, 72*n*
financial crises, 3
limiting foreign currency exposure of
banks, 133
Lyon Summit recommendations, 4-5
members, 3*n*
pegging exchange rates, 73-74
soft pegging, 86

solvency problems, 50n
tiered response by IMF, 95
voluntary approaches, 140-41
G-10 countries, NAB creation, 4n
G-10 working party, 5
G-22 Reports, 96-101
crisis prevention, 96-98
crisis resolution, 98-101
debt suspension, 143n-144n
Gasprom bonds, 119
GDP, Asian crisis, output decline, 42, 42t
General Arrangements to Borrow (GAB),
59
G-7 recommendations, 3, 4
Halifax Summit, 88
large-scale official financing, 114
unanimity to activate, 61n
Genoa Summit (2001), multilateral
development banks, 125
Germany, collective action clauses, 101n
globalization, herding increased, 37n
gold standard, 62
good collateral, 60, 60n
Bagehot rule, 58
goods-market arbitrage, 81, 82
government guarantees, 26-27, 26n
Group of 10, established, 11n
Group of 20, 96n
guarantees
exchange rate risks, 40n-41n
government, 26-27, 26n
implicit, 27
Krugman model, 43n

Halifax communiqué (Group of Seven
1995), 3-4
Halifax Summit (1995), 3, 88-89
reform results, 91
hard pegging
comparing three forms, 77-80
small economies, 84
ways to achieve, 75-76
when appropriate, 85
hedge funds
FSF working group, 11
Thailand, 29, 30n
hedging
Asian crisis, 40n-41n
cost of, 40n
herding, 37n
HIPC Initiative, 88
Hong Kong dollar, 32, 34
attacked, 84
hard pegs, 84n

illiquidity, 56
Calomiris recommendations, 65
IMF
Asian crisis, 7
recognizing, 94-95
contractual approach, 131
creditor panic role, 49
criticisms, 9-10
debt problems, 99-100
financial resources, 61-62, 62n
implicit guarantees, 27
Indonesian bailout, amount of, 33
innovations after Asian crisis, 7-9
Korea bailout, 35
as lender of last resort (LLR), 57-63
classic case for an LLR, 57-58
how Fund differs, 60-62
how Fund resembles LLR, 58-60
recasting the analogy, 62-63
lending into arrears
as binding mechanism, 139
G-22 report, 100n
IIF response, 91
Köln Summit, 102
Rey Report on, 90
letter of intent, 9
Mexican bailout, 2
precarious strategy of, 52-54
reconfiguration proposed, 115
requirements for financing, 9
Thailand bailout, 29, 30-31
reasons given, 31
tiered response, 95
Ukraine aid, 47
implicit guarantees, 27
Indonesia
bailout, 7, 8t
bilateral funding, 60
exchange rates, 30f
IMF requirements, 9, 10
policy conditions, 109
rupiah, depreciation rate, 55n
rupiah policy, 32-34, 32n
Indonesian central bank, short-term
interest rates, 54n
Indonesian rupiah, 39
inflation
capital inflows, 17
exchange rates, 81-82
inflation targeting, 41n, 82, 86n
Institute of International Finance (IIF),
90-91, 91n
Korea's private creditors, 142n

leading indicators, publishing, 107-08
official pressure or coercion, 139
interbank credit, Korea, 35, 35n
interbank debt
  Brazilian crisis, 142, 145n
  Thailand bailout, 31, 31n
  volatility, 123
interbank lending, 28
  Rey Report, 28n
interbank lines, 6
interdependence, effects of, 36-37
interest rate defense
  conventional, 55
  summary of debate, 56
interest rates
  Asian crisis, 54-57
    IMF blamed, 42
  conventional interest rate defense, 55
  Korean short-term debt, 35
  "Laffer Curve," 56
  Mexican, 22
  official versus private loans, 122-23
  path of exchange rate, 56
  sterilization, 17n
  United States, private capital flows, 15,
    15n
Interim Committee (IMF), 93
  Asian crisis, 94-95
  Rubin's views on pegged exchange
    rates, 74, 74n
intermediate option, 86
"intermediate regime," 75n
intermediation, 28
International Accounting Standards
  Committee (IASC), 92
International Association of Insurance
  Supervisors (IAIS), 92
international banking standard, 5
International Capital Markets
  Department, 125
International Monetary and Financial
  Committee (IMFC), 74n
International Organization of Securities
  Commissions (IOSCO), 92
investors
  anticipation of, 37
  capital outflow controls, 136
  foreign, attitudes and actions, 38
  herding, 37n
  spillover effects, 37
  tequila effect, 26, 26n
  wake-up calls, 37
involuntary standstills, 139

IOSCO, 92
  Objectives and Principles of Securities
    Regulation, 128

Japan
  recession impact on Thailand, 29
  Thai foreign currency debts, 7
  Thailand bailout, 31, 31n
  mobilizing support, 31n

Köhler, Horst, 10
Köln Summit (1999), 101-05
  framework, 102-03
    implementing framework, 103-05
  private-sector involvement, 101, 102
  reports, 11
Korea
  bailout, 7, 8t
  bilateral funding, 60
  debt rescheduling, 141-42, 141n-142n
  exchange rates, 30f
  foreign currency creditors, 149
  foreign currency loans, 28n
  IMF requirements, 9-10
  Malaysia compared, 136-37
  policy conditions, 109
  reserves, 95
  rollover options, 148
  socialization of risk, 98
  systemically important, 142
  voluntary or concerted, 141
  vulnerability, 34-35
  won, 34-35, 39
    depreciation, 41

large-scale official financing
  imprudent behavior, 151-52
  institutionalization of, 9
  limiting reliance on IMF, 111-17
    reconfiguring the IMF, 114-17
    risks and costs, 112-14
  prospect of, risks, 112
Latin America, regional monetary
  cooperation, 80
Lawson Doctrine, 18n
lenders of last resort (LLR), 57-63
  classic case, 57-58
  currency boards as, 77-78
  defining, 57
  how IMF differs from, 60-62
  how IMF resembles, 58-60
  Meltzer Report recommendation, 63,
    112
  recasting the analogy, 62-63

Genoa Summit (2001), 125
institutional incongruities, 130
multiple-currency (basket) pegs, 75
Murphy's Law, 52-53

national financial systems, G-22 working
group, 97-98
net reserves, 95
New Arrangements to Borrow (NAB), 4,
59
country crises, 114
Halifax Summit, 88
large-scale official financing, 114
restrictive rules, 60-61
noise-to-signal ratio, 107
nominal rate, 81
North American Monetary Union
(NAMU) notion, 80

offshore financial centers
bank supervision, 88
FSF working group, 11
offshore transactions, Malaysia, 44
Okinawa Summit (200), Köln operational
guidelines, 104
O'Neill, Paul, 125n
on-lending, 64, 64n
Organization for Economic Cooperation
and Development (OECD), 23

Pakistan, 47
Paris Club comparability, 119
voluntary or concerted, 141
"Panglossian investment," 27
Paris Club, 5
comparability, 119
Pakistan, 119, 122, 141
private creditors on, 123
reverse, 123
Köln framework, 102, 104
Partido Revolucionario Institucional
(PRI), 1-2
pegged rates, 72
discouraged, 153
exiting from, 82
large-scale financing, 112
peso crisis
Asian crisis compared, 7-8
currency crisis to debt crisis, 2
origins, 1-5
reforms proposed, 1
See also Mexican crisis
Philippine peso, 32, 39
policy conditions, 9-10

creditor panic, 51
criticized, 9-10
debate over, 43
following Mexican debt crisis of 1980s,
23
Indonesia, 33
Korea, 35
reviewing compliance, 61
Russia, 44
See also conditionality
political factors
election effect, 25n
national solvency, 50
official concern, 122
political shocks, Mexican crisis, 19n, 24n
portfolio investment, Mexican crisis, 19,
20t
Poverty Reduction and Growth Facility
(PRGF), 88, 128
prequalification, 69-71
preconditions for eligibility, 154
presumptive prequalification, 153-55
private capital flows
IMF on, 15, 15n
push and pull factors, 15n
World Bank on, 14-15
private capital flows to developing
countries, 14-16, 14t
private debtors, Rey Report, 5
private sector
Asian and Russian crises, 94
"concerted" involvement, 105
government guarantees criticized, 98
official versus private creditors, 122
phrasing of collective action clause
recommendations, 99n
response to Rey Report, 90-91
short-term borrowing and capital
inflows, 134n
standards and codes, 111
transparency needed, 96-97
voluntary cooperation, disadvantages,
138
private-sector debt, Thailand bailout, 31
private-sector involvement
attempts criticized, 121-22
debates over, 49-50
G-7 finance ministers, 103
Köln Summit
debt management approach, 102
implementing framework, 103-04
operational guidelines, 103-04
rethinking, 138-43, 138n

how the crisis started, 28-31
Malaysia compared, 136-37
policy conditions, 109
probabilities of crisis, 107
public warnings, 108
reserves, 95
systemic implications, 115
tiered response by IMF, 95
time-based expectations, 117
time consistency, 74
trade
Asian crisis limitations, 42n
capital flows related, 17-18
cluster analysis, 38, 38n
effects on Asian crisis, 37-38, 38n
trade credits, 6, 142
trade deficit, Mexico, 23
transparency
and accountability, G-22 working
group, 96-97
dollarization, 83
exchange rates, 76n
Lyon Summit recommendations, 4
reports proposal, 97
treasury bills, Russian (GKOs), 44, 45,
46n
Treaty of Rome (1958), 80
two-corner approach to exchange rate
regime, 80-84
crawling away from the corners, 84-86
Rubin on, 73

UDROP (Universal Debt Rollover Option
with a Penalty), 148-49
Ukraine, 47
debt sustainability, 118-19

voluntary or concerted, 141
unhedged foreign currency debt, 39, 40-
41, 40n
unilateral actions, 99-100
United Kingdom, collective action
clauses, 101n
United States, exchange rate regimes, 72
universality, principle of, 61-62
unresolved issues, overview, 12
US Treasury
crisis prevention, 10-11
Mexican bailout, 2
peso crisis, 2
streamlining of IMF, 116

voluntary cooperation, disadvantages,
138
voluntary debt exchange, 100
vulnerability, detecting, 105-08

wage-price spiral, 81
wake-up calls
investor behavior, 37
Thai crisis, 38
Western Hemisphere, private capital
flows, 14t
wholesale prices, 81
Willard Group. See G-22 Reports
Working Group on Capital Flows, 132-33
Working Party on Financial Stability in
Emerging Market Economies, 91-92
World Bank
contractual approach, 131
focus criticized, 125n
World Financial Authority, 69n

yen-dollar rate, 39

Other Publications from the
**Institute for
International Economics**

* = out of print

POLICY ANALYSES IN
INTERNATIONAL ECONOMICS Series

BOOKS

IMF Conditionality*   John Williamson, editor
1983   ISBN 0-88132-006-4
Trade Policy in the 1980s*   William R. Cline, editor
1983   ISBN 0-88132-031-5
Subsidies in International Trade*
Gary Clyde Hufbauer and Joanna Shelton Erb
1984   ISBN 0-88132-004-8
International Debt: Systemic Risk and Policy
Response*   William R. Cline
1984   ISBN 0-88132-015-3
Trade Protection in the United States: 31 Case
Studies*   Gary Clyde Hufbauer, Diane E. Berliner, and Kimberly Ann Elliott
1986   ISBN 0-88132-040-4
Toward Renewed Economic Growth in Latin
America*   Bela Balassa, Gerardo M. Bueno, Pedro-Pablo Kuczynski, and Mario Henrique Simonsen
1986   ISBN 0-88132-045-5
Capital Flight and Third World Debt*
Donald R. Lessard and John Williamson, editors
1987   ISBN 0-88132-053-6
The Canada-United States Free Trade Agreement:
The Global Impact*
Jeffrey J. Schott and Murray G. Smith, editors
1988   ISBN 0-88132-073-0
World Agricultural Trade: Building a Consensus*
William M. Miner and Dale E. Hathaway, editors
1988   ISBN 0-88132-071-3
Japan in the World Economy*
Bela Balassa and Marcus Noland
1988   ISBN 0-88132-041-2
America in the World Economy: A Strategy for
the 1990s*   C. Fred Bergsten
1988   ISBN 0-88132-089-7
Managing the Dollar: From the Plaza to the
Louvre*   Yoichi Funabashi
1988, 2d ed. 1989   ISBN 0-88132-097-8
United States External Adjustment and the World
Economy*   William R. Cline
May 1989   ISBN 0-88132-048-X
Free Trade Areas and U.S. Trade Policy*
Jeffrey J. Schott, editor
May 1989   ISBN 0-88132-094-3
Dollar Politics: Exchange Rate Policymaking in
the United States*
I.M. Destler and C. Randall Henning
September 1989   ISBN 0-88132-079-X
Latin American Adjustment: How Much Has
Happened?*   John Williamson, editor
April 1990   ISBN 0-88132-125-7
The Future of World Trade in Textiles and
Apparel*   William R. Cline
1987, 2d ed. June 1990   ISBN 0-88132-110-9

Completing the Uruguay Round: A Results-
Oriented Approach to the GATT Trade
Negotiations*   Jeffrey J. Schott, editor
September 1990   ISBN 0-88132-130-3
Economic Sanctions Reconsidered (2 volumes)
Economic Sanctions Reconsidered: Supplemental
Case Histories
Gary Clyde Hufbauer, Jeffrey J. Schott, and
Kimberly Ann Elliott
1985, 2d ed. Dec. 1990   ISBN cloth 0-88132-115-X
    ISBN paper 0-88132-105-2
Economic Sanctions Reconsidered: History and
Current Policy
Gary Clyde Hufbauer, Jeffrey J. Schott, and
Kimberly Ann Elliott
December 1990   ISBN cloth 0-88132-140-0
    ISBN paper 0-88132-136-2
Pacific Basin Developing Countries: Prospects for
the Future*   Marcus Noland
January 1991   ISBN cloth 0-88132-141-9
    ISBN 0-88132-081-1
Currency Convertibility in Eastern Europe*
John Williamson, editor
October 1991   ISBN 0-88132-128-1
International Adjustment and Financing: The
Lessons of 1985-1991*   C. Fred Bergsten, editor
January 1992   ISBN 0-88132-112-5
North American Free Trade: Issues and
Recommendations*
Gary Clyde Hufbauer and Jeffrey J. Schott
April 1992   ISBN 0-88132-120-6
Narrowing the U.S. Current Account Deficit*
Allen J. Lenz
June 1992   ISBN 0-88132-103-6
The Economics of Global Warming
William R. Cline/*June 1992*   ISBN 0-88132-132-X
U.S. Taxation of International Income: Blueprint
for Reform*   Gary Clyde Hufbauer, assisted by
Joanna M. van Rooij
October 1992   ISBN 0-88132-134-6
Who's Bashing Whom? Trade Conflict in High-
Technology Industries   Laura D'Andrea Tyson
November 1992   ISBN 0-88132-106-0
Korea in the World Economy*   Il SaKong
January 1993   ISBN 0-88132-183-4
Pacific Dynamism and the International Economic
System*
C. Fred Bergsten and Marcus Noland, editors
May 1993   ISBN 0-88132-196-6
Economic Consequences of Soviet Disintegration*
John Williamson, editor
May 1993   ISBN 0-88132-190-7
Reconcilable Differences? United States-Japan
Economic Conflict*
C. Fred Bergsten and Marcus Noland
June 1993   ISBN 0-88132-129-X

Does Foreign Exchange Intervention Work?
Kathryn M. Dominguez and Jeffrey A. Frankel
September 1993   ISBN 0-88132-104-4
Sizing Up U.S. Export Disincentives*
J. David Richardson
September 1993   ISBN 0-88132-107-9
NAFTA: An Assessment
Gary Clyde Hufbauer and Jeffrey J. Schott/*rev. ed.*
October 1993   ISBN 0-88132-199-0
Adjusting to Volatile Energy Prices
Philip K. Verleger, Jr.
November 1993   ISBN 0-88132-069-2
The Political Economy of Policy Reform
John Williamson, editor
January 1994   ISBN 0-88132-195-8
**Measuring the Costs of Protection
in the United States**
Gary Clyde Hufbauer and Kimberly Ann Elliott
January 1994   ISBN 0-88132-108-7
The Dynamics of Korean Economic Development*
Cho Soon
March 1994   ISBN 0-88132-162-1
Reviving the European Union*
C. Randall Henning, Eduard Hochreiter, and Gary
Clyde Hufbauer, Editors
April 1994   ISBN 0-88132-208-3
China in the World Economy   Nicholas R. Lardy
April 1994   ISBN 0-88132-200-8
**Greening the GATT: Trade, Environment, and the
Future**   Daniel C. Esty
July 1994   ISBN 0-88132-205-9
Western Hemisphere Economic Integration*
Gary Clyde Hufbauer and Jeffrey J. Schott
July 1994   ISBN 0-88132-159-1
**Currencies and Politics in the United States,
Germany, and Japan**
C. Randall Henning
September 1994   ISBN 0-88132-127-3
Estimating Equilibrium Exchange Rates
John Williamson, editor
September 1994   ISBN 0-88132-076-5
**Managing the World Economy: Fifty Years After
Bretton Woods**   Peter B. Kenen, editor
September 1994   ISBN 0-88132-212-1
Reciprocity and Retaliation in U.S. Trade Policy
Thomas O. Bayard and Kimberly Ann Elliott
September 1994   ISBN 0-88132-084-6
The Uruguay Round: An Assessment*
Jeffrey J. Schott, assisted by Johanna W. Buurman
November 1994   ISBN 0-88132-206-7
Measuring the Costs of Protection in Japan*
Yoko Sazanami, Shujiro Urata, and Hiroki Kawai
January 1995   ISBN 0-88132-211-3
Foreign Direct Investment in the United States,
3rd Ed.   Edward M. Graham and Paul R. Krugman
January 1995   ISBN 0-88132-204-0

**The Political Economy of Korea-United States
Cooperation***
C. Fred Bergsten and Il SaKong, editors
February 1995   ISBN 0-88132-213-X
International Debt Reexamined*   William R. Cline
February 1995   ISBN 0-88132-083-8
American Trade Politics, 3rd Ed.   I.M. Destler
April 1995   ISBN 0-88132-215-6
**Managing Official Export Credits: The Quest for a
Global Regime***   John E. Ray
July 1995   ISBN 0-88132-207-5
Asia Pacific Fusion: Japan's Role in APEC*
Yoichi Funabashi
October 1995   ISBN 0-88132-224-5
**Korea-United States Cooperation in the New
World Order***
C. Fred Bergsten and Il SaKong, editors
February 1996   ISBN 0-88132-226-1
Why Exports Really Matter! *   ISBN 0-88132-221-0
Why Exports Matter More!*   ISBN 0-88132-229-6
J. David Richardson and Karin Rindal
July 1995; February 1996
Global Corporations and National Governments
Edward M. Graham
May 1996   ISBN 0-88132-111-7
**Global Economic Leadership and the Group of
Seven**   C. Fred Bergsten and C. Randall Henning
May 1996   ISBN 0-88132-218-0
The Trading System After the Uruguay Round*
John Whalley and Colleen Hamilton
July 1996   ISBN 0-88132-131-1
**Private Capital Flows to Emerging Markets After
the Mexican Crisis***   Guillermo A. Calvo,
Morris Goldstein, and Eduard Hochreiter
September 1996   ISBN 0-88132-232-6
**The Crawling Band as an Exchange Rate Regime:
Lessons from Chile, Colombia, and Israel**
John Williamson
September 1996   ISBN 0-88132-231-8
**Flying High: Liberalizing Civil Aviation in the
Asia Pacific***
Gary Clyde Hufbauer and Christopher Findlay
November 1996   ISBN 0-88132-227-X
**Measuring the Costs of Visible Protection in
Korea***   Namdoo Kim
November 1996   ISBN 0-88132-236-9
The World Trading System: Challenges Ahead
Jeffrey J. Schott
December 1996   ISBN 0-88132-235-0
Has Globalization Gone Too Far?   Dani Rodrik
March 1997   ISBN cloth 0-88132-243-1
Korea-United States Economic Relationship*
C. Fred Bergsten and Il SaKong, editors
March 1997   ISBN 0-88132-240-7
Summitry in the Americas: A Progress Report
Richard E. Feinberg
April 1997   ISBN 0-88132-242-3

Corruption and the Global Economy
Kimberly Ann Elliott
June 1997   ISBN 0-88132-233-4

Regional Trading Blocs in the World Economic
System   Jeffrey A. Frankel
October 1997   ISBN 0-88132-202-4

Sustaining the Asia Pacific Miracle:
Environmental Protection and Economic
Integration   André Dua and Daniel C. Esty
October 1997   ISBN 0-88132-250-4

Trade and Income Distribution   William R. Cline
November 1997   ISBN 0-88132-216-4

Global Competition Policy
Edward M. Graham and J. David Richardson
December 1997   ISBN 0-88132-166-4

Unfinished Business: Telecommunications after
the Uruguay Round
Gary Clyde Hufbauer and Erika Wada
December 1997   ISBN 0-88132-257-1

Financial Services Liberalization in the WTO
Wendy Dobson and Pierre Jacquet
June 1998   ISBN 0-88132-254-7

Restoring Japan's Economic Growth
Adam S. Posen
September 1998   ISBN 0-88132-262-8

Measuring the Costs of Protection in China
Zhang Shuguang, Zhang Yansheng, and Wan
Zhongxin
November 1998   ISBN 0-88132-247-4

Foreign Direct Investment and Development: The
New Policy Agenda for Developing Countries and
Economies in Transition
Theodore H. Moran
December 1998   ISBN 0-88132-258-X

Behind the Open Door: Foreign Enterprises in the
Chinese Marketplace   Daniel H. Rosen
January 1999   ISBN 0-88132-263-6

Toward A New International Financial
Architecture: A Practical Post-Asia Agenda
Barry Eichengreen
February 1999   ISBN 0-88132-270-9

Is the U.S. Trade Deficit Sustainable?
Catherine L. Mann/*September 1999*
ISBN 0-88132-265-2

Safeguarding Prosperity in a Global Financial
System: The Future International Financial
Architecture, Independent Task Force Report
Sponsored by the Council on Foreign Relations
Morris Goldstein, Project Director
October 1999   ISBN 0-88132-287-3

Avoiding the Apocalypse: The Future of the Two
Koreas   Marcus Noland
June 2000   ISBN 0-88132-278-4

Assessing Financial Vulnerability: An Early
Warning System for Emerging Markets
Morris Goldstein, Graciela Kaminsky, and Carmen
Reinhart
June 2000   ISBN 0-88132-237-7

Global Electronic Commerce: A Policy Primer
Catherine L. Mann, Sue E. Eckert, and Sarah
Cleeland Knight
July 2000   ISBN 0-88132-274-1

The WTO after Seattle
Jeffrey J. Schott, editor
July 2000   ISBN 0-88132-290-3

Intellectual Property Rights in the Global
Economy   Keith E. Maskus
August 2000   ISBN 0-88132-282-2

The Political Economy of the Asian Financial
Crisis   Stephan Haggard
August 2000   ISBN 0-88132-283-0

Transforming Foreign Aid: United States
Assistance in the 21st Century   Carol Lancaster
August 2000   ISBN 0-88132-291-1

Fighting the Wrong Enemy: Antiglobal Activists
and Multinational Enterprises
Edward M. Graham
September 2000   ISBN 0-88132-272-5

Globalization and the Perceptions of American
Workers
Kenneth F. Scheve and Matthew J. Slaughter
March 2001   ISBN 0-88132-295-4

World Capital Markets: Challenge to the G-10
Wendy Dobson and Gary C. Hufbauer,
assisted by Hyun Koo Cho
May 2001   ISBN 0-88132-301-2

Prospects for Free Trade in the Americas
Jeffrey J. Schott
August 2001   ISBN 0-88132-275-X

Lessons from the Old World for the New:
Constructing a North American Community
Robert A. Pastor
August 2001   ISBN 0-88132-328-4

Measuring the Costs of Protection in Europe:
European Commercial Policy in the 2000s
Patrick A. Messerlin
September 2001   ISBN 0-88132-273-3

Job Loss from Imports: Measuring the Costs
Lori G. Kletzer
September 2001   ISBN 0-88132-296-2

No More Bashing: Building a New Japan-United
States Economic Relationship
C. Fred Bergsten, Takatoshi Ito, and Marc Noland
October 2001   ISBN 0-88132-286-5

Why Global Commitment Really Matters!
Howard Lewis III and J. David Richardson
October 2001   ISBN 0-88132-298-9

Leadership Selection in the Major Multilaterals
Miles Kahler
November 2001   ISBN 0-88132-335-7

The International Financial Architecture:
What's New? What's Missing?
Peter Kenen
November 2001   ISBN 0-88132-297-0

DISTRIBUTORS OUTSIDE THE UNITED STATES

Australia, New Zealand, and Papua New Guinea
D.A. Information Services
648 Whitehorse Road
Mitcham, Victoria 3132, Australia
tel: 61-3-9210-7777
fax: 61-3-9210-7788
e-mail: service@dadirect.com.au
http://www.dadirect.com.au

Canada
Renouf Bookstore
5369 Canotek Road, Unit 1
Ottawa, Ontario K1J 9J3, Canada
tel: 613-745-2665
fax: 613-745-7660
http://www.renoufbooks.com

United Kingdom and Europe
(including Russia and Turkey)
The Eurospan Group
3 Henrietta Street, Covent Garden
London WC2E 8LU England
tel: 44-20-7240-0856
fax: 44-20-7379-0609
http://www.eurospan.co.uk

India, Bangladesh, Nepal, and Sri Lanka
Viva Books Pvt.
Mr. Vinod Vasishtha
4325/3, Ansari Rd.
Daryaganj, New Delhi-110002
India
tel: 91-11-327-9280
fax: 91-11-326-7224
e-mail: vinod.viva@gndel.globalnet.
ems.vsnl.net.in

Japan and the Republic of Korea
United Publishers Services, Ltd.
Kenkyu-Sha Bldg.
9, Kanda Surugadai 2-Chome
Chiyoda-Ku, Tokyo 101
Japan
tel: 81-3-3291-4541
fax: 81-3-3292-8610
e-mail: saito@ups.co.jp
**For trade accounts only.
Individuals will find IIE books in
leading Tokyo bookstores.**

Southeast Asia (Brunei, Cambodia,
China, Malaysia, Hong Kong, Indonesia,
Laos, Myanmar, the Philippines, Singapore,
Taiwan, and Vietnam)
Hemisphere Publication Services
1 Kallang Pudding Rd. #04-03
Golden Wheel Building
Singapore 349316
tel: 65-741-5166
fax: 65-742-9356

Thailand
Asia Books
5 Sukhumvit Rd. Soi 61
Bangkok 10110 Thailand
tel: 662-714-0740-2 Ext: 221, 222, 223
fax: 662-391-2277
e-mail: purchase@asiabooks.co.th
http://www.asiabooksonline.com

**Visit our Web site at:
http://www.iie.com
E-mail orders to:
orders@iie.com**